OCEAN BIRDS

OCEAN BIRDS

LARS LÖFGREN

ALFRED A. KNOPF

New York

1984

THIS IS A BORZOI BOOK
PUBLISHED BY ALFRED A. KNOPF, INC.

World copyright © 1984 AB Nordbok,
Gothenburg, Sweden.

Published in the United States by
Alfred A. Knopf, Inc., New York,
and simultaneously in Canada by
Random House of Canada Limited, Toronto.
Distributed by Random House, Inc., New York.
Published in Great Britain by Croom Helm Ltd, London

Typeset by Text Processing Ltd, Clonmel, Ireland.
Colour reproduction by Offset-Kopio, Helsinki,
Finland, and by Reproman, Gothenburg.

Library of Congress Cataloging in Publication Data

Löfgren, Lars.
  Ocean birds.

  Bibliography: p.
  Includes index.
  1. Sea birds.   I. Title.

QL673.L73   1984   598.4   84-47831

ISBN 0-394-53101-9

Manufactured in Italy
First American Edition

OCEAN BIRDS has been originated, designed, and
produced by AB Nordbok, Gothenburg, Sweden, in close
collaboration with the author/photographer.

Editor-in-Chief: Turlough Johnston.

Editor: Jon van Leuven.

Designer: Roland Thorbjörnsson.

Design assistant: Anna-Karin Öbom.

Artwork: Syed Mumtaz Ahmad, Tommy Berglund, Paul
Blake, Anders Engström, Lars Jödahl, Hans Linder,
Lennart Molin, Ulf Söderqvist.

Colour lithography: Nils Hermanson.

Nordbok would like to express sincere gratitude to Mark
Beaman for advice during preparation of the manuscript.
The following illustrations have made use of particular
sources which are cited in the Bibliography: pages 128
(Ashmole and Ashmole, 1967), 138-139 top centre
(Shuntov, 1974), 152 top (Pearson, 1968), 152 centre
(Lack, 1945), 220 (Murphy, 1936), 229 (Woodwell,
Wurster, and Isaacson, 1967).

CONTENTS

PREFACE

The vast oceans with strong winds, high waves, and sometimes severe storms, yet no shelter and nothing but water with a high salt content to rest upon, temperatures ranging from tropical in many areas to subzero in others—such are some of the conditions to which seabirds have adapted during millions of years in the evolution of their properties. Shown here is a Great Shearwater passing through the North Atlantic during its long migration from the Southern Hemisphere.

It is not surprising that our almost universal interest in birds should be directed mainly toward those which are easiest to observe. Being active by day, commonly drawn to open areas, and not very shy of man, birds of the land have become particularly well-known in their habits and often greatly admired for their beauty. But birds that make a home on the vast expanses of ocean seldom come so close to us. Many of these do not, as a rule, even fly near the sea coasts or breed in accessible places. Their ability to survive under conditions that are inhospitable for other animals, as well as their unusual reproductive behaviour, long migrations, and occasional appearance in quite unexpected regions, are part of a way of life which is none the less fascinating because it seems remote.

Seabirds are the last great "adventurers" on earth, and their free-ranging existence is especially alluring from the standpoint of man's own desire for freedom. The flight of the albatross, soaring effortlessly over giant waves, has always captivated sailors and gave rise to an ancient belief that this creature incarnated their souls after death. At the same time, such birds appeal to many other human emotions. Most are inconspicuously coloured, yet their simplicity can be an attractive virtue, as the fabulous little White Tern of the tropics shows with its translucent wings. Among the loveliest seabirds of all, despite its humble hues, is a Sooty Albatross spanning the waters on slender angled wings and long pointed tail. People are frequently amused by penguins that look like a parody of over-fed clowns in dress-coats, or by the naive antics of birds on unspoiled breeding grounds. Again, we may be amazed—or indeed annoyed—to view the insatiable voracity of a gull as it feeds on our favourite beach.

When I began to work aboard merchant vessels in the early 1960s, I had already become a devoted amateur in the field of ornithology, and it was inevitable that my rapport with seabirds grew steadily. This eventually led me to study birds on the oceans almost daily during more than a decade as a radio officer, and later to visit many seabird breeding grounds. Even before setting foot on a ship's deck, I had read about a few records of Great and Sooty Shearwaters on the coast of Sweden, not far from my home. What awakened my curiosity was the fact that these birds breed in the Southern Hemisphere and somehow manage to travel enormous distances, normally to North Atlantic areas other than the Swedish coast. Nor was I the only layman to be filled with wonder. The ranks of bird-watchers are multiplying each year around the world.

Scientists have done much of their basic biological research upon seabirds, some of which are consequently among the best-known bird species. Others, however, belong to the most mysterious of all animals, chiefly due to extreme rarity and oceanic ways of life. There remain unsolved problems in the very identification of seabird species, mapping of distributions, and data on details of migration. My voyages provided an opportunity to observe a large proportion of the varieties of seabirds in every major ocean, but little help could be obtained from good field-guides in those days. Recent publications can now assist the enthusiast greatly in such matters, opening a path to understanding of fundamental aspects of the world of seabirds—as in ecology, behaviour, and breeding.

This book gives the general reader a complete survey of seabirds' biology, taking all the essential features of their lives into account. It is also an attempt to popularize theories and principles of science which are relevant to a study of birds and, in particular, to those of the oceans. Research at the latter level is often of broad interest but confined to a diversity of specialist literature that cannot be grasped fully even by scholars. On the one hand, scientific methods must be clarified in order to overcome the difficulties of observing seabirds and explaining their traits. Most people begin to watch birds with an assumption that the question why an animal does what it does is fairly unambiguous—but some knowledge of evolution and classification will show that concepts like "species" and "causes" demand careful treatment. On the other hand, biological science has grown hugely in recent decades, and experts themselves may find discoveries hard to appreciate in a context as wide as that of seabirds.

To sort out the key facts and ideas about seabirds in a manner acceptable to everybody is not a simple task. By following a logical sequence of topics, minimizing the need of technical jargon, and presenting the details in as many verbal and visual ways as possible, I have hoped to build up a picture that is sufficiently thorough and vital to engage both the long-time investigator and the landlubber who has yet to lay eyes on an ocean bird. In addition, the uncertain and enigmatic aspects of research on seabirds have been noted, stimulating readers to make further studies and new contributions in the future.

Since much of our understanding of the animal world involves the twin roles of inheritance and environment, these are outlined in the first chapter, with particular attention to how the different kinds of seabirds evolved and are now classified. Chapter 2 describes the physical adaptations of seabirds to their varied surroundings for purposes such as feeding, breeding, flying, and defence. In Chapter 3, the distinguishing characteristics of ocean birds are given, for each of their sixteen families in four orders, as well as for smaller groups of importance, and the 290 species are accompanied by their illustration page-numbers for immediate reference. When Chapter 4 and the topic of migration are reached, page-references occur on the maps showing movements of many seabird species.

Chapter 5 is an introduction to the relatively novel discipline of ecology, with its systematic implications for seabirds as members of the whole natural world: their marine habitats and populations, how these are related to factors of climate and land, the feeding methods of ocean birds, and the cycle formed by their lives and deaths. A closer examination of behaviour, in Chapter 6, primarily concerns our explanations of the peculiar ways in which ocean birds act towards each other when they breed and, in general, communicate. Reproduction itself, a complex matter of places, times, physiological events, and actual dangers, is treated in Chapter 7.

The final questions about ocean birds, in Chapter 8, are also central ones: what has man done for, or against, the winged beings of the salt air—and *vice versa*? We have learned to view the specific data on seabirds, from the conditions for their mere existence to the situations in which they truly thrive, in the light of nature as an interconnected totality. But this is only a necessary step toward the realization that human beings, too, are a part of the integrated global ecosystem. The scientific principles and processes of life on earth discussed here are as relevant to us as to seabirds. Both we and they must help to maintain the system in order to survive, and our obligation to do so is greater because we have more power. In the long run, such a system has no room for selfishness, and the fate of many birds is proof that the "long run" can be few years indeed. Thus, I have tried to be reasonably explicit about the future prospects of seabirds in a rapidly changing world.

Soon after my interest in animals was aroused, I took up nature-photography. Ocean birds became a ready object for my camera so that, while working on ships and during later travels, I acquired a sizeable collection of most varieties of seabirds on film. A photograph has the advantage of capturing, not simply an individual at which it is aimed, but an entire assemblage of circumstances in which the individual participates. However, drawings and paintings of birds often have great aesthetic value, and the artist is in many ways free to illustrate phenomena that are difficult or impossible to photograph. Whereas in nature one can find—and film, with luck—innumerable imperfections and gradations, as in the plumage of birds, such art tends to idealize life by exhibiting "typical" average examples of flawless specimens in their prime. The two methods of portrayal, therefore, complement each other and have been combined throughout this book.

Although the result is not meant to be a field-guide for identification of seabirds in every context, all of their basic types and two-thirds of their species are shown under selected conditions, leaving the reader with an ample impression of how they look. It should be kept in mind that many species are very similar and frequently require not only a manual but much experience, or even direct examination in hand, to be distinguished exactly. The emphasis in these pages is rather upon complementing the tools of field-observation. We shall see ocean birds in their living ambience, recognize their unity as well as their contrasts, and notice the beauty which makes them too marvellous for words alone.

A tangible, do-it-yourself approach to seabirds may be hindered by their unsuitability as household pets, game fowl, and the like. Nevertheless, as many as half of the people in the world live within easy reach of the ocean and have probably at least glimpsed birds of this kind, while some of us are fortunate enough to have spent decades on coasts or islands rich in seabirds. My book was prepared before a continual, busy audience of the big gulls and terns which, along with skuas and other random visitors, inhabit the wintry waters between the North and Baltic Seas. When such a sharp-eyed character is sitting just outside the window as you inspect a picture of its opposite sex, favourite food, or worst enemy, the feeling of being involved in its life is hard to avoid.

Severe storms and oil spillages are among the common incidents which also bring us into contact with the death of seabirds and with practical means of benefitting them. In several countries, these means can now be learned from bird-protection societies which are always worth joining. Yet it is surely the ocean-going sailor and long-distance traveller who have the greatest chances of enjoying and studying seabirds as a whole. Even a specific quest may be undertaken, aided by distribution maps and information from local wildlife organizations. No ordinary tourist agency, of course, will tell you where to go in search of a Jackass Penguin, Barau's Petrel, or Marbled Murrelet—and some of the best places for observing seabirds, as in breeding colonies, have rightly become sanctuaries with restricted access. But once you accept the challenges of personally meeting ocean birds, deep rewards await you.

Chapter One
EVOLUTION AND CLASSIFICATION

Birds have attracted the attention of mankind since the earliest times. Even in prehistoric cultures, birds were not only used as a source of food and implements, but were often given a religious significance that is akin to our aesthetic appreciation of birds today. But while humans have always possessed some knowledge of birds, it is only in the last few centuries that scientific methods have been applied to birds, and that a systematic understanding of them has developed.

Natural science was at first interested in describing and classifying organisms. Taxonomy—the formulation of a system of classification, with categories and names—was the chief occupation of ornithologists during the eighteenth and much of the nineteenth centuries. But basic information about the habits of birds was also gathered, and scientific efforts began to shift towards classifying such knowledge. This was accompanied by an even more fundamental trend in biology, from simple fact-gathering to the development of general, explanatory theories. For a classification of facts must rest on a theoretical framework, and explanations of facts can only be evaluated in terms of how well they fit into a larger theoretical picture.

One of the major insights that resulted from this new direction was a realization that all living things are interconnected elements in a complex system that embraces the whole natural world. Every such web of interrelationships is today called an *ecosystem*, and the position of each kind of organism in the web—the role it plays in its ecosystem—is called its ecological niche. To understand seabirds fully, we must not only know about their own intrinsic attributes and habits, but must understand their interactions with other organisms and with their physical environment. Indeed, the character of these processes both at the present time and during the past history of seabirds must be studied. A basic theory that enables us to structure biological information in this way is the theory of evolution by natural selection. We will now examine this theory, as well as the fundamentals of classification; in later chapters, we will give detailed consideration to seabirds in the light of principles like those of evolution and ecology.

Evolution

While we can readily observe the development of an individual organism from fertilized egg to adult, the deeper question of how life itself began remains unanswered. Science maintains that, over a billion years ago, certain physical phenomena came into being by chance, through random combinations of matter and energy on the surface and in the atmosphere of the primitive earth. These phenomena created complex molecules, with the unique ability to extract material from their surroundings and to replicate themselves. Fragile substances that required a special environment, competing with one another for the materials necessary for replication, these molecules experienced selective forces that eliminated some and preserved others. Those that were more efficient in extracting materials from the environment survived and reproduced, but those that were less efficient did not. Although the process must have taken an enormous span of time, the types of competing molecules gradually became more complex: those that continued to exist developed ever greater efficiency in assimilating materials, and in preserving themselves against competitors and hostile environmental conditions. From these ancient molecules, able to replicate themselves yet also able to change, life as we know it evolved, each form of organism being the descendant of older forms.

Organisms that survive and reproduce must be compatible with their environment, obtaining essential energy and materials while coping with enemies and competitors. Such compatibility involves *adaptations*—adjustments to conditions in the environment. These include mutual adaptations by organisms which, in an ecosystem, belong to each other's environment. Individuals that lack any of the necessary adaptations are eliminated and leave no descendants, whereas those that are fully adapted will preserve themselves. As environments undergo gradual changes, organisms gradually acquire new adaptations, or else they perish. It is the dual process of elimination and preservation that constitutes *natural selection*. The increase in complexity of organisms since the first appearance of life, and the exquisite adaptations we see in living things, are both due to natural selection.

Inheritance and change

But how are adaptations acquired? How are organisms able to change, in order to meet new demands made by the environment and to compete more successfully? The attributes of any organism, both structural and behavioural, are largely controlled by *genes*. Genes are coded bits of information, located on long molecular strands known as chromosomes. Chromosomes are present in every living cell, and the information coded in the genes gives rise to the properties of the cell and to the attributes of the entire organism. Like the ancient molecules that were the

Wandering Albatross *(Diomedea exulans)*

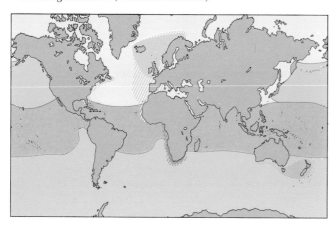

A world map of the distribution patterns of various kinds of sea-birds indicates not only the countless observations which are necessary to establish such patterns, but also many curious features that biological science must explain. Shown above are the distributions of the following:

☐ albatrosses
☐ frigate-birds

This map includes distributions of the three species of gannets:
☐ Northern
☐ Cape
☐ Australian
breeding range of species in each region
☐ Northern
☐ Cape
☐ Australian

Great Frigate-bird, immature *(Fregata minor)*

Peruvian Diving-petrel *(Pelecanoides garnoti)*

The albatrosses and frigate-birds *(photos on this page)* are both perfect gliders, adapted to feeding on food scattered over vast areas. Yet they differ in other characteristics and are adapted to distinctive climates—the albatrosses to windy waters and large waves of higher latitudes, and frigate-birds to the weaker winds of the tropics with air-convection currents on which they can stay circling. A converse phenomenon is shown by diving-petrels *(right)* and alcids, or auks *(opposite top)*. While confined respectively to the Southern and Northern Hemispheres, they resemble each other greatly in general build. This is a result of adaptation to similar ecological niches in those separate regions, exemplifying what is known as *convergent evolution*.

Alcids: an Atlantic Puffin *(Fratercula arctica)* **with Razorbills** *(Alca Torda)*

Seabirds living far apart may become rather different even when they belong to the same type. This is well illustrated by the gannets *(below)*, whose three species are closely related but are rarely confused due to their distinct distributions *(see map opposite)*. Because of *geographical isolation*, some varying features have also evolved, such as the extent of black colour on the wings and tail of adults in each species. Isolation which inhibits the exchange of genes betwen animal populations is a prerequisite for their beginning to differ in inherited properties.

The map at right shows the distributions of

    alcids
    diving-petrels

as discussed on the last page.

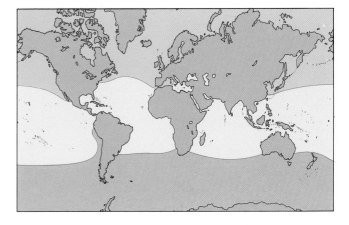

Northern Gannet *(Sula bassana)*

11

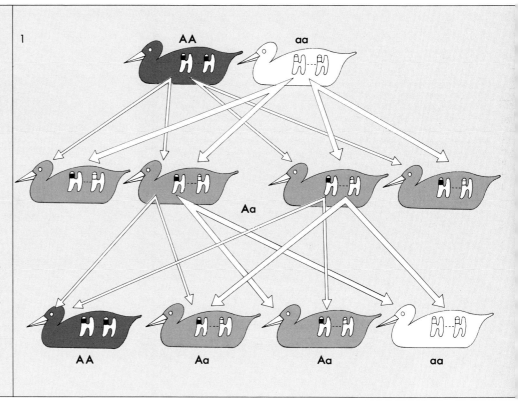

The principles of heredity in sexual reproduction belong to the science of genetics. A seabird, for example, has a fixed number of tiny chromosomes in each body cell. The chromosomes occur in related pairs, as they originate from the father's sperm and the mother's egg which were united by fertilization. Several types of genes make up a chromosome and have special locations on it. Thus, in a pair of chromosomes, there are usually two genes of every type, one from each parent. If the genes are identical, the bird is *homozygous* with respect to this gene type. But if they are variant genes, called *alleles*, the bird is *heterozygous*. These genes condition a property of the bird.

Shown here are the possibilities of inheritance in a breeding sequence. The first birds are homozygous but have different alleles (AA, aa) of the gene type, and they differ clearly in regard to that property. Their pairs of chromosomes can be combined in four ways to produce the second generation of birds. All of the latter are heterozygous (Aa),

precursors of life, chromosomes can replicate themselves. Each time a cell divides, as it does during development from a fertilized egg to an adult, the information coded in the genes is replicated, so that every cell in the body of an organism has the same genes.

But the replication of the chromosomes is not always perfect. A variety of factors can cause small "errors" during the replication of these long chains of genes. The result of such an error is a change in the genetic information, making a change in the properties of the cell. This is particularly important because genes are transmitted from old to new individuals during reproduction. If a genetic error is thus inherited, then the offspring will not be an exact copy of its parent. These genetic changes, known as *mutations*, may have small effects on the attributes of the offspring—but they are always significant, as they alter such attributes and may make the offspring more or less efficient than its parent. If the mutation is deleterious, the organism will be less successful than others in the population, and it or its descendants will eventually disappear. But if the mutation is a favourable one, its possessor will be at least as successful as others, and will leave descendants with the new genetic information.

Organisms are said to belong to the same *genotype* if they contain any identical genes, and to the same *phenotype* if they exhibit any identical attributes. While genes are inherited, attributes are influenced by both genes and the environment. Each organism's attributes determine its abilities to survive and to reproduce, and thereby its success in terms of natural selection.

Sexual reproduction

Evolutionary change can come about in another way than through mutations. Most organisms, including birds, reproduce sexually. The chromosomes in most cells of the body are paired, each member of a pair containing the same types of genes arranged in the same sequence along the chain. But for sexual reproduction, special cells are formed with only one member of each pair of chromosomes. These are the sex cells—the unfertilized egg and the sperm. When they combine to produce a fertilized egg, each sex cell contributes half of the chromosomes, which are again paired after fertilization. If the two parents are not genetically identical, the fertilized egg and the organism that will develop from it are not genetically identical to either of the parents. The genes are now inherited in new combinations.

Since many attributes of organisms are the result of the information in more than one gene, this *recombination* of genes is another source of evolutionary change. Favourable new combinations of genes confer an advantage on individuals that possess them, and so, like favourable mutations, they are perpetuated in subsequent generations. On the whole, sexual reproduction, and the genetic recombination which it makes possible, are very important causes of variation among the individuals in a population. Those organisms that reproduce sexually are most flexible in evolutionary terms. Organisms that can only reproduce asexually, without recombination, amount to a small minority of living things; their rate of evolutionary change is extremely slow, and they are relatively vulnerable to changes in the environment.

Thus, evolutionary change and the acquisition of new adaptations involve changes in the genetic components of organisms. Natural selection has a molecular basis, and is fundamentally a process of change in the frequencies of genes during consecutive generations of living things. This process not only depends on, but also influences, the ability of organisms to reproduce. Differences in *reproductive success* are a main reason why some genes become more frequent than others in a population. Sexual reproduction itself, as an inherited feature, is a primary outcome of evolution.

The species

A group of organisms which have a common set of genes, or *gene pool*, and which are capable of reproducing, makes up a species. Because of genetic differences, as in structure or behaviour, a species is unable to interbreed successfully with other such populations, and is said to be in *reproductive*

with one gene of each allele, and may have an intermediate form of the property *(1)*. Often, however, one allele is completely *dominant* over the other, which is *recessive*, and such birds have the same property as did the homozygous parent with the dominant gene *(2)*. In the third generation, half of the birds are homozygous and half are heterozygous. The different forms—or phenotypes—of birds may also differ in their ability to survive and reproduce, so that the relative frequency of the two alleles is changed in further generations. If one homozygote (say AA) has the best chances, the other allele (a) will be gradually eliminated by natural selection. But sometimes this cannot occur, as heterozygotes are favoured: such "hybrid vigour", or *heterosis*, leads to a more or less stable polymorphism (variety of forms) in the properties of the species.

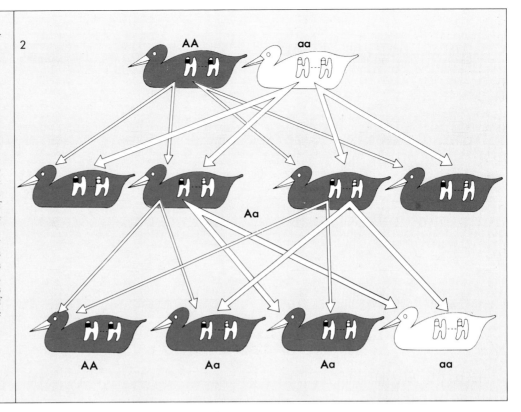

isolation. This isolation has an important evolutionary effect: each species can maintain its own genetic variations, and can evolve adaptations distinct from those of other species.

Competition thus involves not only individuals, but entire populations. The competition between species is an important selective force. Genetic mutations and recombinations that increase the success of one species at the expense of another are preserved, and it is against this background that much natural selection operates. Although the sources of genetic variation—mutation and recombination—are random, the influences of the environment and of competition between individuals and between species are not. As unfavourable variations are eliminated from populations, while favourable ones spread through them, evolutionary change results in an ever-increasing refinement of their adaptations and adjustments to environmental conditions.

In a real sense, then, the basic unit upon which natural selection operates is the species, a group of individuals that are capable of breeding only within the group. It is not always possible, however, to determine the limits of a species. Populations of nearly identical individuals may be separated geographically, as is the case with many seabirds that breed on far-flung islands, so that we cannot tell whether they are capable of interbreeding or not. The environment may act directly upon the attributes of individuals in a population, making them apparently different from other populations, even though they are not very different genetically and are capable of interbreeding with others as a single species. Such populations are usually called *geographical races* or *subspecies*. Despite these ambiguities, which abound among seabirds, the biological concept of the species is a fundamental one in the theory of natural selection.

The origin of species

As a result of continual changes in the environment, and in the selective forces that operate upon organisms, most species change gradually through time. Over the course of many generations, new adaptations arise, with new structu-

ral and behavioural attributes appearing and old ones disappearing. As long as all the individuals that make up a species continue to interbreed, these gradual changes affect all of them. Sometimes, however, part of a species undergoes *geographical isolation*, so that it can no longer exchange genes with the rest of the species. If this isolated population should experience different selective forces in its geographical environment, then genetic differences will gradually accumulate. Finally, the two populations may differ so much that they are incapable of interbreeding even if the geographical barrier that has separated them disappears. What was once a single species is now two species with a single common ancestor. Such a process, by which new species originate, is called *speciation*. Although geographical isolation is not the only proposed means of speciation, it is clearly the most important, and it is the only one that seems to occur in the case of birds.

Hybridization

If two newly evolved species do come together, and begin to compete with one another, natural selection will normally favour the development of still greater differences, as each species adapts to a distinct ecological niche so that competition is minimized. Sometimes, individuals of two species actually meet and interbreed, producing hybrid offspring. The reproductive isolation between closely related species is not absolute, and the mechanisms which hamper interbreeding may fail to operate. If the two parent populations are sufficiently different species, the hybrid offspring will not be favoured by natural selection, and further mechanisms of reproductive isolation will be evolved, diminishing the tendency to hybridize. But populations that have not long been separated may produce hybrids which are not at a disadvantage. Then the isolating mechanisms may continue to break down, the flow of genes between the two populations resumes, and whatever differences had accumulated disappear, showing that these populations still belong to a single species.

13

Altruism and food calls

Properties governing the behaviour of animals such as seabirds are fascinating examples of inheritance. Altruistic behaviour, which benefits other individuals but not necessarily the one performing it, is well-known yet often hard to explain. Thus, with some seabirds like the Arctic Skua (below), when predators approach the chicks, the parents may feign injury by beating their wings irregularly as if unable to fly, making themselves more vulnerable to the enemy and being sacrificed as the chicks escape. It might seem that genes conditioning such distraction displays *would not spread, since birds acting selfishly would have higher survival chances. However, if evolution favours "survival of the fittest", fitness depends largely on success in reproducing. A parent which abandons its chicks to predation (opposite top, 1a) may survive (1b), but has fewer chances of spreading its genes in the next generation (1c). If an altruistic parent (1d) bears a conditioning gene (X) and defends the chicks with its life, they probably inherit the gene and, by surviving (1e), can spread the gene in a further generation (1f). Therefore, such genes may become common due to normal natural selection. Successful reproduction also requires other kinds of altruism, like feeding the chicks and protecting them against weather.*

More puzzling are animals which behave altruistically towards individuals that are not their offspring. Food calls by gulls (opposite, bottom) may attract conspecifics—birds of the same type—and are even varied by some gulls to show the kind of food found. But since birds decrease their chances in life by attracting competitors, how can an altruistic gene for food calls spread?

The answer now suggested is inclusive fitness: *altruism favours the reproduction only of birds that also have the altruistic gene, making these collectively "fittest". Genes often occur in clusters, and if a food-call gene (X) always accompanies another gene for understanding food calls (Y), then only birds having X as well as Y can benefit. For example, an altruistic bird (2a) calls when it sees food, but is ignored by birds with different genes (2b), and the food is taken by conspecific birds with the same genes (2c). These may have greater chances of survival (2d), and their reproduction (2e) makes the altruistic gene (X) more frequent in future generations. A similar explanation could be given for birds which altruistically reveal their own presence to predators by making warning calls to conspecifics.*

Food calls are more complex in reality. Some seabirds benefit directly by summoning conspecifics, to prevent fish from escaping—this is cooperation, not altruism. Certain calls may be not food indicators but threats, when defending or robbing food. The understanding of calls is sometimes learned rather than inherited, although in at least some such cases it depends also on genes. Gull chicks have been proven to understand warning calls of parents even before the eggs are hatched to make learning possible.

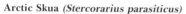

Arctic Skua *(Stercorarius parasiticus)*

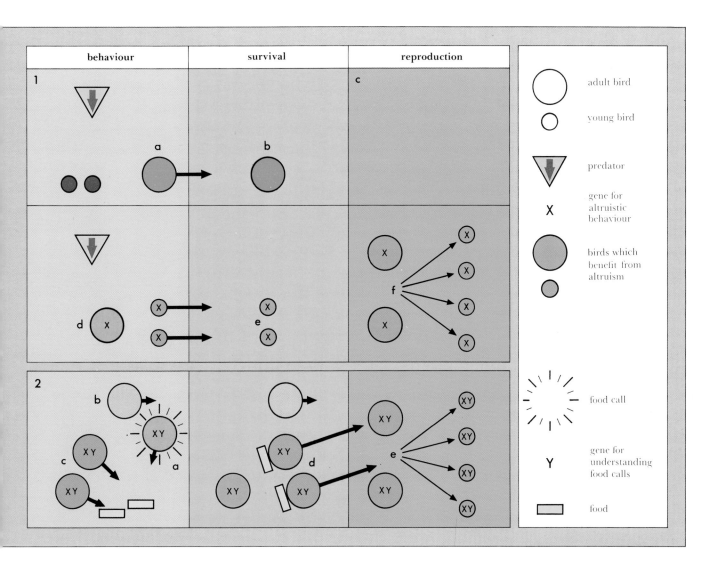

behaviour	survival	reproduction

Southern Black-backed Gull *(Larus dominicanus)*

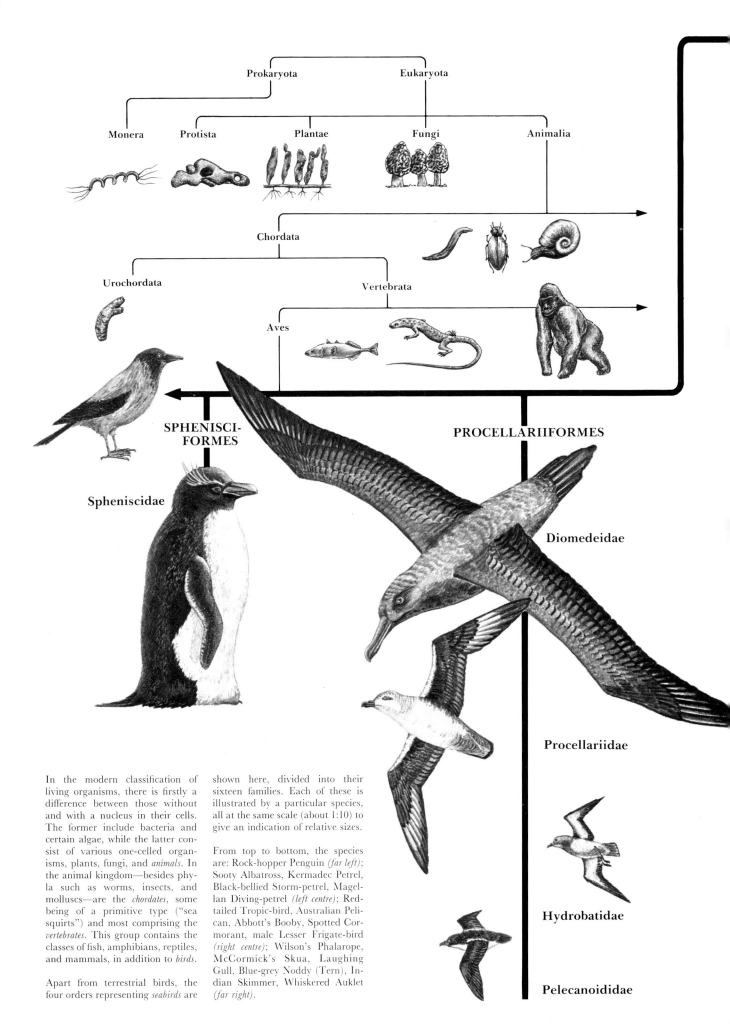

Prokaryota   Eukaryota

Monera   Protista   Plantae   Fungi   Animalia

Chordata

Urochordata   Vertebrata

Aves

**SPHENISCI-
FORMES**

PROCELLARIIFORMES

Spheniscidae

Diomedeidae

Procellariidae

Hydrobatidae

Pelecanoididae

In the modern classification of living organisms, there is firstly a difference between those without and with a nucleus in their cells. The former include bacteria and certain algae, while the latter consist of various one-celled organisms, plants, fungi, and *animals*. In the animal kingdom—besides phyla such as worms, insects, and molluscs—are the *chordates*, some being of a primitive type ("sea squirts") and most comprising the *vertebrates*. This group contains the classes of fish, amphibians, reptiles, and mammals, in addition to *birds*.

Apart from terrestrial birds, the four orders representing *seabirds* are

shown here, divided into their sixteen families. Each of these is illustrated by a particular species, all at the same scale (about 1:10) to give an indication of relative sizes.

From top to bottom, the species are: Rock-hopper Penguin *(far left)*; Sooty Albatross, Kermadec Petrel, Black-bellied Storm-petrel, Magellan Diving-petrel *(left centre)*; Red-tailed Tropic-bird, Australian Pelican, Abbott's Booby, Spotted Cormorant, male Lesser Frigate-bird *(right centre)*; Wilson's Phalarope, McCormick's Skua, Laughing Gull, Blue-grey Noddy (Tern), Indian Skimmer, Whiskered Auklet *(far right)*.

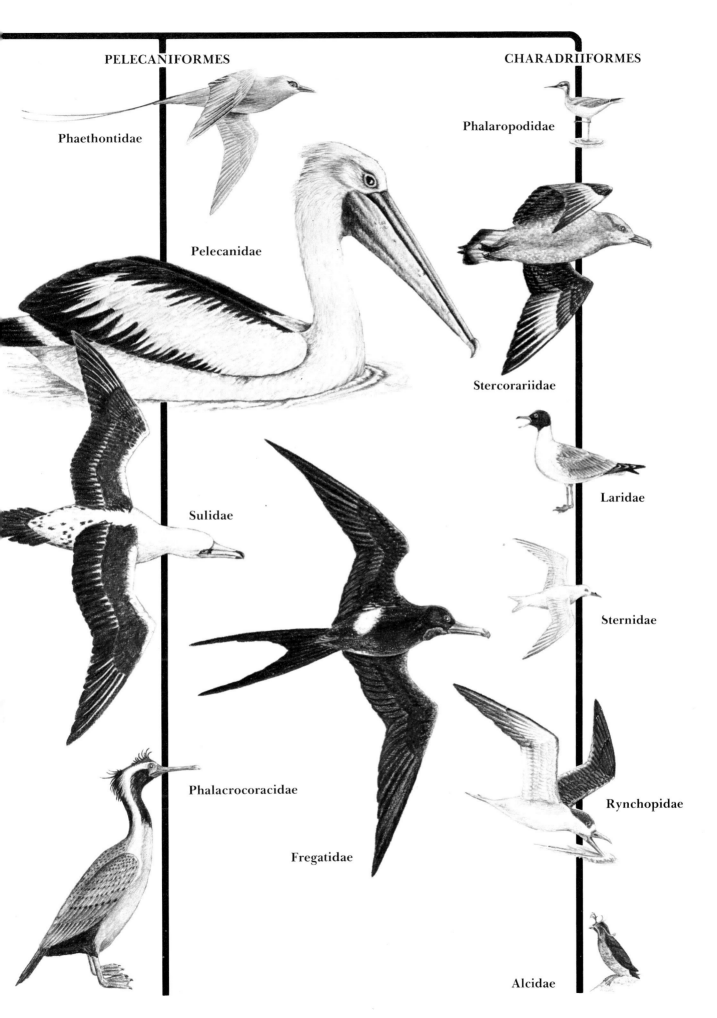

PELECANIFORMES

CHARADRIIFORMES

Phaethontidae

Phalaropodiidae

Pelecanidae

Stercorariidae

Sulidae

Laridae

Sternidae

Phalacrocoracidae

Rynchopidae

Fregatidae

Alcidae

17

Herring Gull *(Larus argentatus argentatus)*

Lesser Black-backed Gull *(Larus fuscus graellsii)*

In the distribution of a widespread species, there are often various populations which differ gradually in their properties, according to whether they live nearby or far apart—exhibiting what are sometimes called *clines.* As birds spread, the distribution may become crescent-shaped around a region which is unsuitable for living, and eventually ring-shaped so that the opposite ends meet. The Herring Gull *(above left)* is such a species. Part of its distribution is also inhabited by the Lesser Black-backed Gull *(above right),* which must be termed a distinct species since the two hybridize very little. Their respective subspecies have breeding ranges that are indicated on the map as follows.

Larus argentatus:
heuglini
argentatus
argenteus
atlantis
michahellis
cachinnans
mongolicus
taimyrensis
vegae
smithsonianus
Larus fuscus:
fuscus
intermedius
graellsii

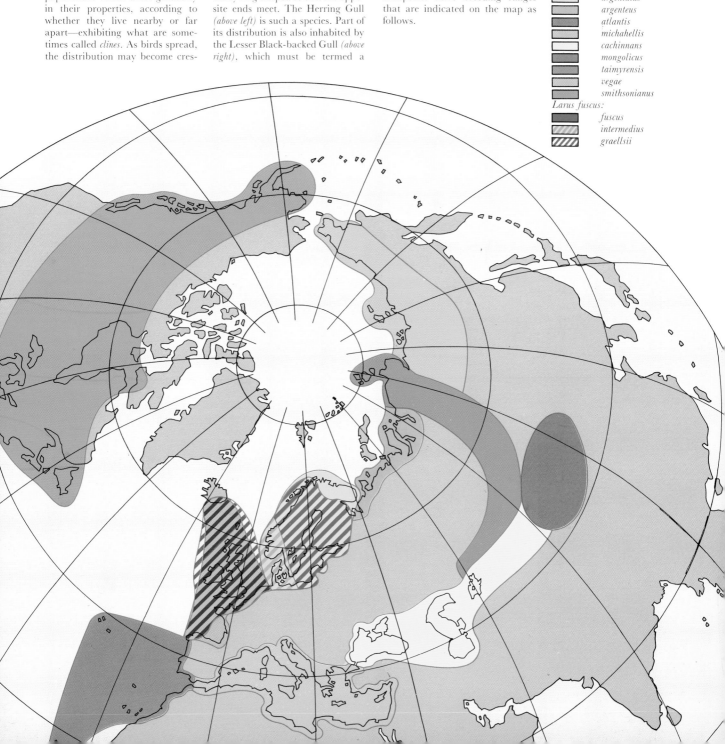

(*Opposite*) Where the ends of such a ring-shaped distribution meet, the bird populations may be too different in properties to interbreed. But interbreeding can occur between the more similar populations elsewhere along the ring, and this may allow a flow of genes (inherited features) around the ring, even from one end population to the other. Herring Gull subspecies differ as in colour of mantle and legs, size and amount and pattern of black and white on wing-tips. Their two main rings of distribution extend around Europe and around the Arctic Basin, with some breaks where very little gene exchange occurs. In northwestern Europe, *L.a. argentatus* and *argenteus* are not enough like their neighbours, *heuglini* and *atlantis*, to imply significant interbreeding with them: for instance, the legs of most adults are flesh-coloured in the former but yellow in the latter. However, the Lesser Black-backed Gull in that area has yellow legs in most adults; and two of its subspecies, *L.f. fuscus* and *graellsii*, are relatively similar to the neighbouring *L.a. heuglini* and *atlantis*, so probably interbreed with them to some extent along borders. Moreover, the subspecies of Herring Gulls in northwestern Europe are rather isolated genetically by the North Atlantic Ocean from the Herring Gulls in America. Yet these birds are all very similar—most adults have flesh-coloured legs in America and eastern

Siberia, too. The European birds probably once spread from America, and some flow of genes may still occur in this direction, as many birds are wind-driven across the Atlantic. In addition, there are other gulls with a close relation to the Herring Gulls, such as the Glaucous-winged Gull which hybridizes with those in western Canada, and the comparatively isolated Thayer's Gull and Iceland Gull. The many forms of gulls indicate that the type spread rapidly and not long ago, adapting to local conditions.

(*Below*) Marine iguanas in the Galapagos Islands are said to be purely herbivorous, but even very specialized animals sometimes turn to other food, and this iguana is competing with a Lava Gull over a dead fish. The iguana's forelimbs seem to have little in common with the wings of birds, yet fossils prove that these organs are *homologous*, having the same origin. Birds evolved from reptiles, in fact from some forms of dinosaurs: while they still lay eggs, their ancestral forelimbs have undergone profound evolution in becoming a means of flight.

Classification

Just as the species is the basic unit of evolutionary theory, so it is the basic unit in the classification of living things. This is true not only of modern taxonomy, but also of the nomenclature used by other cultures. The seabird known to science as the Northern Fulmar (*Fulmarus glacialis*) has been recognized as a distinct species by seafarers of many nationalities and languages. In modern scientific classification, this bird has a formal name of two words. The first word, *Fulmarus*, is the name of the genus to which this species belongs, while the second word, *glacialis*, is applied only to the Northern Fulmar.

This system of two-part names, called the "binominal system", was proposed in the mid-eighteenth century by the great Swedish botanist Carolus Linnaeus, and is still in use today. Every plant and animal species has such a name, usually of Latin or Greek origin, which applies to no other organism. The system is employed throughout the world, enabling all biologists to use a single name for each species. Moreover, many species contain distinct populations with separate geographical ranges. These subspecies or races are designated by a three-part name. Thus, one population of the Northern Fulmar that inhabits the North Atlantic is named *Fulmarus glacialis glacialis*, and is termed the nominate subspecies, while the slightly different population of the North Pacific is named *Fulmarus glacialis rodgersii*. This "trinominal system" was developed in the nineteenth century, after the theory of natural selection had been accepted and it was realized that slightly different populations could often be regarded as members of a single species.

Whether it is composed of subspecies or not, each species is assigned to a genus, the generic name forming the first part of the species' name. Whereas the species has a rather firm

Lava Gull (*Larus fuliginosus*)

Speciation

Museum specimens of two subspecies of the Soft-plumaged Petrel show differences in bill size and structure. Both subspecies breed in Madeira, the one with the smaller bill on mountaintops in the middle of the main island, and the other on the outlying Desertas with about two months' difference in the onset of breeding. Thus, although they occur in the same water areas, they are now reproductively isolated. *As their properties make ecological differences likely, they may well be in a process of* speciation. *Possibly they once competed for food in surrounding seas, leading to differentiation in ecology and bill structure, as birds with mixed*

properties and less specific breeding times would be less successful than the more specialized individuals. The latter would spread their genes to a greater extent, enabling a gradual character displacement to evolve. The two populations have nowadays been reduced through human activities, and are probably too small to have much effect on concentrations of food around the islands. Because they breed not far apart, some birds of one subspecies may start to breed in the colony of the other, and the success of the resulting hybrids will determine the future fate of these populations.

Study of terrestrial birds on such islands has often supported the "principle of competitive exclusion": complete competitors cannot coexist. *If two genetically isolated populations have the same type, place, and time of resource exploitation, and if the resource limits their population sizes, then this competition must be either given up or won—the two will undergo a displacement of characters, or else one of them will become extinct. This explains the important fact in biology that, in each ecologica! niche, we usually find only one species of a given kind of animal such as seabirds. While food is a common limiting factor, other resources can play a similar role, like the supply of suitable nesting sites. This has caused terns to disappear from many breeding islands which have rapidly expanding gull populations in recent years. But species can indeed coexist and use the same resources when population size is being limited by something else. This may be a hard pressure from predators, particularly if these are of less specialized kinds which can shift to different prey. In such a case, a great diversity of species in one ecological niche is easier to understand.*

biological basis, the genus is a more artificial category, and there is frequent disagreement as to the genus to which a particular species belongs. According to current views, the genus *Fulmarus* contains two species—the Northern Fulmar and the Southern Fulmar *(Fulmarus glacialoides)*, a bird of the cold seas of the Southern Hemisphere. The scientific name of a species thus serves as more than a mere name: it tells us something about the relationships of the bird.

Every species of living thing belongs to a genus, which includes its very close relatives if it has any. More distantly related species are placed in other genera. Among the genera containing birds akin to the two Fulmars are the genus *Macronectes*, consisting of the two species of giant petrels of the Southern Hemisphere, and the genus *Pagodroma*, which contains a single species, the all-white Snow Petrel *(Pagodroma nivea)* of the Antarctic. Three further genera *(Daption, Thalassoica, Halobaena)* comprise the other birds that are thought to be most closely allied to the two Fulmars.

More distantly related to them are various genera of shearwaters and petrels, such as *Calonectris* with two species, *Puffinus* with 12 species, *Pterodroma* with 25 species, and *Procellaria* with four species. All of these genera, and others besides them, are placed together in the family *Procellariidae*, whose name is based on the generic name *Procellaria*, and which includes the fulmars, shearwaters, petrels, and prions. Like the genus, the family is a somewhat subjective category; but among the seabirds, there are comparatively few cases in which authorities disagree on the limits of the families.

The family *Procellariidae*, with the albatrosses of the family *Diomedeidae*, the storm-petrels of the family *Hydrobatidae*, and the diving-petrels of the family *Pelecanoididae*, form a large assemblage known as the order *Procellariiformes*, whose name

is likewise derived from the genus *Procellaria*. The four families of this order contain the most oceanic of seabirds, a total of about 98 species that spend almost all of their time at sea and come ashore only to breed.

The *Procellariiformes*, together with the three other orders that contain seabirds—the *Sphenisciformes* (penguins), the *Pelecaniformes* (pelicans, cormorants, and related birds), and the *Charadriiformes* (phalaropes, gulls, terns, auks, and their allies)—and with 23 other orders of birds, make up the class *Aves*. This includes all birds, and is one of the several classes that make up the phylum *Chordata*. The latter, which also includes the mammals, reptiles, fishes, and smaller groups, is one of about 30 phyla that form *Animalia*, the Animal Kingdom, one of the primary divisions of living things.

Taxonomy, the grouping of species (and subspecies) into ever higher categories—genus, family, order, class, phylum, and finally kingdom—allows us to arrange living things in a clear and convenient sequence. The basis for the arrangement of the groups in this system is the degree of relationship between them. A judgement of how closely two species are related involves assumptions about their common ancestry: the more closely two species are related, the more recent is their descent from a common ancestor presumed to be. Such judgements rely heavily on the theory of natural selection and the modern biological concept of species, and form the subject of the field of systematics.

In the next chapter, we shall turn to the attributes of the 300-odd species of ocean birds, a kind of birds that—while adapting to what might seem to be a fairly uniform environment—displays a remarkable diversity of form, colour, ecology, and behaviour.

Chapter Two
THE PROPERTIES
OF OCEAN BIRDS

There are two kinds of answers to the question why a certain animal has the properties that it does. In explaining how an individual comes into being and develops, the combined effects of its inheritance and environment are investigated, as shown previously. What concerns us in this chapter is, rather, how the attributes of seabirds have evolved as a result of adaptive functions and value.

The adaptations of organisms serve two chief purposes: survival and maintenance of the individual, and successful reproduction. Our focus here is primarily upon the first subject and the ways in which seabirds interact with the environment, including other animals, while staying alive. This involves adaptations to the physical surroundings, for feeding, and for defence against enemies, as well as for cooperation among individuals. Success in these respects is essential for reproduction, which will be examined more fully in our discussions of behaviour and breeding, along with the distinctive properties used by seabirds when reproducing.

The physical environment

The oceans cover about seven tenths of the earth's surface. Some parts of the sea are highly productive of living organisms and, in several areas, as much so as the most bountiful regions on land. Yet only about 300 of all the 8,600 species of birds, or 3–4%, are seabirds. Conditions at sea are evidently not as diverse as those on land. Still, important differences between areas of the ocean do exist. To begin with, the steaming tropics contrast in climate with the cold Arctic and Antarctic. The former provide a relatively uniform ambience throughout the year, whereas profound changes occur from summer to winter at high latitudes. In the polar and cold temperate environments, variations of sunlight affect the aquatic life on which seabirds depend— not only by altering the water temperature, but also by determining the amount of photosynthesis that allows primary production in plants. Seabirds must adapt to the temperature itself, whether high or low, with regulating mechanisms that include physical and physiological properties as well as behaviour.

Winds may vary considerably over the oceans. In the low-pressure belt at 40–60° latitudes, strong and regular westerly winds prevail. Storms arise there, no less than in the tropics. Seabirds have to cope with temporary adverse conditions and, in areas with such winds, special adaptation can be seen in flying abilities. Both winds and waves, however, are sometimes not a problem but an aid to birds, which may use them to save energy during flight. In the tropical doldrums, other flight patterns are used as adaptations to weaker winds, for example in the soaring of frigate-birds.

Different, too, are the conditions in areas close to coasts, over continental shelves, and on the deep waters of the open ocean. Seabirds have adapted to these conditions as well, and some species are mainly coastal while others are oceanic. When all such geographical and climatic contrasts are taken into account, we see a more or less corresponding variety in the habitats to which seabird species have adapted. Certain species are confined to particular habitats, but many are comparatively opportunistic, with a wider range of surroundings.

Distinctive marine habitats offer different kinds of food, and there are degrees of specialization in the diets of seabirds, although the opportunists have not evolved particular "weapons" or other properties for feeding on a single type of prey. The prey itself must be able to survive as a rule, and many marine organisms have adaptations for avoiding predation by seabirds. Indeed, some predator–prey relationships occur among seabirds themselves, and the young of certain species are adapted for defence against predatory seabirds. Extensive feeding on eggs during breeding, and piratical stealing of food from other seabirds, are also observable. Thus, a constant aspect of life in the oceanic environment is mutual adaptation by its inhabitants, due to their co-evolution and to common dependence on the primary production of the seas.

General characteristics of birds

Birds of the land and sea exist in great numbers and diverse species in most parts of the world. Why have they been so successful as a group? The answer can probably be found in their ability to fly, and more exactly in their own device for flying—feathers. A basic advantage of flight is that it increases mobility, permitting animals to pursue prey and escape attack with speed and efficiency. The feathers of birds are very resistant to injury, and are replaced regularly, while a few broken wing-quills do not seriously hamper flight. And by laying eggs, a bird avoids carrying extra weight during reproduction, which would waste energy and reduce flying manoeuvrability.

The value of these properties is easily seen by comparing birds with other flying creatures. Bats, for example, have not met with equal success in their variety of species, habitats, and ecological niches. The reproduction of such mammals may seem much less vulnerable than that of birds, whose fragile eggs are exposed and require constant incubation. In addition, seabirds must use a lot of energy in transporting food for their young. However, bats must fly with the burden of carrying offspring while pregnant. The wings of bats are partly supported by the hind legs, restricting the latter for purposes like locomotion. A tear in the wing membrane of a bat will put an end to its flying career. It needs not only to live in a more protected manner than birds do, but also to find safe roosting sites, and the relative scarcity of these could be partially responsible for the lower success of bats.

The evolutionary ancestors of birds were reptiles, namely

World climate

Weather and climate are important factors in the environment to which seabirds have adapted by evolution. They arise mainly from the effects of the sun's warmth, the earth's shape and motion, the atmosphere, and the distribution of land and ocean areas. One result is the extreme seasonal variation of weather at high latitudes. Another is the prevalence of winds toward the east at high, and west at low, latitudes—for the earth spins eastward and its surface moves fastest at the equator. Some regions have fairly constant conditions, such as those of high pressure in subtropical latitudes with rather weak winds and little precipitation, or the trade-wind belts around the equator. But these sometimes have tropical storms, and in the low-pressure belts halfway to the poles it is autumn that brings the strongest storms, releasing much atmospheric energy stored during summer. The western Pacific and northern Indian Oceans have unusually variable wind directions and precipitation through monsoons. Such complexities in world climate are largely reflected by the diversity of seabirds.

Atmospheric-pressure and wind features at the earth's surface are shown on this map for the month of January, as averages during the first half of our century. Such features for July indicate little seasonal difference in many parts of the world, particularly in the Southern Hemisphere with its stabilizing ocean masses. But the northern seas in summer have higher pressures, while the monsoon winds then blow north towards the Asian continent.

H	high-pressure centre
L	low-pressure centre
→	prevailing wind direction

High Arctic zone
Low Arctic zone
Subarctic (Boreal) zone
North Subtropic zone
Tropic zone
South Subtropic zone
Subantarctic zone
Antarctic zone

(1) The external parts and feathers of a bird constitute its topography: *(a)* back, *(b)* neck, *(c)*, nape, *(d)* ear, *(e)* crown, *(f)* cheek, *(g)* forehead, *(h)* eye, *(i)* mandibles of bill, *(j)* chin, *(k)* throat, *(l)* breast, *(m)* belly, *(n)* flank, *(o)* rump, *(p)* legs, *(q)* webs, *(r)* toes, *(s)* tail; *(t)* primary and *(u)* secondary feathers, *(v)* scapulars, *(w)* wing and *(x)* tail coverts.

(2) A bird's respiratory system, seen in this simplified diagram, consists of several air sacs, the anterior *(a)* and the posterior *(b)* ones, as well as two lungs *(c)*, all connected to the main bronchus *(d)* from the throat *(e)*. Two whole cycles of respiration, by inspiring *(A)* and expiring *(B)*, are needed to move the gas through the entire system.

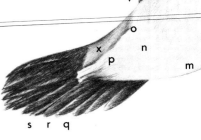

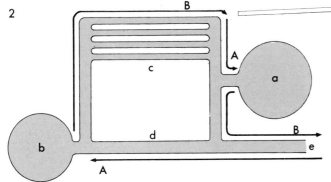

(3) A microscopic view of a bird's flight feather shows its amazing complexity. From the central shaft or rachis *(a)* extends, on each side, a row of barbs *(b)* which bear curved barbules *(c)*. The rearward barbules carry barbicels *(d)* that hook onto their forward neighbours, thus maintaining the feather's meshed structure.

3

some species of small dinosaurs that lived about 150 million years ago. This is confirmed by fossils such as *Archaeopteryx*, a primitive bird with feathers. Feathers were not the only physical adaptation that made flying possible. In fact, a few other early reptiles could fly, and feathers may first have evolved as a means of insulation rather than for flight. Fundamentally, the muscles and skeleton had to change in order to give the airborne animal a functional unity. The strength of breast muscles increased, and the skeleton became very light with air-filled cavities in the bones. The breathing apparatus also improved greatly in its exchange of gases, a development necessary for the energy of flight.

As a whole, the structure of a bird can be said to fulfill two requirements—high power and low weight. There are some limitations of size in birds, due to the methods which they have evolved for flying. Physical laws allow flight only within a particular range of sizes, below about 15 kg (33 lb). Very large flying birds such as albatrosses and condors rely upon an energy-saving soaring technique, while others like the swans remain swimming as they feed. Still, not all birds fly and, of those which have lost flying abilities, some have become quite large in the course of evolution. Among seabirds, the penguins provide good examples, and an Emperor Penguin weighs up to around 45 kg (100 lb). Yet 10–50 million years ago, a kind of penguin existed with a standing height of about 1.5 m (5 ft), nearly as tall as a man.

Further properties that characterize birds include a horny bill and legs with a tarsus, four toes, and claws. Some of these may be regarded as helping to solve the problem of flight, with lightness and functional compatibility of all body features. Excellent vision—which is generally essential to flying animals—as well as colour vision, and an acute sense of hearing, are also typical of birds, whereas the sense of smell is relatively little developed.

Adaptation by seabirds

If the common nature of birds, faced with the worldwide differences in physical conditions and ecological niches, eventually led to the great variation of bird species, the difficulties of such adaptation are clear in the case of seabirds. These birds live and feed on the oceans, but are totally dependent on land for breeding, and some coastal species rely on land for roosting as well. They must cope with two distinctive environments, and perfect adjustment to both may be impossible. Certain species seem to have achieved a compromise between the requirements of land and sea, but many are adapted chiefly to life at sea and are awkward on land. Thus, they are vulnerable to terrestrial predators, and need protected breeding sites. It is for this reason that numerous seabird species breed on offshore islands, isolated headlands, or sandbars.

How birds survive

Let us first consider adaptations to the physical environment. Sea water has a much higher salt content than do the body liquids of birds, and no fresh water is available in the oceans. Even if seabirds normally do not drink sea water, some will inevitably be swallowed along with their food. Moreover, the salt content of the food of seabirds is comparable to that in the birds themselves. Excretion of excess salt is therefore necessary, but is beyond the capacity of the kidneys. This problem is solved, in seabirds, by special salt glands. These are located in the skull, above or in front of the eyes. The excreted liquid, with its high concentration of sodium chloride, normally pours out through the mandible and drips off the tip of the bill. In some petrel species, we

How seabirds get rid of ingested salt was unknown until recently, as their kidneys are much less efficient than those of mammals. The salt glands in a seabird's skull are similar in some ways to mammalian kidneys, but function only when the bird needs to excrete excessive salt—as after intensive feeding at sea. The shape and position of the glands differ somewhat between species, those of a gull being being illustrated below *(a)*. A gland has many parallel lobes, each with thousands of tiny tubes which take in salt from the bird's blood as it circulates past them.

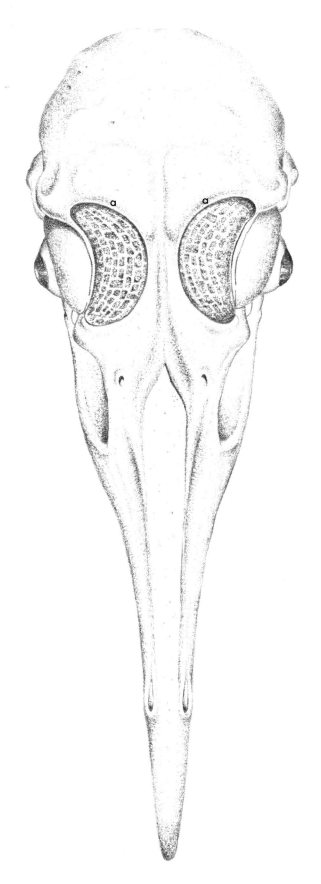

The solution from the salt glands, even more concentrated than sea water, flows to the nasal cavity. How it is usually eliminated by dripping off the tip of the bird's bill is shown by a fulmar petrel. Seabirds are often observed to shake their heads and this can help to throw off the salty drops. Some seabirds also drink fresh water at times, enabling their salt balance to be maintained more easily than through excretion of salt.

even find that birds can eject droplets into the air through their tube-shaped nostrils.

Certain seabirds will indeed drink fresh water if it is available. Many gulls, for example, regularly visit freshwater lakes or streams for drinking and bathing, as do the oceanic kittiwakes during breeding periods. However, strictly oceanic species often have no such habits. Occasionally, sick or exhausted petrels and shearwaters come to rest on ships, and may stay on board for several days, accepting food offered to them, while totally refusing to drink fresh water.

Temperature regulation

All birds lack sweat glands, but evaporation of water in other ways removes heat from their bodies. This process can be increased, to prevent overheating, by means of rapid panting or gular fluttering. Especially on breeding grounds in the tropics, overheating is a great risk. Abbott's Booby of Christmas Island in the Indian Ocean has actually been reported to evert its cloaca in order to increase the surface for evaporative cooling. Yet temperature regulation in seabirds mainly involves insulation against a cold environment. Such is the case particularly for birds that spend much time in the water or in the cooler latitudes. Hence, the body feathers of most seabird species consist of a very dense layer, whose water-resistant properties are improved by oil that is spread out from the preen gland—located just above the base of the tail—during feather-preening. The feathers hold a layer of still air close to the skin, and air is a poor heat-conductor. In very cold conditions, birds may increase this layer's thickness by fluffing out their feathers, especially when motionless. Penguins, tubenoses, and sea ducks also conserve heat with a layer of fat inside the skin.

While body temperature is regulated largely by physical properties and involuntary processes, it is adjusted to some extent by behavioural adaptations, such as seeking shade on breeding grounds in hot climates. These adaptations are quite important for the heat regulation of small chicks, whose survival may require protective behaviour on the part of parents. In cold weather, the parents can cover chicks with their bodies and feathers, whereas shelter from the sun can be offered by the same means in hot weather. Likewise, the young of Emperor Penguins, in the freezing Antarctic winter, huddle together in sizeable groups to avoid loss of heat. The choice of nest sites may also be connected with heat regulation. For instance, the habit of digging burrows to nest in—an interesting illustration of how organisms adjust the environment to themselves, rather than the reverse—is valuable to many seabird species as a protection against weather conditions, as well as against predators.

All seabirds have webs on their feet, although some, like the frigate-birds and phalaropes, have only small webs. When this naked skin comes into contact with cool water or ground, a loss of heat is avoided by a remarkable adaptation: regulation of blood flow through the so-called *rete mirabile* in the legs, a complex network of blood vessels which functions as a heat-exchanger. Here, blood flowing out to the feet is cooled by blood flowing in from the feet, which in turn is warmed. The feet can thus be kept at a temperature close to that of the environment without any heat loss from the body. If a need arises for removal of excess heat, the feet can also be useful by receiving a greater flow of warm blood. In such circumstances, some seabirds even excrete onto their legs and webbed feet, to increase cooling by evaporation of moisture.

Waved Albatross *(Diomedea irrorata)*

Many seabirds have adapted poorly to existence on land, breeding in relatively inaccessible places. Difficulties of locomotion on the ground are apparent in the clumsy "sway-walk" of the Waved Albatross, which it also uses during displays.

Since the evaporation of water *(bottom)* requires energy, it can take heat from body surfaces, thus limiting their temperature in hot conditions. This occurs through sweating in mammals, but the same effect in seabirds is illustrated by the Common Cormorant, which flutters its gular skin to aid evaporation of internal moisture and lower its blood temperature.

Common Cormorant
(Phalacrocorax carbo)

26

Black-browed Albatross *(Diomedea melanophris)*

The webbed feet of seabirds probably evolved as aids to swimming, but they now play many roles and beautifully exemplify the phenomenon of multifunctionality. A subadult Black-browed Albatross *(above)* may brake during flight with its webs, and a puffin *(right)* can use them to steer or to increase its lifting surface at slow speeds. Other seabirds may employ their feet to patter the water while feeding by dipping, or to run over the water and gain speed during take-off. The webs of some seabirds even help to keep their eggs warm during incubation.

(Below) Insulation against colder surroundings—the main problem of temperature regulation for seabirds—often includes keeping their feet inside the body feathers when flying, as with the Iceland Gull.

Atlantic Puffin *(Fratercula arctica)*

Iceland Gull *(Larus glaucoides)*

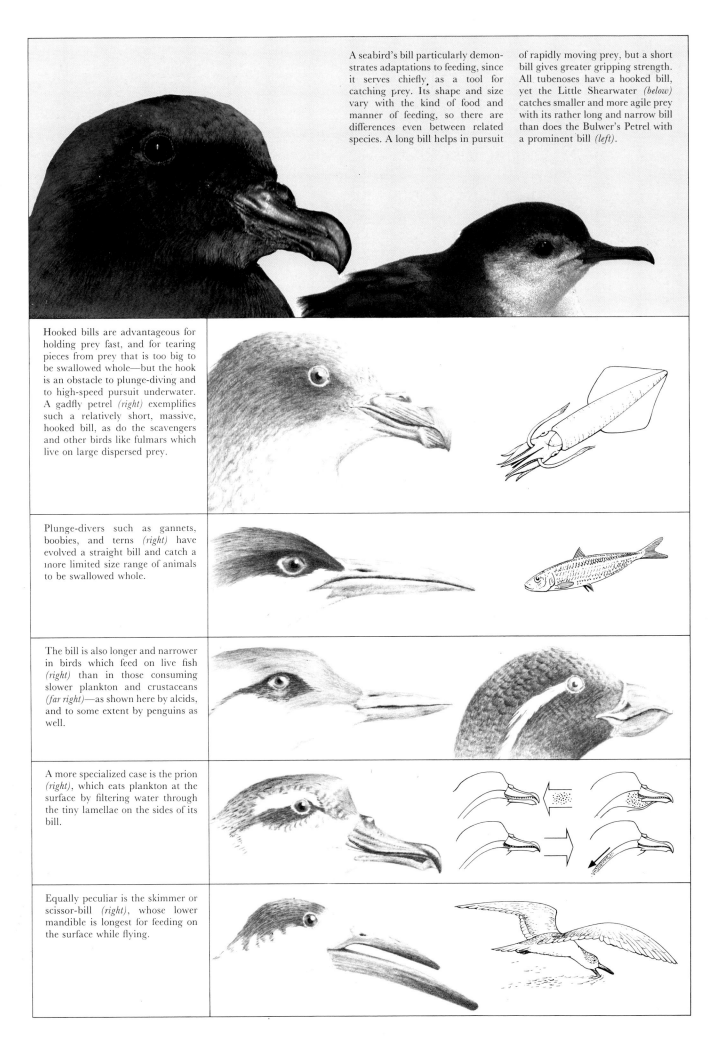

A seabird's bill particularly demonstrates adaptations to feeding, since it serves chiefly as a tool for catching prey. Its shape and size vary with the kind of food and manner of feeding, so there are differences even between related species. A long bill helps in pursuit of rapidly moving prey, but a short bill gives greater gripping strength. All tubenoses have a hooked bill, yet the Little Shearwater *(below)* catches smaller and more agile prey with its rather long and narrow bill than does the Bulwer's Petrel with a prominent bill *(left)*.

Hooked bills are advantageous for holding prey fast, and for tearing pieces from prey that is too big to be swallowed whole—but the hook is an obstacle to plunge-diving and to high-speed pursuit underwater. A gadfly petrel *(right)* exemplifies such a relatively short, massive, hooked bill, as do the scavengers and other birds like fulmars which live on large dispersed prey.

Plunge-divers such as gannets, boobies, and terns *(right)* have evolved a straight bill and catch a more limited size range of animals to be swallowed whole.

The bill is also longer and narrower in birds which feed on live fish *(right)* than in those consuming slower plankton and crustaceans *(far right)*—as shown here by alcids, and to some extent by penguins as well.

A more specialized case is the prion *(right)*, which eats plankton at the surface by filtering water through the tiny lamellae on the sides of its bill.

Equally peculiar is the skimmer or scissor-bill *(right)*, whose lower mandible is longest for feeding on the surface while flying.

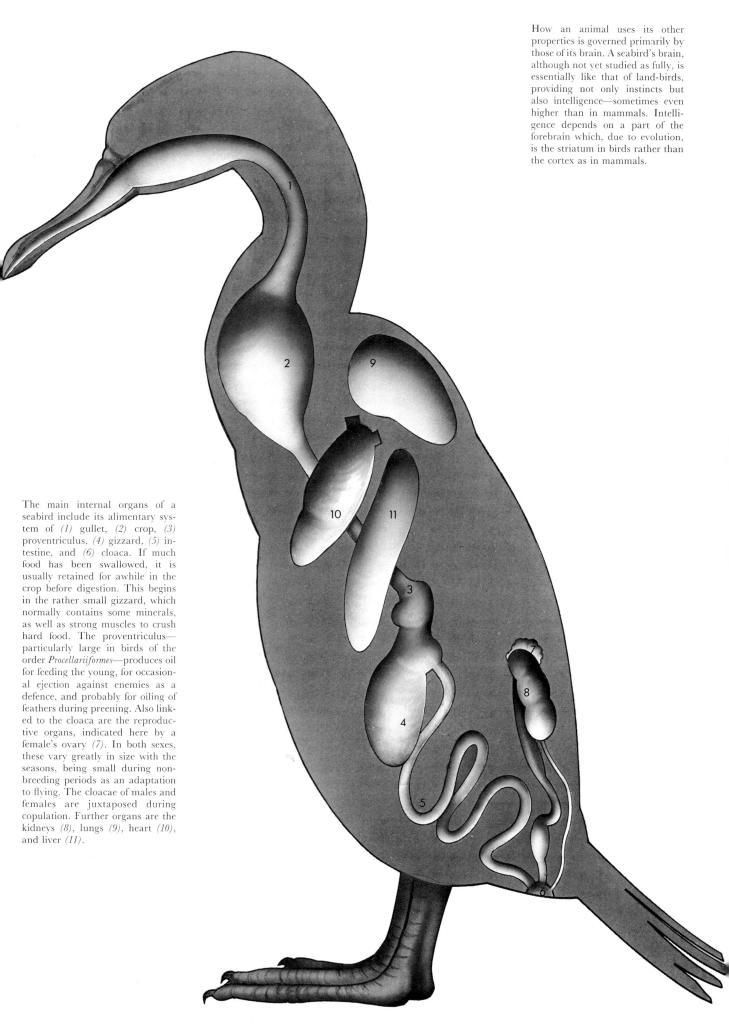

How an animal uses its other properties is governed primarily by those of its brain. A seabird's brain, although not yet studied as fully, is essentially like that of land-birds, providing not only instincts but also intelligence—sometimes even higher than in mammals. Intelligence depends on a part of the forebrain which, due to evolution, is the striatum in birds rather than the cortex as in mammals.

The main internal organs of a seabird include its alimentary system of *(1)* gullet, *(2)* crop, *(3)* proventriculus, *(4)* gizzard, *(5)* intestine, and *(6)* cloaca. If much food has been swallowed, it is usually retained for awhile in the crop before digestion. This begins in the rather small gizzard, which normally contains some minerals, as well as strong muscles to crush hard food. The proventriculus—particularly large in birds of the order *Procellariiformes*—produces oil for feeding the young, for occasional ejection against enemies as a defence, and probably for oiling of feathers during preening. Also linked to the cloaca are the reproductive organs, indicated here by a female's ovary *(7)*. In both sexes, these vary greatly in size with the seasons, being small during non-breeding periods as an adaptation to flying. The cloacae of males and females are juxtaposed during copulation. Further organs are the kidneys *(8)*, lungs *(9)*, heart *(10)*, and liver *(11)*.

Many seabird species have certain properties with clear signal functions, particularly when communicating for reproduction. A striking instance *(left)* is the Red-billed Tropic-bird with its conspicuous tail-streamers.

Plumage may serve as a hunting camouflage by enabling a bird to approach prey which have good vision and are mobile enough to escape. The immature Wandering Albatross *(below)* is mainly brownish above, but its white underwings and face make it harder to detect against the sky and water as seen from below. Seabirds that hunt by plunge-diving are also often white on their frontal parts and undersides, as shown by the South American Tern *(opposite left)*. Many terns have a black cap, probably with some signal function during breeding, but a majority of these acquire a white front at other times.

Red-billed Tropic-bird *(Phaethon aethereus)*
Wandering Albatross *(Diomedea exulans)*

Herring Gull *(Larus argentatus)*

Like this Herring Gull not yet fledged *(above)*, most young gulls have a protective camouflage which makes them hard to detect against the ground. They normally retain it for a long period as immatures after being fledged.

South American Tern *(Sterna hirundinacea)*

Feeding methods

The multifunctional character of many seabird properties is well exemplified by the fact that adaptations often concern the search for food in addition to coping with physical conditions. Birds such as the cormorants use their webbed feet to dive and swim underwater in pursuit of food. Webbed feet are equally useful for running on the water surface during take-off, and are employed for flight in manoeuvres like braking.

Among storm-petrels that frequently trip or patter on the water while feeding, the legs have sometimes become very enlarged. But their muscle power has not evolved correspondingly, and the legs cannot bear the full weight of the bird on land. Various other seabirds exhibit comparable maladaptations to life on land. Thus, many species in the order *Procellariiformes*, the tubenoses, push themselves forward on their bellies over the ground, or walk slowly and awkwardly. Birds that dive and swim much underwater tend to have their feet placed far backward on the body, giving them a rather upright stance when standing and walking upon land. Difficulties in walking are common, and penguins occasionally even propel themselves on their bellies over snow by means of their wings.

Flying abilities may be as poorly adapted to conditions on land as they are well-suited to life at sea. Some seabirds consume highly dispersed food, in localities which are separated by vast areas of ocean: this is made possible in part by a soaring flight over the waves to conserve energy. Many albatrosses, fulmars, and petrels fly in such a way and, with their long narrow wings, represent the perfect gliders. Yet they are clumsy in landing and taking off at breeding grounds, rendering them slow and inefficient in encounters with terrestrial predators.

Techniques of pursuing and catching food differ widely between the seabird types. The structure and size of a bird is, indeed, a reflection of its feeding methods and kind of prey. Gannets and boobies, for instance, dive straight down into the water—sometimes from great heights with enormous speed—to take food, generally fish. For this purpose they have a long pointed bill, binary vision to measure distances accurately, and air-sacs under the skin to cushion their impact on the water surface. At the moment of impact, they become spear-shaped by folding their wings directly backward, a shape permitted by the build of skeleton and muscles.

Of seabirds that dive and swim below the water surface, some use their wings for propulsion underwater as if flying. While large wings are unsuitable in this case, flight in the air is not easy with small wings, which must move at relatively high speeds, and which create problems in landing or taking off. Many shearwaters dive and swim underwater with their wings, whereas the gadfly petrels do not dive and have larger wing areas. Other examples are the auks and diving-petrels. During moult, these birds often lose their flying abilities altogether for a certain period. As we shall see, a compromise between flying and diving with regard to wing area is difficult to reach in heavy seabirds, which therefore either fly and feed at the surface, or dive and remain flightless with small wings. Total inability to fly is a characteristic evolved by penguins, as well as by the Great Auk and the Flightless Cormorant. Although cormorants use their feet underwater, instead of wings, a problem of excessive buoyancy seems to be created by the large wings, as quantities of air are held in the feathers. A cormorant's solution is apparently to soak the wing feathers, its body feathers being waterproof—but such soaking causes additional difficulties in flight, and forces the bird to spend time on land for drying its wings.

In contrast to properties which involve compromises between different requirements are those that arise from simple adaptation to specific needs. In regard to feeding, some seabirds are conspicuous exceptions to the general rule that birds have a poor sense of smell. The tubenoses include species with a fairly keen sense of smell, having adapted to feeding on prey of sporadic local occurrence. Such are the scavenging seabirds that consume large decaying animals, like giant petrels. They must usually fly around a lot in search of isolated meals, and a good olfactory sense is clearly of value to them.

We also find specific adaptations in the sizes of birds and in their bill shapes. The type and size of food worth pursuing are a result of what may be called cost/benefit relations. In the order *Procellariiformes*, a size ratio of more than 300:1 exists between the largest albatrosses and the smallest storm-petrels. This is reflected in their diets, with the former living mainly on squid and the latter on tiny plankton. Birds that are not so specialized, however, have a bill structure that corresponds to their more varied diet. In gulls, the bill tends to be moderately long and slightly hooked, while the body form and flying abilities suit a more general choice of feeding methods. This may include scavenging on a broad range of foods, and plunge-diving like terns, although gulls are less efficient in such techniques than the specialists.

A curious fact about feeding adaptations is that birds have no molar teeth for crushing food, as mammals often do. Instead, they swallow coarse sand or pebbles of appropriate sizes, which are held in the "gizzard", a part of the stomach enveloped by strong muscles, whose rhythmic contractions crush swallowed food. But many seabirds spend their lives mainly over the open oceans: where do they find pebbles? Great Shearwaters have been caught in Newfoundland waters with small stones of volcanic origin in their gizzards, and no such minerals exist in that area. Since they breed in the volcanic islands of Tristan da Cunha in the South Atlantic, and regularly migrate to the North Atlantic, the birds apparently collect these pebbles on their breeding grounds. Like a lot of other migratory seabird species, Great Shearwaters number in the millions. Evidently, a vast transport of minerals across the oceans is managed by birds which, through their deaths, spread stones from diverse regions onto the sea floors and occasionally even to distant land areas!

Problems of reproduction

Seabirds reproduce on land, and must be capable of reaching it from the air or water. Some powers of movement on the ground are also required in most cases, although frigate-birds, for example, usually just perch and take off from their nest sites. The claws on the toes of seabirds are generally rather small and serve little purpose while at sea. But claws give a firmer grip on branches or when walking on land, and may—like strong bills—be essential to the many seabirds that dig burrows.

Feeding at sea, and sometimes at very great distances from breeding sites, means that birds need a reliable way of transporting food to their offspring. Often it is carried in their bills, or lower down in the crop, a part of the lower esophagus. The big pouch of a pelican normally functions as a kind of fishing-net during feeding. Meals or nesting materials are occasionally transported in the pouch, but as a rule the crop is employed to carry food. Among other seabirds, many small alcids have acquired rather large throat-pouches to convey quantities of food from the seas. The most oceanic birds of all—the tubenoses—have evolved a highly specialized organ which is not found in any other birds: the big proventricular oil gland that secretes an energy-rich liquid for feeding the young. This oil, analogous to the milk of mammals, diminishes the "cost" of transporting nutrients over long distances. For oils and fats contain more energy in relation to weight than does the usual food of seabirds, which is composed to a great extent of water.

Reproduction demands coordination in the behaviour and physiological activities of the two sexes, as well as in the behaviour of parents and offspring. This is effected through communication—or signalling behaviour—which may require special organs, structures, or colours. Some seabird species communicate extensively with sounds, and many are quite vocal on breeding grounds, but most are rather silent at sea. Thus, the sound-generating organs can be viewed as a property evolved chiefly for use during reproduction. Sounds are created mainly by vocal cords in the syrinx, near the bifurcation of the windpipe into its two bronchi. Certain species also make sounds by other means, such as bill-clapping. Good examples of communicative structures are the long tail-streamers of skuas and tropic-birds, the bright-red inflated throat-pouches of frigate-birds, and the high and brilliantly hued bill of puffins.

Colour and plumage

Protection of the skin and conservation of heat were probably the chief reasons for evolution of feather-like structures in the ancestors of birds. The body feathers still fulfill these original functions, as well as allowing birds to fly. But there are additional features—such as pigmentation—which enable birds to make use of their feathers, and which in some cases are peculiar to seabirds. Particularly when explaining pigmentation as a result of adaptation, we should keep various possibilities in mind. Feathers may have a certain colour because of its own advantages, or because this colour is the result of a different characteristic with advantages, or simply because no other colour would have adaptive value. Totally unpigmented feathers are whitish, due to their construction and material.

The most common dark pigment in bird feathers is melanin. This substance protects feathers against wearing, rendering them stronger and more durable. Thus many seabirds have black tips, relatively resistant to wear, on wing feathers that are otherwise pale. Dark pigments serve as protection from sunlight, whose rays of greatest energy—like ultraviolet—have an aging and decaying impact upon the skin and feathers. A dark surface absorbs visible light easily and radiates it again as heat energy, whereas a light-coloured surface must reflect it. On the other hand, concealed feathers are often unpigmented and whitish, close to the body and on the inner parts of quills. Many seabirds are white on their undersides, which have least exposure to sunlight. In such cases, this colour may mean only that pigmentation would have no adaptive advantage, just as it has none for the skeleton.

According to a generalization known as "Gloger's Rule", animals living in areas with high humidity tend to be darker than similar animals in drier areas. This phenomenon has never been fully explained, but the reason may be that dark colours help in radiating excessive heat, where the high humidity makes evaporation of water less efficient for cooling. Since they also maximize the absorption of light energy, dark colours increase the body temperature if much sunlight prevails—but a great degree of cloud cover is usually associated with very high humidity, and the balance in animals can favour heat loss over heat gain. Likewise,

whitish colours may preserve body heat in dry and cold regions such as the Arctic and Antarctic. This could even account for concealed feathers which are white on many birds in those regions.

Camouflage

If a white seabird is hard to notice aginst the polar snows, it is equally true that camouflage and the need to hide are a frequent cause of pigmentation in feathers. This may explain a good deal about the colour patterns found in seabirds, although there are often difficulties in determining the most important factor in the evolution of a particular colour, and in deciding whether more than one factor has contributed to that adaptation. Indeed, two main types of camouflage can be distinguished and, as they often resemble each other, both of them are probably responsible for the plumage colours of many seabird species.

One type, a *protective camouflage*, makes a bird more difficult for its enemies or resource competitors to detect. The second type, a *hunting camouflage*, makes it easier for the bird, as a predator, to approach prey without being detected. The relation between these types, of course, depends on the physical surroundings and visual abilities of other animals. Since a bird is very unlikely to interact with the same kind of animal and environment in all situations, there is no reason to expect that a single sort of camouflage would fulfill every requirement. Thus, interesting examples are provided by parts of the plumage in numerous seabirds. Plunge-divers such as terns, gulls, gannets, and boobies are light-coloured on the underside and, commonly, also on the leading edges of the wings and on the head. This is presumably a hunting camouflage which renders the birds less conspicuous against the light sky and water surface, as seen by marine creatures from below.

Varieties of seabird plumage

The colours of seabirds are normally somewhat more dull than those of many land-birds. Three types of colour are dominant—white, greyish, and dark brown to blackish—occasionally in diverse patterns of the plumage. The following general cases should be discussed before we consider groups of birds within a species.

Medium to light greyish above, and whitish below

When the sun or sky illuminates a bird with greyish upperparts, and its whitish underparts remain in shade, both sides acquire the same greyish appearance: the bird is "countershaded" and blends with lightish or greyish backgrounds. Such conditions occur on sandy shores, mud banks, and water areas with much cloud cover or fog, especially in combination with weak winds which give the water a light-greyish tone. Just as the world's navies have found that greyish colours are the best camouflage for vessels, this pattern functions chiefly as a protective camouflage in birds. It may guard them not only against predators, but also in resource competition against other birds of the same or different species. The pattern is very common among shore-dwellers, for birds of the land as well as seabirds. Many of the latter live in temperate latitudes, where the low-pressure belt makes clouds and fogs frequent, while far fewer tropical and Arctic or Antarctic species have this pattern.

Dark brown to black above, and light below

A darker contrasting plumage also permits countershading. Although the pigmentation on the upperparts of birds is partly explained by sunlight protection and resistance to

Razorbill *(Alca torda)*

Black-faced Cormorant *(Phalacrocorax fuscescens)*

Northern Gannet *(Sula bassana)*

Brown Booby *(Sula leucogaster)*

Many seabirds which swim and hunt underwater are very dark above and white below, the Razorbill and the Black-faced Cormorant *(opposite)* being illustrative. Similar colour patterns often occur on fish, and the multifunctional purpose of such a hunting and protective camouflage is likely in both cases, for seabirds are also vulnerable to aquatic predators.

The colour pattern of brown to black above, with white on the undersides, is found in numerous seabird species such as the Brown Booby *(above)*.

Among the many seabird species which are mainly all-dark is the Grey Gull *(right)*.

The gannet is mainly white when adult and dark when immature, with intermediate forms as in the subadult *(opposite, bottom right)*. Various reasons have been sug-

gested for the evolution of a mainly white plumage in such seabirds. For example, "phaneric colouration" of an adult would make it conspicuous and summon conspecifics when it finds food, which might be a "benefit to the species". However, this colour could also summon competitors of other species, while genetic mutation might allow a bird to retain immature plumage in adult life and have a further advantage of not summoning competitors. Instead, there may simply be little advantage for adults in having their feathers pigmented.

Grey Gull *(Larus modestus)*

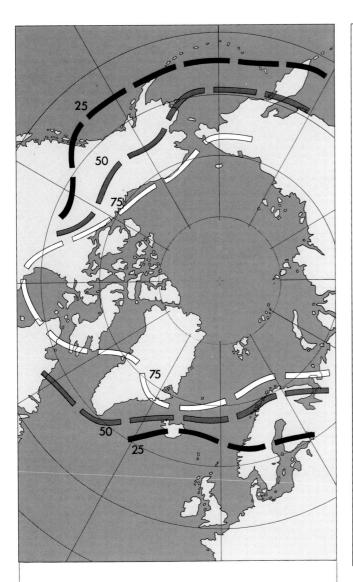

Polymorphism is still often hard to explain, but genetic and environmental factors mentioned in Chapter 1 indicate several basic reasons. In the diagram opposite, thicker or broken arrows show a relative advantage or disadvantage in the inheritance of some traits. (1) Different genes in a species may be neutral *with no relative advantage for survival or reproduction. Thus, if genes causing different morphs are not eliminated, the species may continue to be polymorphic. (2) Sometimes the heterozygotes, carrying different alleles of a gene, are more successful in life and reproduction than homozygotes. Then no alleles will be eliminated, and the species may have a* stable polymorphism *with constant proportions of various birds. (3) If a new mutant gene occurs, it may have advantagaeous effects and spread in the population until most individuals possess it. Polymorphism exists during this period of* species evolution, *although such a slow process may seldom apply to the colouring of seabirds. (4) The mutant gene may instead give individuals a disadvantage. But if the latter is small—especially when the mutant allele is recessive and has effects only in homozygotes—there will be a* slow elimination *of the mutant. The resulting polymorphism may even be stable due to rates of mutation and elimination. (5) A species with a wide geographical distribution, adapting to different local environments, may produce a uniform subspecies in each area. Gene flow across the borders can make each area's population somewhat* polytypic *with further variations. The occurrence of different morphs may even change gradually in frequency from one end of the distribution to the other. Such is the polymorphism in certain seabirds like the Arctic Skua and Common Guillemot, although it is not quite clear whether they are adapted to local conditions in their end-areas.*

Polymorphism

Some seabird species are termed polymorphic *because they have two or more different forms, or morphs, of colouring. Extreme polymorphism is illustrated by the Arctic Skua, which varies continuously from all-dark colouring to all-white undersides. The light phase occurs in increasing percentage towards the north (see numbers on the map above), suggesting geographic differences in natural selection pressures. Other factors seem to conflict: the females apparently prefer dark males, yet light-phase birds begin to breed earlier in life and they may have a greater lifetime breeding success than the dark birds. Some environmental conditions have evidently changed with time, and this species as a whole could be evolving towards light birds, whose proportion is slowly growing in the north.*

wear, as mentioned already, this plumage may in addition serve as a protective and hunting camouflage. For example, underwater swimmers are seldom greyish and tend to be dark, often black, on their upperparts. In the upper layers of sea water, their background looks dark from above, so they can blend in with it. Moreover, the sea surface looks quite light from below and, when these birds are swimming or resting upon it, their light underparts can prevent detection by marine predators such as large fish or leopard seals.

Generally dark brown to black

Apart from protection against sunlight and wear, dark pigmentation of the whole plumage is a protective camouflage for species that rest on dark ground or feed along dark-coloured shores. This is equally true of many chicks and immatures, as they probably need time to learn skills for avoiding predators, so that such camouflage is of greater value to them than to adults—and it has been found among some gulls that the immatures are more shore-dwelling than the adults. A similar advantage may exist for dark birds that are active at night, depending on the amount of light from the moon and stars. However, a case such as that of gulls and terns, in which the rather dark species occur primarily in the tropics, can be explained as adaptation for protection from sunlight and for heat regulation in humid areas, not as an example of camouflage in dark surroundings.

Generally white

In the whitish environments of the Arctic and Antarctic, white colours of animals may serve for either protective

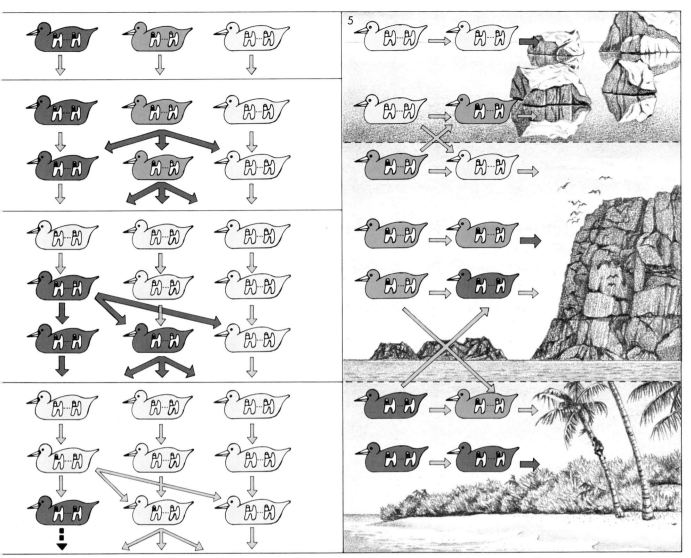

camouflage or heat regulation, and there is controversy as to which of these factors has been of greatest importance in evolution. A few white species of seabirds live in the same regions—for instance some Arctic gulls, the Snow Petrel of the Antarctic, and a colour-phase of the Giant Petrel. More broadly, if birds of different sizes are compared, it is found that small ones with wholly or mainly white plumage are rare. But a number of very large birds are chiefly white: examples among seabirds are some pelicans, gannets, and adult Wandering Albatrosses. This does not seem to be connected with differences in climate, so heat regulation is probably not involved, but the need for protection may well depend on the size of the bird. A case of special interest is the all-white colour of the White Tern, whose highly translucent wings should be valuable as a hunting camouflage against light skies and water surfaces.

Plumage distinctions within a species

Some detailed differences between individuals in a species are related to reproduction. Particularly important are those between the sexes, the main age groups, and the periods of breeding or non-breeding.

Males and females

It is fairly common among birds for the males to differ from females in colour, structure, or size, and the males are often more colourful than females. Seabirds offer comparatively few such sexual differences of colour, but notable examples do occur. In frigate-birds, the males are generally dark, and females of most species tend to have some light colour on their underparts. The most spectacular distinction is a bright red throat-pouch exhibited by males during courtship, whereas females may show coloured eye-rings. Sexual differences of these kinds are usually connected with communication in displays, mate selection, and pair bonding. The pupil sizes differ between sexes of the Blue-footed Booby, and females are somewhat darker than males in the Wandering Albatross.

Very clear distinctions, with gaudy males, chiefly involve species with promiscuous relations between the sexes. This happens primarily when the males of a species do not participate in the rearing of offspring, and when only a few of the displaying males are selected by females for copulation. No such free and competitive type of reproduction exists among seabirds. As a rule, both parents contribute to rearing the offspring and, in many species, they remain faithful to each other or to nest sites, year after year. Phalaropes, which feed on the seas for nine or ten months of the year, but breed in Arctic marshes and ponds, reveal a peculiarity: the females depart from breeding areas soon after laying eggs, and leave incubation to the males. Here, the females are the most colourful, an exception to the normal rule in birds.

Adults and immatures

In all seabird species, the plumage develops from the moment when the eggs are hatched until the young are fledged and able to fly. Many species, breeding on open grounds, have downy young with a protective camouflage which makes them inconspicuous, as noted earlier. The

Red-footed Booby *(Sula sula)*
Common Guillemot *(Uria aalge)*

The Red-footed Booby *(above)* is an instance of polymorphism with a dark and a light phase. On dark-phase birds, the tail is also dark in the Galapagos Islands, although normally light elsewhere as in the Caribbean.

Polymorphism in the Common Guillemot consists of a bridled form as well as a non-bridled one. The first is rather rare in the southernmost parts of the range of the species, but it becomes gradually more frequent towards the north where about half of all birds are bridled in some colonies. This form, however, is less common in northern Iceland, where the species coexists with the Brünnich's Guillemot.

Pomarine Skua *(Stercorarius pomarinus)*
Galapagos Penguin *(Spheniscus mendiculus)*

Another example of extreme polymorphism is the Pomarine Skua,
which has a continuous variation
from all-dark colouring to all-white
undersides. Both light *(top right)*
and dark phases of this species may
be seen in winter quarters.

The Galapagos Penguin *(bottom
right)* follows a general rule that
immatures are duller in colour than
adults among penguins. Brighter
colours of an adult like this one
probably have some signal functions during breeding. Such age
differences of colour prevail in all
orders of seabirds except the *Procellariiformes*.

The male and the female Blue-footed Booby differ in apparent pupil size, because the female has dark pigment around her pupils. She is also somewhat larger than the male, but has a slightly shorter tail.

fledged immatures are very similar to the adults in some species, but different in others, and in most such cases they have duller colours.

Among penguins, the immatures tend to differ from adults in being duller, lacking the colours and structures which have signal functions in adults during breeding. Among the tubenoses, immatures are generally similar to adults, but have duller colours in many albatross species and, in a few, they take several years to develop full adult plumage. Adults and immatures are similar in other families of this order, except that immatures are darker in the two species of Giant Petrels. Numerous species are nocturnal on breeding grounds, and communicate mainly through sounds at night, with little need for visual communication. In all families of the order *Pelecaniformes*, differences related to age are found, the immatures normally being duller and darker, and sometimes more barred or spotted, although immature frigate-birds generally are lighter than adults. In the order *Charadriiformes*, the immature phalaropes are similar to non-breeding adults, but in other families—such as the gulls and terns—there are rather striking distinctions from adults: the immatures are duller, darker, more barred, or equipped with other kinds of plumage for protective camouflage against terrestrial backgrounds. The differences are less clear in alcids, and many species have immatures whose plumage is similar to that of the adults in winter.

Annual breeding periods
Particularly in higher latitudes with varying environmental conditions, many seabird species breed with an annual cycle, and this is often accompanied by changes in plumage. Thus,

a number of species in the order *Charadriiformes* possess a duller, more streaked, barred, or patchy plumage during non-breeding periods. Brown and Chilean Pelicans, as well as cormorants, exhibit analogous differences. One reason may be that conspicuous breeding plumages signal sexual readiness to mates. Such estimations of fitness are essential to success in reproduction, apart from the directly communicative functions of plumages during breeding. Another factor is probably the seasonal difference in ecological niche, and consequently in diet, which occurs during the reproductive cycle in some species—like the marsh terns—as they breed in terrestrial habitats but winter at sea.

Moult
All feathers of a bird are subject to wear. In flight, they rub against each other, hit various obstacles, and suffer minor accidents. Predators and competitors may inflict damage, while the sun and weather have an aging effect. Thus, the survival chances of a bird would diminish rapidly after it acquired feathers if they were not regularly replaced. During the process of moult, old feathers are dropped and new ones are acquired. A few other reasons for moult can be found in the need of some birds to have a special plumage when breeding.

Many problems must be solved by birds in connection with moult, and diverse "strategies" have been established in the course of evolution. A common strategy is to moult only a few feathers at a time, as a few missing feathers are not crucial for survival. In the case of quills in the tail and wings, such moulting often occurs in an orderly sequence. But some species lose all of the flight feathers at once, as in numerous alcids which thereby become flightless for up to two months. This does not markedly impair their feeding, since they dive and swim for food below the water surface, a method which is used even by penguins with rather small flippers.

Most birds breeding annually also have an annual moulting cycle, and this is the general rule for the schedule of moult. Some birds moult the body feathers twice each year, in conjunction with annual changes in plumage characteristics. However, a few species have cycles longer than a year, like the gannet which moults only three or four of its primary wing feathers each year. Certain tropical species with non-annual breeding cycles have less clear moulting cycles. Frigate-birds, for example, never moult when feeding their young, and the rearing of young takes at least a year or more. The amount of time used for moulting is related to food availability, and some bird species in high latitudes moult rather quickly in two to three months, although periods of three to five months are more common since these minimize the effect on powers of flight and hunting.

The time of year for moulting has a close association with both breeding and migration. Expenditure of energy on feathers as well as on care of offspring is disadvantageous, because excellent flying ability is needed when gathering food for the young. Therefore, moult during breeding is very unusual, despite its occurrence in a few tropical species. Impaired flight during long migratory journeys is equally unsuitable, and species with such a migration tend to moult during the static winter months, which also determine the birds' location when moulting.

Peculiar moulting cycles are often exhibited by immature birds before they come into phase with adults, since they are normally born at times when adults are not moulting. In some species, particularly of tropical semi-annually breeding birds, there are whole subpopulations with notable differences in moulting. Penguins, too, are unusual in that they feed heavily for a time after breeding—to attain a reserve layer of fat—and then go ashore to fast while moulting, replacing all of their feathers in three to four weeks.

Care of the body

Physical properties and their adaptations to the environment have been emphasized in this discussion so far. We may now focus upon adaptations in behaviour, a topic to be explored in other respects later. It should be remembered that not all of the activities taking place within an organism can be called behaviour. Processes of physiology also have important adaptive functions but are not behavioural.

Preening and oiling
The plumage needs frequent care for efficient heat regulation, proper flight, and making feathers durable and water-resistant. Various small interlocking parts of the feathers often become dislocated, minor injuries are incurred, and the finer structures must be restored. Sometimes, ectoparasites infest the plumage as well. Preening activities are an essential countermeasure. A bird grasps a feather in its bill, nibbling from the base to the tip or drawing the feather through its bill in one movement, to remove dirt and smooth the barbs so that they lock together. Often, the feathers are preened one by one in a systematic fashion through the entire plumage. Considerable time is spent on feather care—normally around two or three hours each day in breeding birds, and occasionally longer as, for instance, during moult.

Oiling is an associated activity, involving the oil gland (or preen gland) which is located above the base of the tail and

produces an oily secretion. The bird presses out some of the oil with its bill, and transfers it to the diverse feathers, sometimes also by rolling the back of the head onto the gland and then onto parts of the plumage. This gland is particularly well-developed within the orders *Procellariiformes* and *Pelecaniformes* and in numerous other aquatic birds. It is the only external gland in birds, except for certain small glands in the outer ear passages. The oil serves to make the plumage supple and waterproof, an essential property for aquatic birds as a whole. The oil also contains a substance that is converted to vitamin D by the influence of sunlight, and some of the oil is swallowed accidentally during preening or is absorbed by the skin. This process is still under investigation and possibly varies according to the species, but it is known that some birds acquire the symptoms of rickets when this gland is removed.

Birds often perform oiling while they are bathing, and the oil is probably spread more evenly if the plumage is damp. Bathing itself is an important activity in feather maintenance, as are scratching, stretching, and plumage-shaking. Scratching is an aid to care of the skin, and stretching can stimulate the circulation of body fluids, although the latter may not completely explain such acts as stretching the wings backward and yawning. A more curious kind of behaviour is sun-bathing with outstretched wings, seen especially in the order *Pelecaniformes*. This can be easily understood for the cormorants, which must dry their soaked tail and wing feathers after diving: they do so in cloudy weather as well as sunshine, and only their body feathers are waterproof. Yet no one knows exactly why young frigate-birds that have never been near water are also sun-bathers. Production of vitamin D in oiled feathers has been suggested, but measures against external parasites could be involved. Frigate-birds have poorly developed oil glands and very little oil on their plumage—they do not require a waterproof plumage, as they descend onto the water only by accident.

Some seabird species engage in mutual preening. This plays a significant role in pair bonding, although there may be additional functions involved. One of these is probably the removal of parasites, which are difficult for a bird to reach on its head, especially the top, in spite of frequent scratching by the feet or rubbing against other parts of the plumage. Such cooperation is facilitated by the fact that birds engage in feather care mainly when standing on the ground or on floating objects, or while swimming on the sea. However, the aerial seabirds also direct some care to plumage when in the air. They employ their feet for head-scratching, and use of the bill can create truly acrobatic manoeuvres. Almost all feathers except the quills of the wings and tail may be tended in this way. While doing so, the birds simply glide without flapping their wings, an ample proof of their marvellous balance and flight control.

Weather protection
Strong winds and storms are normal phenomena in seabird environments, and birds show various adaptations to them. Dispersal and migratory movements, in general, are a kind of adaptive behaviour related to environmental conditions of longer duration. For temporary protection, many seabirds seem to avoid storm centres by flying parallel to the waves, a course that makes them travel in a circle around such centres. When resting in strong winds, both on land and on the water, a bird normally faces into the wind in order to prevent heat loss or dislocation of feathers, and to be prepared for an easy take-off. During storms, the more coastal species often seek comparatively sheltered areas, as in bays or behind rocks.

Grey-headed Gull (*Larus cirrocephalus*)

Tufted Puffin (*Lunda cirrhata*)

The great reserve capabilities in the plumage of birds are revealed by this Grey-headed Gull, whose feathers are so worn that it might seem unable to fly at all. Also, a white sub-terminal wing patch is normal for the species, but has been almost completely worn away here, while the black wing-tips are retained—a good example of the greater wearing resistance of pigmented feathers.

Like this Tufted Puffin *(above)*, the puffins in general develop a less brightly coloured bill during the winter.

(Below) An immature Magnificent Frigate-bird, sun-bathing its underwings, looks almost foolish to the human eye. This behaviour must have some valuable function, although the latter is still little understood.

Magnificent Frigate-bird (*Fregata magnificens*)

Audubon's Shearwater (Puffinus l'herminieri)

(Above) When resting on the ocean, seabirds often gather in groups, which may be large indeed. The birds commonly engage in both preening and bathing, as do some of these Audubon's Shearwaters in the Galapagos Islands.

(Right) That cormorants do not have oiled and waterproof wing feathers—in contrast to their body feathers—is probably an adaptation to diving, as their buoyancy might otherwise have been too great. The soaked wing feathers, however, must be dried after a dive, and here a Pygmy Cormorant sits drying its outstretched wings in the well-known fashion.

Pygmy Cormorant (Halietor pygmaeus)

Seabirds frequently become wind-driven under adverse conditions, and even oceanic species may appear close to coasts in great numbers as a result. Sometimes the birds are driven ashore in abundance by severe winds, and have acquired names like "storm-petrels" or "gale-birds" in various regions and languages. They may also fly very low over the water during storms, directing their movements to avoid breakers. Storm-petrels of some species use their feet to jump on the water while gliding against the wind. Wilson's Storm-petrel seems to manage quite well in storms by this method, as it is seldom wind-driven to coasts.

Resting and sleeping

As a form of behaviour, resting is an energy-saving adaptation. It may occur when food has been taken in and energy is diverted to digestion, or when the body must recover after physical exhaustion and during periods of sickness. Many seabird species are adapted for feeding only at night or by day, and they spend other hours resting. Resting is often combined with preening and feather care. The choice of resting sites is varied, and some birds—especially the more pelagic ones—rest while floating on the sea. Numerous terns, gulls, and boobies seem to prefer floating objects if these are available. Relatively coastal species tend to rest on land, thereby avoiding cold water and soaking of feathers, as well as avoiding marine predators.

The term "roosting" covers both resting and sleeping, and it is usually applied to birds which have particular roosting sites. Coastal seabirds such as pelicans, cormorants, gulls, and terns often have sites to which the birds traditionally return after feeding flights, and some of these sites are known to have been employed for decades. Certain birds also return to breeding colonies for roosting, notably during breeding periods but, in some species, almost throughout the year. Birds may roost in their own territories or nests, yet many species have separate areas for roosting in the vicinity of colonies.

Birds are light sleepers, and the extent to which seabirds actually sleep at sea is poorly known. Frigate-birds, though never normally resting on water, occasionally spend days far out at sea, and it remains a mystery whether they sleep while flying, as swifts do. Easier to observe are the many coastal species which evidently sleep for short periods on their roosting sites. These usually rest the head on the back with the bill inserted beneath the scapulars, but sometimes they sleep with the bill forward and the head resting between the shoulders. Penguins sleep with the bill hooked behind the wing.

The flight of seabirds

That birds have numerous advantages over land animals due to their ability to fly has already been noticed. Relatively little energy is needed to travel long distances between local

(Above left) Seabirds cannot reach their head parts with the bill during preening, but normally scratch these with the feet—as does this Simeon Gull—or rub the head against the back for oiling of head feathers. The head of this species, unlike many gulls, is white during breeding, and at other times it becomes heavily streaked, even almost all-black.

(Right) On breeding islands where seabirds have much spare time,

they often spend a few hours daily in preening. Here an Atlantic Puffin goes through its wing feathers.

(Opposite) A Chilean Pelican meticulously works through its plumage during preening. It has a much brighter plumage when adult than as an immature, and such differences are rather normal in the order *Pelecaniformes*. Its neck is white in winter but black when breeding.

food resources, the efficiency of approaching and attacking prey while avoiding predators is increased, and more extensive migrations enable birds to cope with highly variable seasonal conditions. Depending on their general ecology, the seabird species have different properties of flight, which can be explained largely by some basic principles of aerodynamics.

Using the wings and tail

One important type of flight is gliding, in which the bird moves forward without beating its wings. The kinetic energy of this movement is obtained by losing some potential energy of height, so the bird must descend while gliding. Thus, the movement will eventually come to a stop at the ground or sea level—unless the bird compensates for the height loss by adding some energy, as when soaring in updrafts of hot air. With another type, active flight, the bird adds energy through muscle activity by beating its wings. Flying forward with vertical up-and-down wingbeats is known as *normal* flight, whereas horizontal back-and-forth wingbeats allow what is sometimes called *helicopter* flight. The latter is used by various species for taking off and landing, but many species within the order *Procellariiformes* cannot perform it. When a bird stands still in the air by hovering, the wingbeat resembles normal flight if the wind is strong, or some compromise between normal and helicopter flight if the wind is weak, and becomes helicopter flight if there is no wind at all. Among seabirds, hovering is employed extensively by several tern species when foraging, and occasionally by certain other birds such as gulls and Long-tailed Skuas.

The amount of wing area per unit of body weight is a key factor in flying. With gliding flight, a larger relative wing area permits a longer distance of gliding in relation to height loss. However, as the wing's area increases, its strength generally decreases and its air friction increases. But if the ratio is comparatively small, the bird requires a greater speed even to attain flight, and its most economical flight speed must be faster as well. A further factor in gliding efficiency is the shape of wings, long and narrow ones being better than short and broad wings. This is clearly illustrated by albatrosses and frigate-birds, the finest gliders among seabirds, although some fulmars and petrels also glide rather efficiently. A frigate-bird has a wing-span of over two metres, yet its weight of about 2–3 lb (1–1.5 kg) is fantastically low for such a large bird. Indeed, the feathers weigh more than the skeleton, and the whole creature seems designed for gliding.

Most seabirds are not so specialized for gliding, despite its energy-saving advantages. Taking off, landing, and feeding are other needs for which compromises in techniques of flight have evolved. Some of the birds in the same order as albatrosses, such as the Sooty and Little Shearwaters, are also adapted to diving and swimming below the sea surface, and use their wings to propel themselves underwater, with

American White Pelican *(Pelecanus erythrorhynchus)*

For soaring, the shape of wings is no less important than their area in relation to body weight. Long, narrow, pointed wings are ideal, as in albatrosses—but they are poor for manoeuvring and many such birds have great trouble in landing or taking off. Better adapted to terrestrial habits is the American White Pelican *(above)* with shorter and broader wings, which also enable it to soar fairly well on rising air currents.

The generalist gulls can easily take off directly upward, and some other aerial seabirds such as terns and frigate-birds do so with equal skill. But many, like this Double-crested Cormorant *(right)*, must make runs on the water during take-off.

Double-crested Cormorant *(Phalacrocorax auritus)*

Flightless Cormorant (*Nannopterum harrisi*)

(Above) The Flightless Cormorant cannot fly with its small wings, but still has a rather large tail, which is useful for steering when—as is normal with cormorants—the bird swims underwater by means of its feet.

(Left) This Laughing Gull in "helicopter flight" has its wings in a backward stroke, with the primary feathers spread so that each tip acts like a propeller's.

Laughing Gull (*Larus atricilla*)

relatively small wing areas in relation to body weight. This ratio is smallest in the auks and diving-petrels, which are still more specialized for diving. These require very high speeds to take off from the water, and minor imperfections in their flight feathers may prevent flying altogether. Nor can they land easily on breeding grounds, manoeuvre well in the air, or fly during moult. They often choose breeding grounds with steep slopes or cliffs, where updrafts help them to take off and land. There, too, the alcids frequently use their webbed feet in flight, as an aid to steering and as a means of increasing their lifting area at low speeds. Albatrosses are similarly dependent on updrafts in the choice of breeding grounds, being unable to employ a helicopter flight method. Apparently, an effective compromise in the use of wings for both flying and underwater propulsion is hard to achieve in birds weighing over 2 lb (1 kg), and evolution has followed another course in some large seabirds—total loss of flying ability—as with the penguins, the now extinct Great Auk, and the Flightless Cormorant.

The length and shape of the tail reveal much about flight in different species. Generally, a long tail is most useful because of its sizeable lifting surface for efficient landings and take-offs. But manoeuvring in the air is not as important for birds that dive and swim underwater: these tend to have relatively short tails, adequate for steering in the water. Birds swimming with their wings can also use their feet for steering, although cormorants are propelled by their feet and cannot use them simultaneously for efficient steering, thus needing a long tail for steering underwater. A deeply forked tail, in frigate-birds and many terns, provides superior manoeuvring powers, since it can be spread out to varying degrees and moved up or down on each side. Less valuable for flight control, but allowing rapid upward and downward shifts in direction, is the wedge-shaped tail. This is also rather common among seabirds, sometimes being combined with elongated central tail-streamers, as in tropic-birds and skuas. In gannets and boobies, the tail is pointed and probably helps to reduce drag when plunge-diving into the

water at high speeds. Between those two extreme shapes of tail, seabirds show intermediate types—shallowly forked, square, round, or slightly wedged—which usually involve minor specialization in the movements of the bird.

Energy from the air

In soaring flight, a bird utilizes rising air to compensate for the height loss when gliding. This is often done in circles within a "bubble" of relatively warm, light air. Frigate-birds are the master soarers, often reaching great heights as they remain at sea for long periods in the air. But these are the only birds which benefit much from the weak updrafts at sea, where air convection currents are limited due to the rather uniform temperatures. More extensively used by seabirds are the updrafts on breeding grounds, with regular rising winds near cliffs and slopes, of considerable importance for the choice of nesting sites.

Birds at sea can also gain energy through a kind of "dynamic soaring". With an alternating flight pattern, they rise fairly high into the air above the wave-crests and down into the troughs between waves. Because of the waves, and air friction against the water, the direction and strength of the wind vary with height over the sea, and birds make intricate use of these differences to maintain flight. Albatrosses do so most expertly and may glide far while rarely beating their wings. Many other species in the order *Procellariiformes*—fulmars, petrels, and shearwaters—employ this technique with less perfection. Even some gulls may use this technique when flying parallel with the waves.

Small updrafts over the waves are used as well by seabirds. Waves may travel long distances when unhindered by land, and swells occur in all open oceans regardless of the winds. A wave moving faster than the wind presses the air upward ahead of it, creating an updraft that a bird can "ride" on. Often the wind blows against a swell and, even if strong, can make it hard for a human to notice, yet seabirds sense and use these updrafts. Indeed, they not uncommonly ride on the bow waves of ships in this way, and albatrosses can be seen

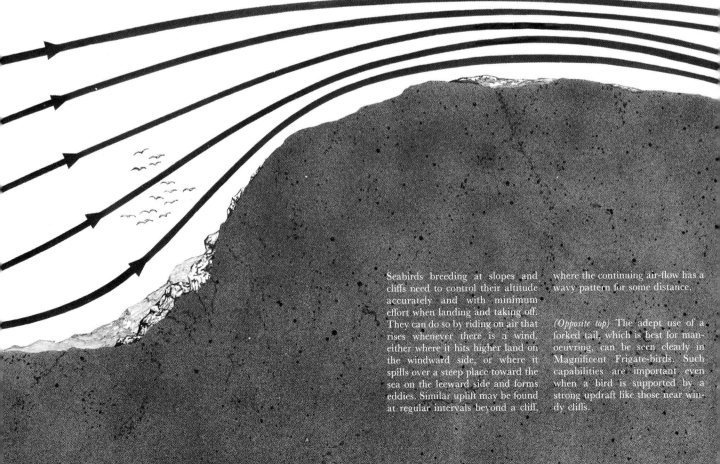

Seabirds breeding at slopes and cliffs need to control their altitude accurately and with minimum effort when landing and taking off. They can do so by riding on air that rises whenever there is a wind, either where it hits higher land on the windward side, or where it spills over a steep place toward the sea on the leeward side and forms eddies. Similar uplift may be found at regular intervals beyond a cliff,

where the continuing air-flow has a wavy pattern for some distance.

(Opposite top) The adept use of a forked tail, which is best for manoeuvring, can be seen clearly in Magnificent Frigate-birds. Such capabilities are important even when a bird is supported by a strong updraft like those near windy cliffs.

Magnificent Frigate-bird *(Fregata magnificens)*

Dynamic soaring

The soaring flight of albatrosses has been much admired, but it took long to explain how they maintain movement over the sea with minimal wing-beating. Such "dynamic soaring" depends on the fact that the wind speed is decreased by friction near the ocean surface. (1) At its highest altitude, the bird may be moving against the air but receiving relatively little uplift. (2) It then turns to descend with the wind, converting the potential energy of height into gliding speed. (3) As the wind slows, the bird goes even faster relative to the air. (4) Usually it glides into a wave trough where the wind is slowest, and turns against the wind at the front of the wave. (5) As it rises above the crests, an increasing and opposed wind speed lifts it powerfully. (6) Though losing forward momentum, the bird can keep soaring until the decreasing relative air speed ceases to lift it sufficiently and the cycle starts again.

(Right) By temporarily moving one wing forward and the other backward, a Fulmar shows its skill in taking advantage of the various wind patterns and strengths over the waves during dynamic flight, when the bird swoops through the air in long arcs.

(Below) The Blue-footed Booby, like many other *Pelecaniformes*, often adopts a V-formation when flying in a group.

Northern Fulmar *(Fulmarus glacialis)*
Blue-footed Booby *(Sula nebouxii)*

Birds flying in a V-formation are assisted by eddy-currents of air from their wings. This simplified view shows a time-sequence of movement (from darker to lighter). On each side of the formation's leading bird (1) is an eddy (a) which meets the next bird (2) to uplift it (b). The latter bird gives a similar uplift to the following one, and so on. Birds avoid the inside of the V where such eddies are usually opposed and create turbulence (c).

(3) The updraft also increases a bird's forward thrust, because it adds to the flow of air past the wings. These are tilted down at their leading edges, and the down-beat produces both upward and forward effects of suction and of pushing against the air. Shown here are the resulting forces of flight, which counteract the forces of gravity and air resistance. Such active horizontal flight involves forces like those on a bird that glides without beating its wings.

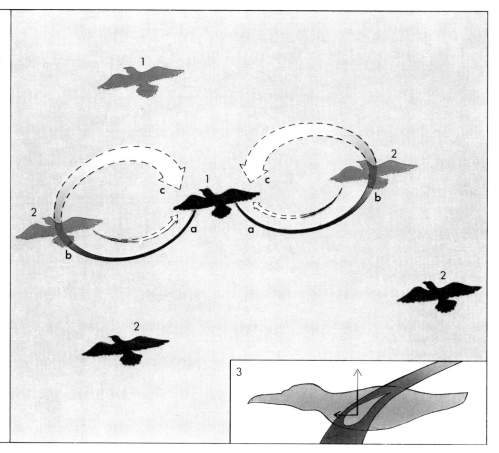

cruising ahead of swells in totally calm weather. In areas where the winds vary in direction, the swells frequently do too, and a combination of updrafts with dynamic soaring may allow birds to follow a wavy flight pattern by swooping in great arcs. Again, the tubenoses excel in this technique, which is one of their many marvellous adaptations to a truly pelagic life. Certain gulls, gannets, and boobies show a similar technique at times, although normally combining it with regular wingbeats. These birds, and pelicans, may also ride ahead of heavy swells along shores.

Why some seabirds have a habit of flying in V-formations is an old source of wonder. Pelicans, gannets, boobies, and cormorants do this extensively, while gulls and a few other birds are more occasional and less skilled at it. The method enables all birds behind the leader to save energy, but not because of any "lee effect" as in riding a bicycle. Behind the wings of each bird is a downward draft of air, at whose sides is a compensating updraft, and the following bird flies in the upward part of the vortex thus created. Just as airplanes can save 5–10% of fuel by flying in such formations, the trailing birds in a V minimize their effort, exhibiting a further adaptation for efficient use of energy in the animal world.

Chapter Three
THE SEABIRD SPECIES

A systematic presentation of the various kinds of seabirds can be as valuable to readers unfamiliar with many of them as it is to the scientist investigating their relationships in detail. Here we shall follow the customary sequence of zoological classification to describe all orders and families of seabirds. After each family is given a list of its species with reference to the pages where they are illustrated, apart from mention elsewhere in this book.

The controversial problems of deciding whether geographically isolated populations of birds with small differences in properties should be treated as separate species, or only as subspecies, have been pointed out already. Steering a middle course between the "lumpers" and the "splitters" among taxonomists, we will provide the most general view of such matters at present. But in numerous cases the final word on classification has not been said, and indeed the abundance of widespread seabirds with genetically isolated populations offers a fruitful area for the study of speciation. While the evolution of such animals is very slow, and slightly different populations are often named merely for convenience, there is a current tendency towards gathering some separate forms into a single species. Interesting examples now being discussed are the closely related forms of the Manx and Audubon's Shearwaters in the genus *Puffinus*, and the geographically separated populations in a subgenus (*Cookilaria*) of gadfly petrels. Similarly, revisions at higher levels of classification are tending toward fewer and larger genera and families.

Limits of knowledge

Even today, it is probably not true that the world's entire range of seabird species and geographical populations is known to science. New ones have been found during recent decades by seabird observers, and several other species remain poorly documented. Notably in the Pacific and the Indian Oceans where some islands and water areas are not yet fully explored, and in the order *Procellariiformes* whose seabirds—often highly pelagic in habits, nocturnal on breeding grounds, and breeding on distant islands near mountaintops or in forests—are not the easiest to observe, it seems likely that a few additional species remain to be discovered.

An instance of what we need to learn is Macgillivray's Petrel, known only from a single specimen: a fledgling taken in October on Ngau Island of the Fiji group during the last century. Also dating from that time are four skins, probably found on Réunion Island, which add to three records in the mid-twentieth century as the sole evidence for the Reunion Petrel. Again from that period came the first of our few records of Heinroth's Shearwater, in the Bismarck Archipelago where two were observed by the present author in December, 1971. The Magenta Petrel was long known from one specimen, taken in 1867 south of Pitcairn Island—but two very similar petrels were caught in nets on January 1, 1978, in the Chatham Islands, and it presumably breeds there in small numbers. Such rare cases occur among some subspecies or isolated populations as well. For example, two specimens taken north of Solomon Island attest a subspecies of the Tahiti Petrel, named "Beck's Petrel", which was originally treated as a separate species.

Of the most recently identified species, the former "Giant Petrel" has been divided into two, while Barau's Petrel is another discovery from Réunion. Jouanin's Petrel, though common in the northern Indian Ocean, was described as late as 1955—and its breeding grounds are not yet known, a problem which arises for certain other seabird species too. Thus, Elliot's Storm-petrel abounds in Peruvian and Galapagos waters, but a nest has never been reported, despite the collection of a female with an egg almost ready to be laid near the Pescadores Islands off the Peruvian coast. This species, however, is separated into two races, one of them probably breeding somewhere in the Galapagos Islands. Markham's Storm-petrel, familiar along the Humboldt Current, also breeds in an unknown area, although females with fully formed eggs in their oviducts have been collected at sea near the Peruvian coast, and an immature which could fly was once taken in the Chilean desert 30 miles (50 km) from the port of Iquique. A comparable case is Hornby's Storm-petrel, even if its breeding habits are partly revealed by a few mummified nestlings found in holes in the desert of northern Chile.

The same problem has now been solved for several species of seabirds. Nobody knew where the Marbled Murrelet breeds until it was seen to do so in holes in tall cedars or other large trees, sometimes rather far from the ocean—an additional instance of nocturnal activity which makes such birds hard to observe. Only since 1965 have we known a breeding area of Hutton's Shearwater, a race of the Manx Shearwater, in the New Zealand mountains at 4,300 ft (1,300 metres) above sea level. New breeding grounds for geographical populations of recognized species are detected occasionally, as happened not long ago with the Great Shearwater in the Falkland Islands, apart from its previously located breeding sites on Tristan da Cunha and Gough Islands. In certain cases, the distribution of a species may indicate that it has secret breeding grounds far away from its presently known ones. An example is the Grey-backed Shearwater, which definitely breeds in the New Zealand area but is simultaneously common along the Chilean coast, whose southern islands are largely uninvestigated. Such tubenoses, however, often take a long time to reach sexual maturity, and the immatures wander widely while the adults are breeding, so a different explanation is possible.

Jackass Penguin *(Spheniscus demersus)*

Black-footed Albatross *(Diomedea nigripes)*

Wandering Albatross *(Diomedea exulans)*

Oceans and their islands

Knowledge of world marine geography plays a constant role in the description of seabird species, notably as regards the distributions and movements of birds. Land near the sea, or surrounded by it, can be as complex in form as regions far from the sea, and island groups may often seem like worlds in themselves. Dependence of seabirds on land for breeding makes coastal areas important for some species, but others—particularly the more pelagic ones—find many oceanic islands essential as breeding grounds. All major island groups or oceanic islands have seabirds breeding on them, and in certain cases the birds maintain enormous colonies, especially in the more productive seas. On a geologic time-scale, old islands disappear and new ones arise, while coastlines change in shape and whole oceans may be joined or separated. Most seabirds evolved 50–100 million years ago and they have succeeded in adapting to continual alterations in marine geography since then.

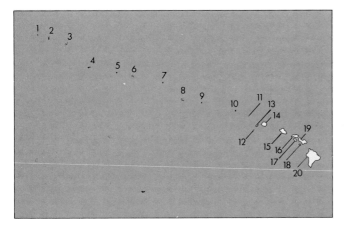

(A) The Hawaiian Islands, a subtropical mid-ocean group, abound in seabirds such as petrels, boobies, terns, and tropic-birds. The Laysan and Black-footed Albatrosses have their chief breeding ground there. The Manx Shearwater and Hawaiian Petrel breed in small numbers in volcanic crater walls on the main islands.

(1) Kure, *(2)* Midway, *(3)* Pearl and Hermes Reef, *(4)* Lisianski, *(5)* Laysan, *(6)* Maro Reef, *(7)* Gardner Pinnacles, *(8)* French Frigate Shoal, *(9)* Necker, *(10)* Nihoa, *(11)* Lehua, *(12)* Kaula, *(13)* Niihau, *(14)* Kauai, *(15)* Oahu, *(16)* Molokai, *(17)* Lanai, *(18)* Kahoolawe, *(19)* Maui, *(20)* Hawaii.

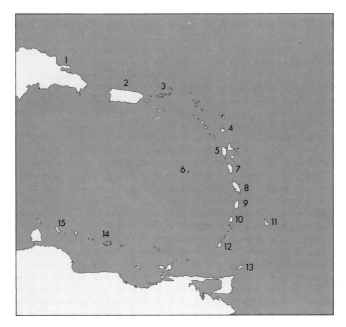

(B) The smaller tropical islands of the Antilles belong to the West Indies in the Caribbean near the South American mainland. Seabirds breed all over the area and some isles, like those named Aves, have great colonies.

(1) Hispaniola
(2) Puerto Rico
(3) Virgin Islands
(4) Antigua (in Leeward Islands)
(5) Guadeloupe
(6) Aves, or Bird Island
(7) Dominica
(8) Martinique
(9) Saint Lucia
(10) Saint Vincent
(11) Barbados
(12) Grenada (in Windward Islands)
(13) Trinidad and Tobago
(14) Islas de Aves, Los Roques
(15) Curaçao

(C) The world map shows principal islands in the following regions.

Eastern Pacific Ocean
(1) Pribilof Is.
(2) Aleutian Is.
(3) Hawaiian Is.
(4) Revilla Gigedo Is.
(5) Clipperton I.
(6) Line Is., with Christmas I.
(7) Galapagos Is.
(8) Phoenix Is.
(9) Marquesas Is.
(10) Fiji Is.
(11) Samoan Is.
(12) Tonga Is.
(13) Cook Is.
(14) Society Is., with Tahiti I.
(15) Tuamotu Archipelago
(16) Austral Is.
(17) Oeno I.
(18) Henderson I.
(19) Pitcairn I.
(20) Ducie I.
(21) Easter I.

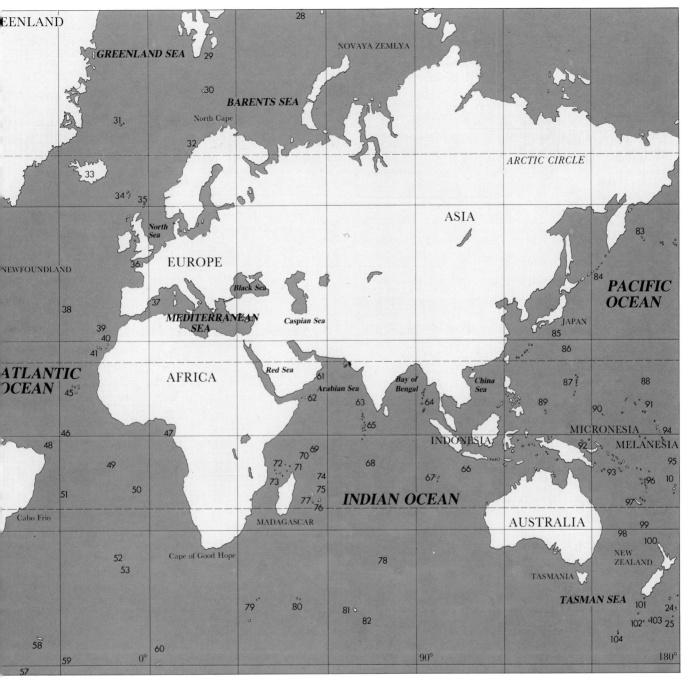

(22) Kermadec Is.	*(45)* Cape Verde Is.	*(68)* Chagos Archipelago	*(91)* Marshall Is.
(23) Chatham Is.	*(46)* St. Paul Rocks	*(69)* Seychelles Is.	*(92)* Bismarck Archipelago
(24) Bounty Is.	*(47)* São Tome and Principe Is.	*(70)* Amirantes Is.	*(93)* Solomon Is.
(25) Antipodes Is.	*(48)* Fernando de Noronha I.	*(71)* Providence I.	*(94)* Gilbert Is.
(26) Juan Fernandez Is.	*(49)* Ascension I.	*(72)* Aldabra Is.	*(95)* Ellice Is.
(27) Mocha I.	*(50)* St. Helena I.	*(73)* Comoro Is.	*(96)* New Hebrides Is.
	(51) Trinidade and Martin Vaz Is.	*(74)* Agalega Is.	*(97)* New Caledonia I.
Arctic and Atlantic Oceans	*(52)* Tristan da Cunha Is.	*(75)* Cargados Carajos Is.	*(98)* Lord Howe I.
(28) Franz Josef Land	*(53)* Gough I.	*(76)* Mauritius I.	*(99)* Norfolk I.
(29) Spitsbergen Is.	*(54)* Falkland Is.	*(77)* Réunion I.	*(100)* Three Kings Is.
(30) Bear I.	*(55)* Staten I.	*(78)* Amsterdam and St. Paul Is.	*(101)* Stewart I. and Snares Is.
(31) Jan Mayen I.	*(56)* South Shetland Is.	*(79)* Marion and Prince Edward Is.	*(102)* Auckland Is.
(32) Lofoten Is.	*(57)* South Orkney Is.	*(80)* Crozet Is.	*(103)* Campbell I.
(33) Iceland	*(58)* South Georgia I.	*(81)* Kerguelen Is.	*(104)* Macquarie I.
(34) Faeroe Is.	*(59)* South Sandwich Is.	*(82)* Heard and MacDonald Is.	
(35) Shetland Is.	*(60)* Bouvet I.		
(36) Channel Is.		**Western Pacific Ocean**	
(37) Balearic Is.	**Indian Ocean**	*(83)* Komandorski Is.	
(38) Azores Is.	*(61)* Kuria Muria Is.	*(84)* Kurile Is.	
(39) Madeira I.	*(62)* Socotra I.	*(85)* Tori Shima Is.	
(40) Salvage Is.	*(63)* Laccadive Is.	*(86)* Bonin and Volcano Is.	
(41) Canary Is.	*(64)* Andaman Is.	*(87)* Marianas Is., with Guam I.	
(42) Bermuda Is.	*(65)* Maldive Is.	*(88)* Wake I.	
(43) Bahama Is.	*(66)* Christmas I.	*(89)* Palau I.	
(44) Lesser Antilles	*(67)* Cocos-Keeling Is.	*(90)* Caroline Is.	

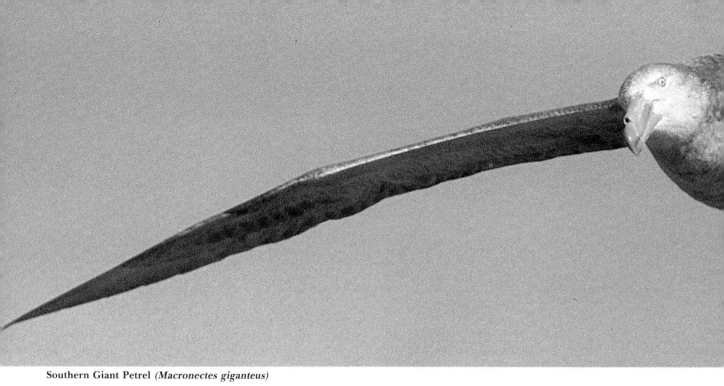

Southern Giant Petrel *(Macronectes giganteus)*

Northern Fulmar *(Fulmarus glacialis)*

Cory's Shearwater *(Calonectris diomedea)*

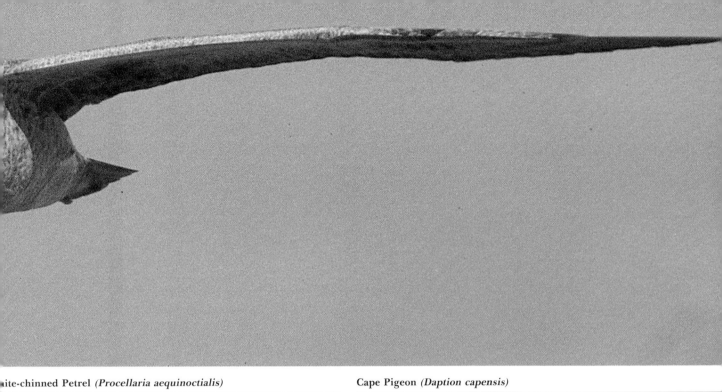

White-chinned Petrel *(Procellaria aequinoctialis)*

Cape Pigeon *(Daption capensis)*

The rarest species

Further instances of our ignorance about many otherwise well-known seabirds can be given in regard to their distribution at sea, exact migratory routes, and general habits. Yet even the chance of studying them no longer exists for a few seabirds which have become extinct through the activities of man in historic times. Both the famous Great Auk (or Garefowl), *Alca impennis*, and the Spectacled Cormorant, *Phalacrocorax perspicillatus*, disappeared in the middle of the nineteenth century. Presently, it is believed that the Guadalupe Storm-petrel, *Oceanodroma macrodactyla*, has passed into oblivion as well: it once bred on Guadalupe Island, but none has been seen since 1911 in spite of searches by naturalists there.

Some species, although less enigmatic, have extremely small populations. Indeed, the most scarce bird species on earth include a number of seabirds. The following are known to have populations so small that they are in danger of becoming extinct:

Galapagos Penguin, endemic to the Galapagos Islands, with a few thousand individuals.

Short-tailed Albatross, breeding on the Tori Shima Islands south of Japan, with an estimated total population of around 200 birds, slowly increasing.

Cahow, or **Bermuda Petrel**, breeding on Bermuda with about 30 pairs, increasing slowly due to strong protective measures.

Black-capped Petrel, closely allied to the Cahow, today breeding on mountaintops in Hispaniola with a few thousand birds, threatened by man and introduced animals. It once bred in the Lesser Antilles; a few pairs may still do so. An all-dark subspecies—the Jamaica Petrel—once bred in Jamaica but is probably extinct.

Abbott's Booby, breeding with quite low success on Christmas Island in the Indian Ocean, now numbering about 1,500 pairs.

Flightless Cormorant, in the Galapagos Islands, with less than 800 pairs.

Likewise, the Ascension and the Christmas Frigate-birds are confined to the islands which provide their names, respectively with 1,000–1,500 and less than 2,000 pairs. The Lava Gull in the Galapagos Islands has at most 400 pairs, and the Audouin's Gull in the Mediterranean has a few thousand birds in small local populations, while the status of the Relict Gull in central Asia is uncertain. Many local populations of generally common species are also in serious danger, and local subspecies of some seabirds are remarkably scarce.

Not all rare birds are necessarily threatened. They may have survived in tiny populations for a long time on scattered islands in unproductive seas. Yet they require careful observation, as current human activities on the oceans produce rapid ecological changes. Several species of seabirds are known to breed at a very low rate and, since many have a great life-span, it may take years before a decline in numbers is detected when their reproduction has been disrupted. By bearing such difficulties in mind, we can better appreciate the information which science does possess about seabirds.

Birds along sea coasts

Exactly which types of birds should be called seabirds can never be quite clear, because of the numerous borderline cases. There are conditions that connect oceanic and terrestrial ecosystems and enable coastal birds to survive on organisms in marine food-chains. Whether these are termed seabirds is often a matter of convenience, and the species that live in such ways belong to four groups: the divers (or loons), grebes, sea ducks, and sheathbills. One species from each group is illustrated here. The four species of divers are skilled underwater swimmers and catch fish. They live in the Northern Hemisphere, and many breed or winter along coasts. Grebes occur in both hemispheres, and some species visit sea coasts at least in winter to eat fish and crustaceans. Among the sea ducks are eiders, scoters, Long-tailed Ducks (Oldsquaw), and Harlequin Ducks. These eat shellfish and crustaceans, notably in winter, and dive well—like other ducks such as mergansers and scaup which visit coasts. The two species of sheathbills live in the Southern Hemisphere, mainly in the Antarctic, scavenging on all kinds of seafood.

(Above) Shown at top is the Western Grebe, *Aechmophorus occidentalis*, a representative of the various grebes frequenting sea coasts.

At bottom is the American Sheathbill, *Chionis alba*, which breeds singly, often among boulders near a colony of penguins.

▨ Breeding area

■ Breeding area

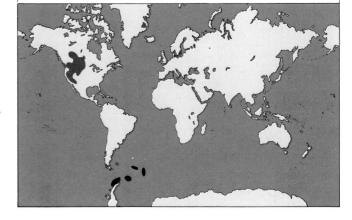

(Below) The upper birds are Steller's Eiders, *Polysticta stelleri*, one of four species of eiders in the Arctic and Subarctic regions, all living along sea coasts.

At bottom is the White-billed Diver, or Yellow-Billed Loon, *Gavia adamsii*, a large representative of the family of divers. It occurs chiefly in the high Arctic.

Order *Sphenisciformes*

All penguins belong to the family *Spheniscidae*, comprising 18 species in six genera. The name "penguin" originates either from Celtic *pen* (head) and *gwyn* (white), or from Latin *pinguis* (fat). In English, it was first applied to the Great Auk or Garefowl of the North Atlantic, and later to the birds now called penguins when these were discovered. The two types of birds are generally similar in appearance, with a stout body, feet displaced backwards and giving an upright stance on the ground, rather large size, dark upperparts and white underparts. Penguins are flightless. Most characteristic are the very reduced wings—termed "flippers" in penguins—which are adapted for propulsion underwater while diving. However, the Great Auk still had reduced flight-feathers, and penguins have lost them completely, the flippers being very stiff and covered with small scale-like feathers. The body also has a dense coverage of short feathers that is important in heat regulation, as is a layer of fat under the skin. The latter varies considerably in thickness during the year, and a particularly heavy layer is built up by Emperor Penguins at the onset of breeding, which takes place on the Antarctic ice in winter and involves long periods without feeding.

Until recently, predators of penguins occurred only in the sea—leopard seals, sharks, and killer whales—so that the birds have not yet evolved any escape reactions to humans on land. Their fearlessness, curiosity, and comical gait can be enjoyed by visitors at breeding grounds, while their reluctance to go back into the water after some time on land is often evident. Otherwise, their whole structure reflects an aquatic life, the short stiff tail and rearward feet enabling them to steer an inflexible body with a short neck, and the general bulkiness with heavy bones making them float low on the water, usually with just the head protruding above the surface. They may travel rather fast underwater, and swimming speeds of 10–15 knots (5–8 metres/second) are not uncommon. They often jump clear of the water like porpoises when breathing at such high speeds, and sometimes they land by gaining momentum from below and jumping a few feet onto the ice or rocks. Penguins can be rather hard to identify in the water, but adults tend to have some bright colours, clear patterns, plumes or crests on the head, which serve for recognition, although immatures are mostly duller in colour.

Penguins are confined to the Southern Hemisphere, inhabiting relatively cool waters, mostly around the latitudes of 40–60° S. Fewer species occur in the Antarctic area proper, and one—the Galapagos Penguin—is found very near the equator, this and the Humboldt Penguin taking advantage of the cool Humboldt Current. Some species comprise enormous populations: for example, the Adélie Penguin has breeding colonies of more than a million pairs. Such colonies, often called "rookeries", are generally located on islands, although certain large ones exist on the Antarctic continent. All penguins breed in colonies, but the less common species do so in rather small congregations. In the far south, most breed in the open, sometimes with pairs very close together, whereas the northerly breeding penguins may dig burrows, find natural holes, or hide under rocks and bushes, with a wider scattering of pairs. Depending on the species, one to three eggs are laid, incubation taking around 33–40 days in the smaller species and about two months in the largest.

As a rule, penguins breed annually in the southern summer—yet this activity is more frequent for the Galapa-

Pink-footed Shearwater *(Puffinus creatopus)*

Pink-footed Shearwater *(Puffinus creatopus)*

**Manx Shearwater, Balearic subspecies
*(Puffinus puffinus mauretanicus)***

Great Shearwater *(Puffinus gravis)*

gos Penguin, and its timing is quite peculiar for the two largest species. The King Penguin breeds twice every three years, thus alternating summers with winters, while the Emperor Penguin breeds in winter as we have seen. Birds of the latter species stand upright, close together, with the single egg resting on the feet and covered by skin in a kind of pouch between the legs. Many penguins are noisy on breeding grounds, their calls providing communication not only between the sexes but also between parents and young, which recognize one another partly through sounds.

When not breeding, penguins disperse widely at sea. Some swim fairly far northward, and the Magellan Penguin—breeding near the lower tip of South America—often reaches Brazil, occasionally up to Cabo Frio. Most species follow a less regular pattern, frequently travelling east or west from their breeding grounds, as well as toward the north during winter. They live mainly on fish, squid, and crustaceans. The larger species tend to have a longer, more pointed bill and prefer to eat agile fish and squid, while some species are comparatively specialized for a crustacean diet. With the gradual extermination of whales, much "krill" and particularly the *Euphasia superba* has become available for other animals, and this increased food supply—besides a ban on persecution by humans—has enabled many kinds of penguins to expand their numbers in the southern seas.

The genus *Aptenodytes* contains the two largest species of penguins. They look similar, but the Emperor weighs most, up to 100 lb (45 kg) and averaging around 65 lb (30 kg), while its yellowish head-patches are paler and less defined. Immatures are duller, with a black bill.

King Penguin	*Aptenodytes patagonica* Ill. pp. 176-177
Emperor Penguin	*Aptenodytes forsteri* Ill. pp. 212-213

In the genus *Pygoscelis* are three species, of similar size and lacking colourful feathers, but differing in the characteristics of bill and head. All are very numerous, and the latter two often breed in adjacent colonies.

Adélie Penguin	*Pygoscelis adeliae* Ill. pp. 140, 186-187
Gentoo Penguin	*Pygoscelis papua* Ill. p. 68
Chinstrap Penguin	*Pygoscelis antarctica* Ill. p. 140

To the genus *Eudyptes* belong six species, only the last two being widespread. Sizes are again similar, and the bill is rather stout, more or less brightly coloured, with clearly visible plates. Adults, and occasionally immatures, have a crest with yellowish or orange plumes. The head is otherwise black, except that the Royal Penguin often has whitish sides on its head and throat. Identification of these penguins is difficult without a knowledge of small details, although differences in their distribution can be helpful. Generally, they desert their breeding grounds for about five months of the year. Some, notably the Rock-hopper Penguin, occur in very large colonies. Most lay two eggs, yet of unequal sizes, the larger one alone being incubated.

Fiordland Crested Penguin	*Eudyptes pachyrhynchus*
Snares Crested Penguin	*Eudyptes robustus*
Erect-crested Penguin	*Eudyptes sclateri* Ill. p. 177

Royal Penguin	*Eudyptes schlegeli*
Rock-hopper Penguin	*Eudyptes crestatus* Ill. pp. 16, 223
Macaroni Penguin	*Eudyptes chrysolophus* Ill. p. 140

The sole species of the genus *Megadyptes* has yellow irises and head features, the latter also including gold and black.

Yellow-eyed Penguin	*Megadyptes antipodes*

The genus *Eudyptula* comprises two species, which some authorities propose to unite as one. These are the smallest of all penguins, weighing up to 4.5 lb (2.1 kg) and averaging about 2.5 lb (1.1 kg). They lack bright colours, having dark to slate-grey upperparts and white underparts, with a black bill. They are nocturnal on breeding grounds and nest in burrows.

Little Penguin	*Eudyptula minor* Ill. p. 198
White-flippered Penguin	*Eudyptula albosignata*

Of the genus *Spheniscus* are four species, whose ranges are largely distinct. Their rather similar structure and colouring include dark upperparts and white undersides, separated by a black line below a white zone across the breast and sides, with a light crescent around the sides of the head and—in adults—usually some pink at the base of the bill.

Jackass Penguin	*Spheniscus demersus* Ill. p. 55
Humboldt Penguin	*Spheniscus humboldti* Ill. p. 222
Magellan Penguin	*Spheniscus magellanicus* Ill. p. 111
Galapagos Penguin	*Spheniscus mendiculus* Ill. p. 39

Order *Procellariiformes*

The four families of this order, *Diomedeidae* (albatrosses), *Procellariidae* (fulmars, typical petrels, prions, shearwaters), *Hydrobatidae* (storm-petrels), and *Pelecanoididae* (diving-petrels), are often collectively called "petrels" or "tubenoses". The latter term, and an alternative name "*Tubinares*" for the order, refer to the peculiar tubular nostrils of all these birds. Why such nostrils evolved is not quite clear, but several theories have been proposed. The shape may be related to the fact that tubenoses are among the very few birds with a fairly good sense of smell. There may be some connection with the process of excreting salt from the salt glands, as certain petrels are known to eject salty droplets into the air through their tubular nostrils—yet the liquid drips off the tip of the bill in various species.

A further suggestion is that cavities inside the tubular nostrils enable these birds to sense changes in air pressure, and thus to gauge air-current speeds. This could partly account for their adept use of differences in wind velocity during flight. While this theory has not been adequately tested to date, their nasal chambers do contain valve-like structures which may function as an anemometer. A tubenose's bill is always hooked and consists of separate horny plates. Since penguins also have such a plated bill, as well as some comparable marine adaptations and habits, the two orders are thought to be distantly related.

At sea, all species except the diving-petrels live chiefly in the air. They fly with great skill, and occasionally rest on the water or feed by surface-swimming and diving, their highly water-resistant plumage being characterized by a strong musky odour. Few species can walk easily on land, and many are polymorphic in their colouring. However, males and females, like adults and immatures, are similar in colour, except in the giant petrels and some albatrosses. Numerous species have pink or yellow legs or feet, and most albatrosses and a few shearwaters have coloured bills.

Nearly a hundred species belong to this order, with very diverse ecological adaptations. All are decidedly marine, and none prefer a true coastal habitat, though some tend to choose continental shelf areas. They are generally adapted to a definite climatic zone, and every zone from the Arctic to the Antarctic pack-ice is exploited by these birds. Corresponding to their ecological niches is a broad range in size, from the impressive albatrosses to the tiny storm-petrels, as well as in food which includes fish, cephalopods, crustaceans, plankton, and whale offal. Certain species scavenge on dead organisms, among which are other seabirds and marine mammals. Many feed at night, particularly in oceanic areas. A majority of species are found in the Southern Hemisphere, and notably few exist in tropical parts of the Atlantic or in the North Atlantic Ocean. When not breeding, most species cover enormous distances, some dispersing widely and others migrating in fixed directions. Many cross over to the opposite hemisphere or—staying in the belt of west winds in the southern oceans—circumnavigate the Antarctic.

Breeding colonies are huge in some species of tubenoses. Here they are nocturnal as a rule, and communicate much through sounds. Nesting in burrows or natural holes is common, but a few larger species breed in the open. Only one egg is laid, and the parents incubate it in shifts of several days over a comparatively long time: around six weeks for the smallest storm-petrels, and two months or more for the bigger species. The chick, covered with thick down at hatching, is brooded by one parent for some days, and is then visited and fed by both parents at increasing intervals. Rearing takes as long as two months in the storm-petrels, and three to five in larger species. Before it fledges, the chick becomes very fat and may ultimately weigh about 20 percent more than adults. When feathers grow, it loses weight and continues to be visited by its parents, although at increasingly longer intervals. At last it takes to sea, normally during the night in nocturnal species, and probably never again has contact with the parents. Not infrequently, its first task is a long migration to a wintering area. The immatures of most species lead a free-ranging life at sea for several, often five to ten, years before they return to land and start breeding, usually in the colony where they were born.

The extreme rarity of a few species in this order makes them perhaps the least numerous living birds on earth. Tubenoses have suffered heavily from human actions, such as actual persecution of the Short-tailed Albatross, introduction of animals like rats, cats, and mongooses, or environmental destruction. Nonetheless, many species are still quite common and the most abundant wild bird in the world may be among them. Ornithologists now tend to believe that it is the Wilson's Storm-petrel, which probably includes some hundreds of millions of individuals, although populations at that scale are very difficult to estimate.

Albatrosses

The family *Diomedeidae* comprises 13 species in two genera. Their name derives from one which was first applied in English to frigate-birds and originated from the Spanish word *alcatraz* for pelicans. The smaller species are often called "mollymawks", a corruption of the Dutch *mal* (foolish) and *mok* (gull)—but they have also been known as "gony" or "goony", an English dialect word for a simpleton. Such terms presumably owe to these birds' clumsiness and lack of fear of man.

Characteristic of albatrosses are their large size, long narrow wings, and short tail. While at sea, they tend to remain in the air and rarely flap their wings as they adeptly use wind patterns over the waves. In totally calm weather without swells, they become virtually unable to fly, although such conditions seldom occur in the areas they inhabit. Nine species are found in the windy southern oceans, three in the North Pacific, and one in the Humboldt Current off Peru and around the Galapagos Islands. As they probably have difficulty in crossing the equatorial doldrums, there is no normal migration between the hemispheres, but a few records exist of some southerly species in the Northern Hemisphere.

All species except the Waved Albatross of the Galapagos Islands breed at the time of the southern summer and northern winter. They breed in rather open terrain, preferably on islands with updrafts on a windy side which help the birds to become airborne. Some species build a fairly high nest, and the two largest breed only every second year. Sexual maturity is reached in six to nine years, the average life-span being long and, occasionally, perhaps up to 60–80 years. Breeding birds are more or less faithful to their mates from year to year. During pair formation, spectacular displays with outstretched wings can be seen. Immatures forming pairs for the first time may start displays at the end of the breeding season in the year before they actually begin to breed. The most important food seems to consist of cephalopods, though other prey such as fish are also taken and some albatrosses scavenge, for example on offal thrown from ships.

In the genus *Diomedea* are eleven species, including the two largest. Most of them exhibit light colouring on the body and underwings, but the Black-footed Albatross is nearly all-dark and the Waved Albatross, apart from its light head and neck, has a somewhat finely barred, darkish body. Three species—the Wandering, Royal, and Short-tailed Albatrosses—show varying degrees of white on their upperwings. While several species with a light body, dark mantle, and dark tail are rather similar, they differ in the colour of the bill, the extent of grey on the head and neck, and the amounts and patterns of dark margins on the underwings. Immatures are duller and darker than adults in a majority of the species.

Wandering Albatross	*Diomedea exulans*
	Ill. pp. 10, 30, 54, 231
Royal Albatross	*Diomedea epomophora*
	Ill. p. 175
Waved Albatross	*Diomedea irrorata*
	Ill. pp. 26, 182
Short-tailed Albatross	*Diomedea albatrus*
Black-footed Albatross	*Diomedea nigripes*
	Ill. p. 55
Laysan Albatross	*Diomedea immutabilis*
	Ill. p. 210
Black-browed Albatross	*Diomedea melanophris*
	Ill. pp. 27, 209, 222

White-necked Petrel *(Pterodroma externa)*
Leach's Storm-petrel *(Oceanodroma leucorhoa)*

White-necked Petrel *(Pterodroma externa)*
Fork-tailed Storm-petrel *(Oceanodroma furcata)*

Cook's Petrel *(Pterodroma cooki)*   Cook's Petrel *(Pterodroma cooki)*

Jouanin's Petrel *(Bulweria fallax)*

Buller's Albatross	*Diomedea bulleri*
Shy Albatross	*Diomedea cauta*
	Ill. p. 110
Yellow-nosed Albatross	*Diomedea chlororhynchos*
	Ill. p. 143
Grey-headed Albatross	*Diomedea chrysostoma*
	Ill. p. 141

The genus *Phoebetria* contains two very similar, all-dark species. These are probably the most graceful of all albatrosses in flight, with long narrow wings and a long wedge-shaped tail.

Sooty Albatross	*Phoebetria fusca*
	Ill. pp. 16, 141
Light-mantled Sooty Albatross	*Phoebetria palpebrata*

Fulmars, petrels, prions, shearwaters

The family *Procellariidae* is large and diverse, comprising 12 genera and around 60 species. They vary in size as from the small prions to the Giant Petrels and, except in the latter case, immatures look like adults. Some of the big species breed in the open, but most nest in burrows, natural holes, or crevices, and the majority are nocturnal on breeding grounds. All oceans, climatic zones, and types of food attract them. These birds fall into four main groups: the fulmar petrels (with 8 species in six genera, including the great range of sizes between Blue and Giant Petrels), the prions (with 6 very similar species in one genus), the shearwaters (with 18 species in three genera, relatively similar in overall structure), and the gadfly petrels (with around 28 species in two genera).

(Top) The Great Auk, *Alca impennis*, now extinct, once lived in the North Atlantic, ranging from Iceland to some wintering places in Spain and Florida. Also known as the Garefowl, it grew to about 30 inches (75 cm) in length, and was most closely related to the Razorbills and some guillemots. Sailors killed it for food, and collectors had a further role in wiping it out around 1844. Great Auks were adapted to conditions like those of penguins in the Southern Hemisphere. These two types of birds illustrate the phenomenon of convergent evolution, being similar in general structure and looks although unrelated.

(Right) Representative of the order *Sphenisciformes* is a Gentoo Penguin, *Pygoscelis papua*. This very common bird breeds among the rocks and boulders on islands in the Subantarctic seas, forming great colonies.

Among the fulmar petrels, the genus *Macronectes* was believed until recently to contain just one species, but two have been recognized as breeding separately—within sight of each other—on at least the islands of Macquarie, Marion, and Crozet. They are as large as the smaller albatrosses, the head being modest in size, with a very long nasal tube on a powerful bill. Colours vary from dark brown to all-white, though the latter occurs only in the southern species. Inhabiting the southern oceans from the Antarctic coast to temperate waters, the southern and northern species at sea tend to occur on opposite sides of the Antarctic convergence during breeding periods. These are the sole birds in the order which feed and walk well on land. Sometimes called "vultures of the sea", they scavenge on all kinds of carcasses—such as dead sea mammals, birds, and fish—and often kill chicks or even adult birds of other species. Their diet also includes live fish, cephalopods, barnacles, amphipods, and krill, while they frequently follow ships and feed on refuse thrown overboard. Seamen and whalers know them as "Nelly", or as "Stinker".

Northern Giant Petrel	*Macronectes halli*
Southern Giant Petrel	*Macronectes giganteus*
	Ill. pp. 58, 140

The genus *Fulmarus* also has two species, which are very closely related and inhabit rather cold waters. One occurs in Antarctic seas, and its plumage is light-coloured. The other has a dark phase as well, and ranges over both the North Pacific and North Atlantic. In the latter region, it has spread remarkably through southerly areas since the eighteenth century, probably due to the release of offal by increased fishing and to better protection on breeding grounds. These birds scavenge freely and often follow ships.

Northern Fulmar	*Fulmarus glacialis*
	Ill. pp. 25, 51, 58, 166
Southern Fulmar	*Fulmarus glacialoides*
	Ill. p. 141

The four remaining genera of fulmar petrels, each with a single species, live in southern oceans and have quite diverse characteristics. The Cape Pigeon, or "Pintado Petrel", is unmistakeable with its black and white chequered upperwings. It is very common, frequently following ships in large numbers, while a few stray birds have even been recorded in the Northern Hemisphere. The Snow Petrel is the only petrel with an all-white plumage, and it sometimes breeds as far as 50 miles (80 km) inland in the Antarctic—showing a notable ability to locate nest entrances covered by snow—although at sea it inhabits the pack-ice zone. The Antarctic Petrel, too, occurs mainly in this zone, being easily recognized by dark upperparts except for white on the tail and wing-quills. The small Blue Petrel is similar to the prions, with grey upperparts and a dark W-pattern across the wings, but differs in having a white tail-tip, a dark crown, and dark sides on the neck.

Cape Pigeon	*Daption capensis*
	Ill. p. 59
Snow Petrel	*Pagodroma nivea*
	Ill. p. 141
Antarctic Petrel	*Thalassoica antarctica*
	Ill. p. 140
Blue Petrel	*Halobaena caerulea*
	Ill. p. 141

Two of the rarest birds in the world are shown here. Both petrels were once believed to be extinct but have been rediscovered.

(Below) The Bermuda Petrel, *Pterodroma cahow*, also called the Cahow, breeds on islets at Bermuda and occurs pelagically in the western North Atlantic subtropical waters. *(Right)* The Magenta Petrel, *Pterodroma magentae*, has a very uncertain status. Some individuals recently caught in mist-nets on the Chatham Islands are the only ones recorded in this century.

White Pelican *(Pelecanus onocrotalus)*

Red-billed Tropic-bird *(Phaethon aethereus)*

Brown Pelican *(Pelecanus occidentalis)*

Birds of the second group, prions of the genus *Pachyptila*, are all so similar as to be almost indistinguishable in the field. Extremely small, bluish-grey above and white below with dark W-patterns over the wings, they have a dark tip on a wedge-shaped tail. Lamellae on the sides of the bill allow the prions to filter sea water for tiny planktonic organisms, occasionally "hydroplaning" by floating on the water and paddling rapidly forward with their wings outstretched and the bill downward. *Euphasia* krill are eaten, and prions may occur in huge flocks where food is abundant. As whales have the same diet, prions tend to accompany these and are used as an indicator for hunting by whalers, who call them "whale-birds" or "ice-birds". They inhabit fairly cool waters of the Southern Hemisphere, chiefly in Antarctic and Subantarctic areas, although some disperse towards more temperate waters in winter. Breeding takes place in burrows or natural holes. The species differ in size, in the shape and size of bills, and partly in the zones of surface water which they occupy.

Broad-billed Prion	*Pachyptila vittata*
	Ill. p. 141
Salvin's Prion	*Pachyptila salvini*
Dove Prion	*Pachyptila desolata*
Thin-billed Prion	*Pachyptila belcheri*
Fairy Prion	*Pachyptila turtur*
Fulmar Prion	*Pachyptila crassirostris*

In the third group, the genus *Procellaria* comprises four species, rather large and heavily built birds with a massive but relatively light bill. The Brown Petrel is least dark in colour, the others being very similar to one another, mainly blackish-brown and hard to distinguish in the field. They live in the Southern Hemisphere, although Parkinson's Petrel probably crosses the equator regularly in the eastern Pacific.

Brown Petrel	*Procellaria cinerea*
	Ill. p. 141
White-chinned Petrel	*Procellaria aequinoctialis*
	Ill. pp. 59, 174
Westland Petrel	*Procellaria westlandica*
Parkinson's Petrel	*Procellaria parkinsoni*
	Ill. p. 118

The genus *Calonectris* has two species of shearwaters, speckled brownish above and white below, with a comparatively long bill and large size.

White-faced Shearwater	*Calonectris leucomelas*
Cory's Shearwater	*Calonectris diomedea*
	Ill. pp. 58, 107

It is in the genus *Puffinus* that we find typical shearwaters with a rather long and slender, mostly dark, bill. They may be all-dark, or dark above and light below, and some have different colour-phases. Their wings tend to be narrow and straight, while the majority dive and swim below the sea surface to an extent when feeding. The name "shearwater" refers to their flight pattern of sweeping up and down over the waves, occasionally hitting the water with a downward wing-tip. Certain species occur in enormous numbers, and the quantity of chicks taken for food in New Zealand and Australia has made the Sooty and Short-tailed Shearwaters known as "mutton-birds" there. Shearwaters live in all climatic zones except the pack-ice, and many species show long complex migrations between the hemispheres. Some are very widespread and have separate geographical populations, although the tropical ones have much smaller populations than do species adapted to cooler waters. They breed in both hemispheres, choosing burrows and natural holes or crevices, where they are nocturnal except for the Galapagos population of Audubon's Shearwater. Many prefer offshore—not true pelagic—habitats, and most are social at sea, feeding in groups and sometimes gathering in big "rafts". Fish and crustaceans are principal foods, cephalopods having much less importance than for petrels of similar size. Shearwaters do not normally follow ships, but a few may take advantage at times of the wind over bow or stern waves.

Pink-footed Shearwater	*Puffinus creatopus*
	Ill. p. 63
Pale-footed Shearwater	*Puffinus carneipes*
	Ill. p. 111
Great Shearwater	*Puffinus gravis*
	Ill. pp. 62, 131
Wedge-tailed Shearwater	*Puffinus pacificus*
	Ill. p. 80
Grey-backed Shearwater	*Puffinus bulleri*
	Ill. p. 195
Sooty Shearwater	*Puffinus griseus*
	Ill. p. 142
Short-tailed Shearwater	*Puffinus tenuirostris*
	Ill. pp. 110, 208
Christmas Shearwater	*Puffinus nativitatis*
	Ill. p. 80
Manx Shearwater	*Puffinus puffinus*
	Ill. pp. 63, 76
Little Shearwater	*Puffinus assimilis*
	Ill. pp. 28, 211
Audubon's Shearwater	*Puffinus l'herminieri*
	Ill. pp. 43, 150
Heinroth's Shearwater	*Puffinus heinrothi*

Finally, of the gadfly petrels, the genus *Pterodroma* contains around 25 species, all with a black bill that is short, stout, and prominently hooked, and many with a pointed tail. Their flight pattern is characteristic: rapid swoops above the wave-crests on stiffly angled wings, sometimes including a few duck-like wing-beats. Most are medium in size, blackish to brown or grey above, and lighter on the underparts. Many are polymorphic and some are all-dark. They inhabit every ocean, but tend to avoid the very cold Arctic and Antarctic waters. The number of species is small in the North Atlantic, and greatest in tropical and subtropical areas, while a majority can be found in the Pacific. These birds are quite pelagic, seldom occurring near continental coasts—a result of their food preference for cephalopods—and many of them disperse widely across the oceans. Breeding commonly takes place in the interior of islands on mountains far from the sea, and is usually nocturnal in burrows or natural holes, despite a few diurnal species which breed in the open on Pacific islands. They do not follow ships.

Great-winged Petrel	*Pterodroma macroptera*
	Ill. p. 142
Kerguelen Petrel	*Pterodroma brevirostris*
	Ill. p. 140
Reunion Petrel	*Pterodroma aterrima*

Solander's Petrel	*Pterodroma solandri*
	Ill. p. 196
Murphy's Petrel	*Pterodroma ultima*
	Ill. p. 81
Kermadec Petrel	*Pterodroma neglecta*
	Ill. pp. 16, 81
Trinidade Petrel	*Pterodroma arminjoniana*
	Ill. p. 81
Soft-plumaged Petrel	*Pterodroma mollis*
	Ill. p. 20
Magenta Petrel	*Pterodroma magentae*
	Ill. p. 69
Tahiti Petrel	*Pterodroma rostrata*
	Ill. p. 80
Phoenix Petrel	*Pterodroma alba*
	Ill. p. 81
Schlegel's Petrel	*Pterodroma incerta*
	Ill. p. 102
White-headed Petrel	*Pterodroma lessonii*
	Ill. p. 140
Mottled Petrel	*Pterodroma inexpectata*
	Ill. p. 215

Five further species in this genus form a distinct group. Rather similar in colour, size, and build, they generally replace one another in different ocean areas.

White-necked Petrel	*Pterodroma externa*
	Ill. p. 66
Hawaiian Petrel	*Pterodroma phaeopygia*
	Ill. p. 227
Black-capped Petrel	*Pterodroma hasitata*
Bermuda Petrel	*Pterodroma cahow*
	Ill. p. 69
Barau's Petrel	*Pterodroma baraui*

Also included is a subgenus of rather small, very similar birds called "*Cookilaria*" petrels. They are mainly white on underparts and in front, greyish on upperparts, with a more or less clear and dark W-pattern over the wings. Occurring only in the Pacific, they make up several distinct geographical populations, whose classification is uncertain. The following species are now generally accepted:

Cook's Petrel	*Pterodroma cooki*
	Ill. p. 67
Stejneger's Petrel	*Pterodroma longirostris*
Black-winged Petrel	*Pterodroma nigripennis*
	Ill. p. 81
Chatham Island Petrel	*Pterodroma axillaris*
Bonin Petrel	*Pterodroma hypoleuca*
Gould's Petrel	*Pterodroma leucoptera*
	Ill. p. 80

The other genus of gadfly petrels, *Bulweria*, comprises rather small, all-dark birds with a short, stout bill and a long, wedge-shaped tail.

Bulwer's Petrel	*Bulweria bulwerii*
	Ill. pp. 28, 203
Jouanin's Petrel	*Bulweria fallax*
	Ill. p. 67
Macgillivray's Petrel	*Bulweria macgillivrayi*
	Ill. p. 80

Storm-petrels

The family *Hydrobatidae* has around 21 species in eight genera. Their name may have arisen from the belief of mariners that a storm was imminent when these birds appeared near a ship. Like other birds in the same order, they are prone to being driven ashore during severe storms. Moreover, they often gather in ships' wakes while hard winds are blowing—perhaps because the water is calmer there—to feed on organisms brought toward the surface by propellers. Only some species have the habit of following ships, but this also happens regularly in calm weather. Wilson's Storm-petrel, in particular, may be seen behind ships in large numbers, occasionally even feeding when galley refuse is thrown overboard and falls partly on drops of oil which the birds can suck into their mouths from the sea surface.

Storm-petrels are divided into two subfamilies which, respectively, have three genera breeding only in the Northern Hemisphere—except for the Markham's and Hornby's species—and five genera breeding chiefly in the Southern Hemisphere. The latter birds possess longer legs and shorter, broader wings than the former. Their legs reflect an adaptation for pattering on the water surface as they feed, gain speed to take flight, or keep up against the wind in strong gales. Thus they can manage rather well even in storms, and are blown to shore much more rarely than the northern birds. The name "petrel" originates from this appearance of walking on the water like St. Peter. However, the muscle power in their long legs is not great enough to support the full weight of these birds on land, and they have difficulty in moving about on breeding grounds.

In general, storm-petrels are small and often all-dark, dark with a white rump, or mainly dark above and white below, the bill being small, hooked, and black. Some fly erratically, or in a bouncing pattern like butterflies, and they resemble swallows when travelling above the waves. Their principal foods are planktonic organisms, larvae of various types, and small crustaceans. They occur in all seas, and species in both subfamilies migrate to the opposite hemisphere during non-breeding periods. The tropical species tend to have much smaller populations than those breeding in cooler latitudes. On breeding grounds, all except the Galapagos Storm-petrel are nocturnal, and choose burrows or crevices. They begin to breed at an age of 4–5 years, unusually late for such small birds, but their life-span is long and probably averages about 20 years. Like all other birds in this order, they lay only one egg. At times of adverse weather, the eggs or young may be left unattended for as long as 10–11 days and, in the Antarctic, Wilson's Storm-petrel occasionally even has to find its way back to the nest hole through snow.

The southern subfamily, *Oceanitinae*, contains these birds:

Wilson's Storm-petrel	*Oceanites oceanicus*
Elliot's Storm-petrel	*Oceanites gracilis*
	Ill. p. 194
Grey-backed Storm-petrel	*Garrodia nereis*
	Ill. p. 141
White-faced Storm-petrel	*Pelagodroma marina*
White-bellied Storm-petrel	*Fregetta grallaria*
	Ill. p. 80
Black-bellied Storm-petrel	*Fregetta tropica*
	Ill. p. 16
White-throated Storm-petrel	*Nesofregetta albigularis*
	Ill. p. 80

Cape Gannet *(Sula capensis)*
Peruvian Booby *(Sula variegata)*

Blue-footed Booby *(Sula nebouxii)*
Brown Booby *(Sula leucogaster)*

(Above) The Fluttering Shearwater is a form of the Manx Shearwater, which is a very widespread bird with at least eight geographically separated populations. It is thus a good example of a "polytypic" species with differentiated properties. Many of these populations have been treated as distinct species in the past, but according to present trends they are generally viewed as subspecies. Their breeding areas are shown on the map.

(a) The Balearic Shearwater is a rather polymorphic subspecies, some individuals being mostly dark but with light underwings, and others having variable degrees of white on their underparts (see photo page 63). Also in the Northern Hemisphere are: (b) the Manx

Shearwater proper, (c) Levantine, (d) Newell's, (e) Black-vented, and (f) Townsend's Shearwaters. In New Zealand, the (g) Fluttering and (h) Hutton's Shearwaters breed in separate colonies and are genetically isolated.

(Opposite) Skuas probably evolved in the Northern Hemisphere. But the Great Skua, Catharacta skua, has spread to the Southern Hemisphere where it is now found widely. Six recognized forms are known to occur with separate populations, whose breeding areas are shown on the map. They include (A) the skua proper and (B) the hamiltoni. A rather small bird, (C) maccormicki, breeds in the Antarctic. This should now be regarded as a distinct species—McCormick's Skua—for it coexists with the form (D) lönnbergi in the South Shetland Islands and the two hybridize very little. The forms (E) chilensis and (F) antarctica coexist with greater hybridization on part of the Argentine coast, and they deserve at least

the status of "semispecies". They may evolve into two clearly different species if the hybrids prove to be relatively unsuccessful.

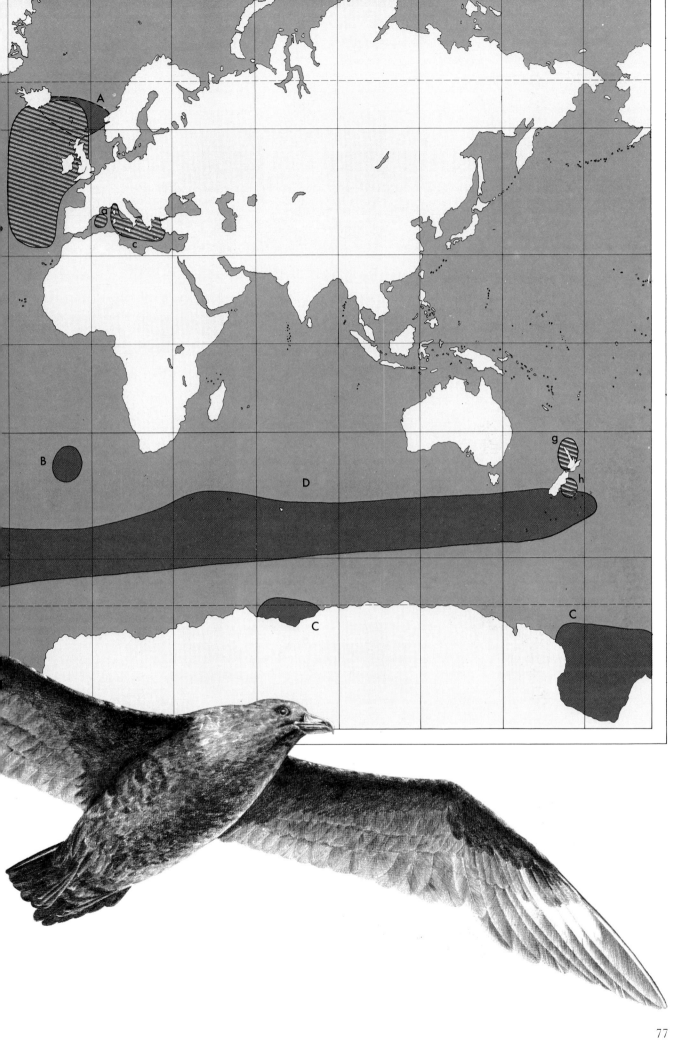

Shag *(Phalacrocorax aristotelis)*
Great Frigate-bird, male *(Fregata minor)*

In the northern subfamily, *Hydrobatinae*, are:

British Storm-petrel	*Hydrobates pelagicus*
Least Storm-Petrel	*Halocyptena microsoma*
Galapagos Storm-petrel	*Oceanodroma tethys*
	Ill. p. 210
Madeiran Storm-petrel	*Oceanodroma castro*
	Ill. p. 211
Leach's Storm-petrel	*Oceanodroma leucorhoa*
	Ill. p. 66
Guadalupe Storm-petrel	*Oceanodroma macrodactyla*
Swinhoe's Storm-petrel	*Oceanodroma monorhis*
Tristram's Storm-petrel	*Oceanodroma tristrami*
Matsudaira's Storm-petrel	*Oceanodroma matsudairae*
Markham's Storm-petrel	*Oceanodroma markhami*
Black Storm-petrel	*Oceanodroma melania*
Ashy Storm-petrel	*Oceanodroma homochroa*
Hornby's Storm-petrel	*Oceanodroma hornbyi*
	Ill. p. 198
Fork-tailed Storm-petrel	*Oceanodroma furcata*
	Ill. p. 66

Long-tailed Skua, immature *(Stercorarius longicaudus)*
Grey Phalarope *(Phalaropus fulicarius)*

Diving-petrels

The family *Pelecanoididae* comprises four species in one genus, *Pelecanoides*. As their English name indicates, they dive and swim underwater, using their small wings for propulsion. Well-adapted for such movement, they are small in size, with a short neck and tail, the legs being far back and laterally compressed, while their colouring is black above and white on the underparts. The hooked, black bill is rather wide at the base and has a distensible pouch below the lower mandible. The Peruvian species weighs about twice as much as the others. The sexes are similar, as are immatures and adults.

These birds do not normally range very far from land. They occur in fairly cool waters, mainly between 35° and 55° S, but the Peruvian Diving-petrel frequents the cool Humboldt Current farther north. It was once quite common, yet diminished greatly in numbers after the depletion of guano, in which it used to dig burrows. The population sizes of diving-petrels are now considerably smaller than that of the very similar Little Auk in the Northern Hemisphere. Their food consists primarily of small fish and crustaceans. Like so many other tubenoses, they breed nocturnally in burrows or natural holes, and may begin in their second year, relatively early among birds in this order. The single egg is incubated for about eight weeks, and the young becomes fledged after another 50–60 days. The chick has little down when hatched, and the adults brood it for one to two weeks—unusually long for tubenoses, which normally leave the chick after a few days. Foraging near the coast, the adults visit the chick comparatively often without risking starvation for either it or themselves during longer periods.

Peruvian Diving-petrel	*Pelecanoides garnoti*
	Ill. pp. 10, 204
Magellan Diving-petrel	*Pelecanoides magellani*
	Ill. p. 16
Georgian Diving-petrel	*Pelecanoides georgicus*
Common Diving-petrel	*Pelecanoides urinatrix*

Seabirds of Melanesia

The Pacific Ocean covers more than a third of the globe, and gadfly petrels are especially common among seabirds there. The pelagic birds illustrated on these pages can be found in the western tropical Pacific, and most of the species shown also breed in this area. They are, in fact, confined to the Pacific except for some which occur in other oceans (1, 5, 11, 13, 15, 16 below). Notably absent from this area are types of seabirds familiar along coasts of continents, such as the widespread gulls.

(1) Wedge-tailed Shearwater
(2) Christmas Shearwater
(3) Gould's Petrel
(4) Macgillivray's Petrel
(5) White-bellied Storm-petrel
(6) White-throated Storm-petrel
(7) Tahiti Petrel
(8) Murphy's Petrel
(9) Phoenix Petrel

(10) Black-winged Petrel
(11) Trinidade Petrel
    (light phase)
(12) Kermadec Petrel
    (dark phase)
(13) Lesser Frigate-birds
(14) Spectacled Tern
(15) Black-naped Tern
(16) Sooty Terns

Pacific Gull *(Larus pacificus)*
Sooty Gull *(Larus hemprichi)*

White-eyed Gull *(Larus leucophthalmus)*

Ring-billed Gull *(Larus delawarensis)*

Order *Pelecaniformes*

This order actually contains six families: *Phaethontidae* (tropic-birds), *Pelecanidae* (pelicans), *Sulidae* (gannets and boobies), *Phalacrocoracidae* (cormorants), *Anhingidae* (darters or anhingas), and *Fregatidae* (frigate-birds). Darters are not treated here, as they feed in inland waters or estuaries. The remaining families comprise about 50 species with many similar properties, although differing greatly in feeding methods and related adaptations.

All such birds have webs between their four toes, and the hind toe is pointed forward. The bill shape varies widely, but is often more or less hooked—while relatively straight in gannets, boobies, and tropic-birds. The nostrils tend to be sealed as an adaptation for diving, and all except tropic-birds have the throat (gular) region naked, this being fluttered for cooling in hot weather. Many of the birds exhibit bright colours on their naked skin, bill, or feet, and in some cases on their feathers. Generally, they communicate little by sounds and largely through their colours and stereotyped, conspicuous behaviour, which suits their diurnal habits since they are not nocturnal on breeding grounds. Tail shapes are as diverse as the feeding adaptations and flight properties, while sizes range from the small cormorants to the massive pelicans. Certain species show differences between geographical populations, yet a clear polymorphism in a single population occurs only with the Red-footed Booby and the Little Pied Cormorant. Strong contrasts exist between the sexes in a few instances, notably the frigate-birds, and almost always between adults and immatures, the latter being duller, darker, or more mottled.

In terms of ecological adaptation, fish is by far the most important food, although tropic-birds also eat squid extensively. Most species prefer coastal or offshore habitats, but many pelican and cormorant species often feed inland in freshwater areas as well, and others breeding on oceanic islands feed in rather pelagic waters. The highly oceanic tropic-birds stay far from land during non-breeding periods, as do gannets, boobies, and occasionally frigate-birds during long intervals. Apart from some cormorants in icy Antarctic waters, the majority of species occur in tropical to temperate regions. They are relatively stationary as a rule, yet some disperse very widely and a few are truly migratory. However, no long-distance migrations between high latitudes in either hemisphere occur within the order. Certain species have quite small populations, while others are extremely numerous as was, formerly, the Guanay Cormorant.

These birds breed in the open, except that the tropic-birds nest in natural holes or crevices, and none dig burrows. Most are colonial, the choice of nest sites varying from flat ground to steep cliffs or trees and bushes. Breeding is usually annual, and more frequent in some tropical species, but the frigate-birds lay only one egg about every second year. It is particularly the most oceanic species which lay a single egg; many others produce two to four eggs. The young are hatched naked, again with the exception of tropic-birds, and normally they stay in the nest, reaching inside the gullets of the parents to get food.

Tropic-birds

The family *Phaethontidae* comprises three species in the genus *Phaethon*. Their name reflects confinement to the warm tropical and subtropical seas, while mariners have also called them "bosun-birds", because their tails resemble the boatswain's marlin-spike. This refers to the long central streamers in the otherwise wedge-shaped tail, which are white except in the Red-tailed Tropic-bird. Immatures lack these and are more barred in appearance than adults, whose beauty is due in part to their mainly white plumage with a black bar across the eye and black markings on the wings. The coloured bill is long and pointed, and in general structure they resemble boobies, although having a much more elaborate flight with quick, strong wing-beats and rarely gliding. They are not very social, and often occur singly at sea, resting on the water during the daytime with their tails cocked upward.

Tropic-birds feed chiefly at twilight and, like boobies, plunge-dive from up to 50–70 feet (15–20 metres) above the water. Squid, which come up to the surface when it gets relatively dark, are an important food in addition to fish. The impact caused by plunge-diving, as in boobies and pelicans, is lessened with a cushion of air-cells in the front of the body. Deep oceanic waters are a preferred habitat, and many of these birds stay in impoverished subtropical seas where almost no other seabirds normally feed for longer periods. All three major oceans are inhabited, but the Red-tailed Tropic-bird is not found in the Atlantic. Breeding—usually on islands and occasionally in steep cliffs—is more frequent than annually at some places, and does not involve large dense colonies although the birds are then fairly gregarious. The single egg is laid in a natural cavity, even in tree-holes, and incubation takes six to six and a half weeks. The chick is fed by both parents for 12–15 weeks and becomes very fat before it fledges.

Red-billed Tropic-bird	*Phaethon aethereus*
	Ill. pp. 30, 71, 170
Red-tailed Tropic-bird	*Phaethon rubricauda*
	Ill. p. 17
White-tailed Tropic-bird	*Phaethon lepturus*
	Ill. p. 230

Pelicans

The family *Pelecanidae* has eight species in one genus, *Pelecanus*. Its name derived from the Greek *pelekys* (axe), which the long bill of these birds was once thought to resemble. The bill, with a great distensible pouch below the lower mandible, is among the most characteristic features of pelicans. They also have a large body, a long neck, short legs, and broad rounded wings. The species differ little in size, and sexes are similar in colouring, but adults usually have some pink or yellow on the bill or pouch—or on the head or neck—whereas immatures are duller and generally brownish. The biggest pelicans weigh as much as 26 lb (12 kg) and have amazing appetites. Crustaceans may be eaten, yet fish is the main diet and various sizes are taken, due to the peculiar method of scooping up fish in the bird's pouch.

Pelicans are very sociable, often flying in lines or V-formations and sometimes soaring in groups to great heights. Individuals of certain species cooperate when feeding, by swimming in lines to drive the fish ahead and scoop them up simultaneously. The Brown and Chilean Pelicans also plunge-dive from up to 35–50 feet (10–15 metres) above the sea. The latter species once existed in hundreds of thousands and was an important producer of guano, but has now diminished considerably although it is still quite common. Other species, too, have suffered from human activities such as water pollution and the drainage of lakes and marshes.

To an extent, the different species of pelicans live in separate geographical areas, yet some breed in the same region. Others migrate to the same places, over distances which may be rather long while not crossing the equator. The birds are generally limited to tropical or temperate zones, and in most species the bulk of the population occurs in freshwater lakes, estuaries, and lagoons. Brown and Chilean Pelicans, however, inhabit only marine areas and do not breed together—they differ mainly in size, and are regarded as subspecies by some authorities. A few other species occasionally breed on islands along sea coasts, feeding in the ocean and, normally, in its shallower waters and tidal areas.

All pelicans breed annually in colonies. The choice of nest site varies, even within a given species, depending on what is available near feeding areas. Some build a nest of sticks in trees, bushes, or mangroves, and others employ reeds in swamps, or use materials like mud and weed to build nests on the ground of hillsides or flat islands. From two to four eggs are laid as a rule, but up to six may occur. Incubation, by both sexes, takes around four weeks and the young fledge in about ten weeks, feeding by thrusting their bills down into the adult's gullet. In some species that breed on open ground, the young huddle together in crèches. Young birds can be noisy whereas the adults tend to be rather silent.

geographical area, and they are migratory although the Australian ones do not travel far. Boobies are tropical or subtropical, and three species are pantropical, occurring in all the major oceans. Abbott's Booby is quite rare, yet the other species in the family are numerous, and the Peruvian Booby abounds in the millions. Northern Gannets have increased steadily in the North Atlantic during the past century.

Breeding takes place in colonies, extremely dense with some species. Most species breed on the ground, building a nest of weed or sticks, but nesting in trees or bushes is not unknown. A few boobies in tropical colonies breed more often than annually. The Peruvian Booby uses mainly guano for its nest, and may lay about three eggs whereas one or two are laid by other species. The eggs are incubated under the webbed feet of the parent, which—having no brood patches—rests its body weight on the tarsi, regulating the blood flow in the feet to a suitable temperature during this period of 42–47 days. Fledging time varies widely according to the food supply, and is normally 10–12 weeks, taking up to 17 weeks in impoverished tropical seas. Both parents incubate and feed the young. The Red-footed Booby feeds its young for some time after fledging, unlike the gannets whose young are usually very fat when they become fledged, scramble down to the sea, and swim away from the breeding island.

White Pelican	*Pelecanus onocrotalus*
	Ill. p. 70
Pink-backed Pelican	*Pelecanus rufescens*
Grey Pelican	*Pelecanus philippensis*
Dalmatian Pelican	*Pelecanus crispus*
Australian Pelican	*Pelecanus conspicillatus*
	Ill. p. 17
American White Pelican	*Pelecanus erythrorhynchus*
	Ill. pp. 46, 174
Brown Pelican	*Pelecanus occidentalis*
	Ill. pp. 70, 163, 230
Chilean Pelican	*Pelecanus thagus*
	Ill. pp. 45, 218, 234

Northern Gannet	*Sula bassana*
	Ill. pp. 11, 34, 206
Cape Gannet	*Sula capensis*
	Ill. p. 74
Australian Gannet	*Sula serrator*
Blue-footed Booby	*Sula nebouxii*
	Ill. pp. 40, 51, 75, 166, 182
Peruvian Booby	*Sula variegata*
	Ill. pp. 74, 163, 219
Abbott's Booby	*Sula abbotti*
	Ill. p. 17
Masked Booby	*Sula dactylatra*
	Ill. pp. 158, 191, 210, 218, 231
Brown Booby	*Sula leucogaster*
	Ill. pp. 35, 75, 235
Red-footed Booby	*Sula sula*
	Ill. pp. 38, 178, 179, 218

Gannets and boobies

In the family *Sulidae* are nine species of the genus *Sula*. The latter was originally a Scandinavian word for birds whose name "gannet" derived from an old Germanic term for a goose—and the Northern Gannet was long called "Solan Goose". The name "booby" is due to Spanish *bobo* (a stupid fellow), applied to these birds because they look foolish on the ground. Gannets and boobies are fairly large, ranging from the male Red-footed Booby to the Northern Gannet about four times as large. They have long pointed wings and tail, a torpedo-shaped body, and a conical pointed bill. Although males are usually smallest, the sexes are otherwise similar. Immatures differ markedly from adults and tend to be brownish, but gradually acquire adult plumage over a few years.

These birds occur chiefly in offshore areas. They live mainly on fish by plunge-diving, often from great heights which, occasionally, enable gannets to reach as deep as 30 feet (9 metres) underwater. While feeding in groups, they may dive simultaneously in order to enhance success. During local migration they frequently travel in groups, sometimes in lines or V-formations. The Red-footed Booby seems to feed at night, probably on squid, but also in daylight on flying fish. As for distribution, the gannets inhabit relatively cool waters, each species in a separate

Cormorants

The family *Phalacrocoracidae* contains 29 species in three genera, although the largest genus is sometimes taken to include the other two which are relatively similar. The name "cormorant" is a corruption of Latin *corvus marinus* (sea-crow), this term being suggested by the size, black colour, and rounded wings of such birds. They have a heavy body and long sinuous neck, a long slender hooked bill, legs placed far back, and large webbed feet, while the tail is long, stiff, and normally wedge-shaped. They swim quite low in the water with their necks appearing above the surface. Many are mainly black, often with a bluish or greenish sheen, but others are blackish above and white below, those with white undersides occurring only in the Southern Hemisphere. Sexes look alike, despite some seasonal differences as ornaments and—during breeding seasons—a more perfect, glossy plumage. Immatures are much duller and browner than adults.

Cormorants vary in habitat from exclusively marine species to those occurring both inland and at sea coasts, to those mainly or solely found in freshwater areas. All depend

Patagonian Black-headed Gull *(Larus maculipennis)*

Andean Gull *(Larus serranus)*

Silver Gull *(Larus novaehollandiae)*

Brown-headed Gull
(Larus brunnicephalus)

87

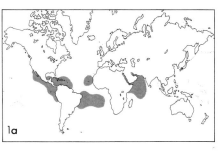

1a

1b

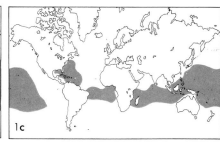

1c

2a

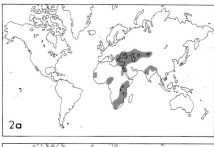

2b,c

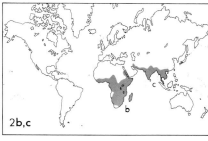

2d

2e,f

2g

2h

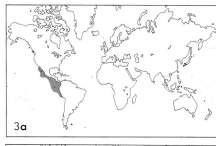

3a

3b

3c

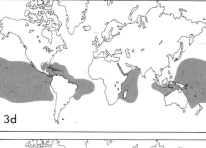

3d

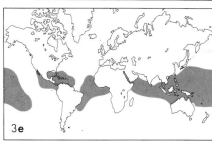

3e

3f

Shown here are the distributions of all tropic-birds, pelicans, boobies, and—in another order—nearly half of all gull species. These four families contain different types of birds, yet both comparisons and contrasts can be made between their living regions. For example, the first three are relatively tropical, while the tropic-birds and boobies are far more oceanic than pelicans and gulls. There is also a generally increasing tendency, from the first to the last family, for species to exist whose individual distributions are limited to rather small areas. Of the gulls not included here, about half are equally restricted—the rest being very widespread, particularly in the Northern Hemisphere.

(1) Tropic-birds: *(a)* Red-billed, *(b)* Red-tailed, *(c)* White-tailed.

(2) Pelicans: *(a)* White, *(b)* Pink-backed, *(c)* Grey, *(d)* Dalmatian, *(e)* Australian, *(f)* American White, *(g)* Brown, *(h)* Chilean.

(3) Boobies: *(a)* Blue-footed, *(b)* Peruvian, *(c)* Abbott's, *(d)* Masked, *(e)* Brown, *(f)* Red-footed.

(4) Gulls: *(a)* Bonaparte's, *(b)* Thayer's, *(c)* California, *(d)* Heermann's, *(e)* Western, *(f)* Iceland, *(g)* Lava, *(h)* Andean, *(i)* Grey, *(j)* Southern Black-backed, *(k)* Dolphin, *(l)* Audouin's, *(m)* Slender-billed, *(n)* Mediterranean, *(o)* Great Black-headed, *(p)* Relict, *(q)* Chinese Black-headed, *(r)* Japanese, *(s)* Slaty-backed, *(t)* Pacific, *(u)* Black-billed, *(v)* Red-legged Kittiwake.

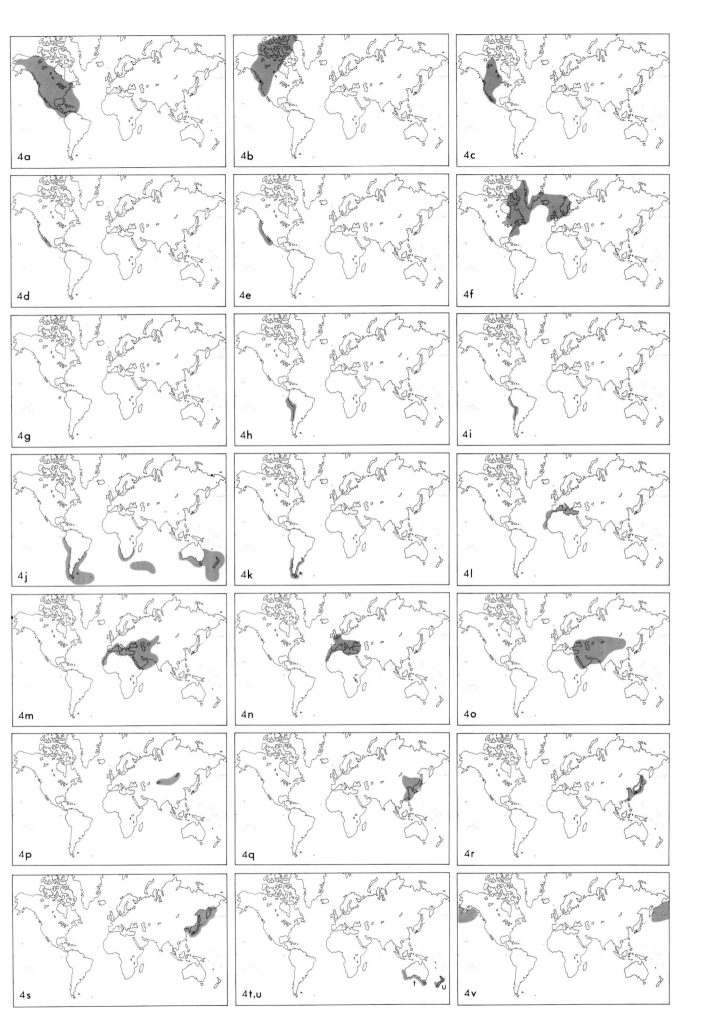

Black Tern *(Chlidonias nigra)*

Common Tern *(Sterna hirundo)*
Crested Tern *(Sterna bergii)*

on land for resting and drying their wings, so they are often seen perching on rocks, trees, or buoys. They feed chiefly on fish; some eat crustaceans as well. Their very social habits include feeding and resting together, flying in long lines or V-formations, and colonial breeding. Most live in the Southern Hemisphere, and some migrate or disperse over modest distances. A few range rather far south in the Antarctic, but the majority remain in temperate or tropical latitudes. Certain species are exceedingly abundant, and two—the Guanay and Cape Cormorants—have been of economic importance as guano producers.

The nests of cormorants are built on rocky islets, on cliff ledges, or in trees. Diverse materials are used, such as seaweed or sticks, although the guano-producing species employ mostly guano. Normally two to four eggs are laid, and both parents incubate for 27–30 days. Since the birds have no brood patches, their webbed feet are placed on the eggs and serve for heat transfer, as is also the case with gannets and boobies. The young become independent after 10–12 weeks, occasionally after having moved around in the colony and gathered in groups. The inconspicuously coloured immatures are a main reason why cormorants are often very hard to identify.

Double-crested Cormorant	*Phalacrocorax auritus*
	Ill. pp. 46, 159
Olivaceous Cormorant	*Phalacrocorax olivaceus*
	Ill. p. 227
Little Black Cormorant	*Phalacrocorax sulcirostris*
Common Cormorant	*Phalacrocorax carbo*
	Ill. pp. 26, 192, 202
Japanese Cormorant	*Phalacrocorax capillatus*
White-necked Cormorant	*Phalacrocorax lucidus*
Indian Cormorant	*Phalacrocorax fuscicollis*
	Ill. p. 131
Cape Cormorant	*Phalacrocorax capensis*
Socotra Cormorant	*Phalacrocorax nigrogularis*
Bank Cormorant	*Phalacrocorax neglectus*
Brandt's Cormorant	*Phalacrocorax penicillatus*
	Ill. p. 215
Shag	*Phalacrocorax aristotelis*
	Ill. pp. 78, 180
Pelagic Cormorant	*Phalacrocorax pelagicus*
	Ill. p. 215
Red-faced Cormorant	*Phalacrocorax urile*
	Ill. p. 215
Magellan Cormorant	*Phalacrocorax magellanicus*
Guanay Cormorant	*Phalacrocorax bougainvillii*
	Ill. pp. 126, 131
Pied Cormorant	*Phalacrocorax varius*
	Ill. pp. 159, 167
Little Pied Cormorant	*Phalacrocorax melanoleucus*
Black-faced Cormorant	*Phalacrocorax fuscescens*
	Ill. pp. 34, 159, 167
Rough-faced Cormorant	*Phalacrocorax carunculatus*
Kerguelen Cormorant	*Phalacrocorax verrucosus*
Blue-eyed Cormorant	*Phalacrocorax atriceps*
	Ill. p. 141
King Cormorant	*Phalacrocorax albiventer*
Red-legged Cormorant	*Phalacrocorax gaimardi*
	Ill. p. 150
Spotted Cormorant	*Phalacrocorax punctatus*
	Ill. p. 17
Long-tailed Cormorant	*Halietor africanus*
Javanese Cormorant	*Halietor niger*
Pygmy Cormorant	*Halietor pygmaeus*
	Ill. p. 43

Flightless Cormorant	*Nannopterum harrisi*
	Ill. p. 47

Frigate-birds

The family *Fregatidae* has five species in the genus *Fregata*. Their piratical habits are also responsible for the name "man-o'-war birds". When soaring at a height, they are easily recognized by their long angled wings and long, deeply forked tail. Colours are chiefly dark brown, partly glossy greenish or bronze, the underparts of body and head often being white—mainly in females and immatures. They are the only seabirds with pronounced differences in colour between the sexes, as the males are mostly all-dark and the females have some white on the underparts, while the female Ascension Frigate-bird is mostly all-dark and the male Christmas Frigate-bird has some white below. A spectacular difference is the bright red throat-pouch in males, which is inflated to an enormous size during display. Adults tend to differ clearly from immatures as well, but no regular annual variation appears in adults. Although females are notably larger than males, the frigate-birds weigh remarkably little in comparison to their size: only about 2.2–3.3 lb (1–1.5 kg), yet with a wing-span over 6.5 feet (2 metres), reflecting their ability to soar.

Having a very small oil gland and little waterproof plumage, frigate-birds never settle on the water and, if they accidentally land there, they must become airborne quickly to avoid soaking their feathers. The legs are quite short and only partly webbed, while the bill is long and hooked. Usually near seabird colonies, they pursue other birds and, by gripping the tail or a wing, force these to disgorge food, which they generally catch in mid-air. Frigate-birds also snatch eggs and chicks in seabird colonies, and seize small turtles on beaches when these hatch and make their way down to the water. At sea, frigate-birds catch flying fishes in the air, and take various prey from the surface without settling on it. They seldom range very far from land, and tend to rest in bushes or trees during the night, but occasionally they are seen far out at sea and probably then spend all their time in the air. They are confined to tropical and subtropical zones, the Ascension and Christmas Frigate-birds living on single islands, and the Great and Lesser Frigate-birds occurring in every major ocean.

Breeding is in colonies and normally near those of other seabirds. Frigate-birds build a nest of sticks in trees or bushes, and may breed on the ground if higher vegetation is lacking. Their breeding cycle is complex. Both parents incubate and the single egg is hatched after 40–50 days. The young can fly after 4–5 months but, in one well-investigated species, the male parent participates in feeding for only 3–4 months and then leaves to complete his moult. The female continues to feed the young for 2–6 months after it can fly, while it gradually acquires skill in feeding itself. As frigate-birds never moult during breeding, the female can breed only once every 1.5–2 years.

Ascension Frigate-bird	*Fregata aquila*
Christmas Frigate-bird	*Fregata andrewsi*
Magnificent Frigate-bird	*Fregata magnificens*
	Ill. pp. 42, 49, 158, 162, 171
Great Frigate-bird	*Fregata minor*
	Ill. pp. 10, 78, 167, 170, 219, 23
Lesser Frigate-bird	*Fregata ariel*
	Ill. pp. 17, 81

Order *Charadriiformes*

This quite diverse group of more or less aquatic birds and shore-birds is usually divided into three suborders. In *Charadrii* are jacanas and waders, which do not live at sea, and the family *Phalaropodidae* (phalaropes) with three species of seabirds. In *Lari* are the families *Stercorariidae* (skuas), *Laridae* (gulls), *Sternidae* (terns), and *Rynchopidae* (skimmers). The suborder *Alcae* contains one family, *Alcidae* (alcids or auks), bringing the total of seabird species in the order to around 120.

These birds have several common properties in spite of their great differences. The nostrils are open, the hind toe is weakly developed or absent, and there are normally twelve tail-feathers and eleven primary wing-feathers. As a rule, coloured or spotted eggs are laid, the newly hatched chicks are covered with coloured or patterned down, and they can lead an active life shortly after hatching. Adults in most species show clear seasonal differences in plumage. Further anatomical similarities exist, but the distinctive traits of each family will be treated in turn below.

Phalaropes

In the family *Phalaropodidae*, one species—Wilson's—is rarely found at sea, whereas the other two are truly oceanic during their non-breeding periods of about ten months per year, and breeding occurs in freshwater areas of the Arctic tundra. The name "phalarope" comes, through Latin, from Greek words meaning "coot-footed". These birds are small and have slightly webbed, lobed toes, resembling sandpipers but not normally feeding along shores. Rather, they swim on the surface and spin round while picking up food, mainly insect larvae in fresh waters or plankton at sea. Their duck-like plumage is dense and waterproof, enabling them to float buoyantly. It is also beautifully coloured during breeding, otherwise being chiefly greyish above and white below. Phalaropes are highly migratory, and the two oceanic species tend to winter in upwelling areas such as the Humboldt Current, off western and southwestern Africa, in the northwest Arabian Sea, and north of New Guinea. They sometimes gather in great flocks over plankton slicks. On the whole, Grey Phalaropes stay over slightly cooler waters than does the Red-necked species. During migration, they are often wind-driven ashore in storms, being known as "gale-birds" in Newfoundland.

Their breeding biology is extraordinary, partly reversing the roles of the sexes. The female, with a more richly coloured nuptial plumage, arrives first on the breeding grounds in June, defends a territory, displays, and courts the males. She may mate with several males, and incubation of the four eggs is left entirely to the male. The eggs hatch in around three weeks and the young—feeding themselves under surveillance by the male, who sometimes feigns injury if predators approach—become independent after about three more weeks. They leave the grounds soon afterward, but the females leave even earlier, and the adults stay for at most two months in breeding areas. The Grey Phalarope generally breeds farther north in the Arctic than does the Red-necked.

Grey Phalarope	*Phalaropus fulicarius*
	Ill. p. 78
Red-necked Phalarope	*Lobipes lobatus*
	Ill. pp. 154, 155
Wilson's Phalarope	*Steganopus tricolor*
	Ill. p. 17

Skuas

The family *Stercorariidae* comprises two very large species in the genus *Catharacta*, and three smaller species in the genus *Stercorarius*, although sometimes all species are grouped into the latter alone. In North America, the smaller species are generally called "jaegers", from a German word for a hunter in allusion to their piratical habits, while the Great Skua is called "bonxie" in certain areas—but the name "skua" is probably of onomatopoeic origin. These birds are rather like gulls in overall structure, yet are more robust and powerful, showing a very vigorous and rapid flight, with a notable ability to manoeuvre in pursuit of other birds which, through persistent harassment, they force to disgorge whatever food is being carried in the crop. They tend to be mainly brownish in colour, and some are more or less white underneath. The shafts or basal parts of the primary feathers are white to an extent, forming a light patch on the wing. Three species—the McCormick's, Pomarine, and Arctic Skuas—are polymorphic with highly variable plumages. The beak is hooked and the central feathers of the wedge-shaped tail are elongated during breeding: very much so in the adults of the three smaller species, forming long streamers in the Long-tailed Skua. The sexes are similar, but immatures differ from adults in being chiefly brownish, as a rule mottled or barred, though gradually becoming lighter with age in the light-phase individuals of the family.

The piratical habits are known scientifically as "klepto-parasitism", or living off other animals by stealing food from them. However, these birds have further means of feeding and are fairly opportunistic in nature. They take eggs and chicks of other birds on breeding grounds, and they may even kill full-grown immature or adult birds. Weakened birds, exhausted migrating land-birds, and floating dead animals are often eaten, while particularly the larger species scavenge extensively. The three smaller species (jaegers) are quite remarkable in their variation of diet between breeding and non-breeding periods: the Pomarine and Long-tailed Skuas, and some populations of the Arctic Skua, breed in the Arctic tundra and rely greatly on rodents when rearing the young, also taking terrestrial birds—mostly chicks—and insects, berries, and carrion. Away from breeding grounds, the Arctic Skua does much piratical feeding, unlike the Long-tailed Skua. The Pomarine and Great Skuas frequently follow ships, eating galley refuse thrown overboard, a habit that is conspicuous among the tubenoses as we have seen.

These birds are extremely widespread, visiting all climatic zones and oceans, although breeding only in high latitudes and—if flying over unproductive subtropical seas—crossing them rapidly during migration. Most migrate long distances, the Arctic and Long-tailed species going to the Southern Hemisphere, as do some Pomarine Skuas, while the majority of the latter stay in tropical and subtropical seas during winter. Immature McCormick's Skuas migrate to the northern Pacific and Atlantic Oceans in the austral winter. Breeding occurs in only one hemisphere except for the Great Skua, and it takes place on the ground—occasionally in colonies but, if so, with well-spaced nests. The birds breeding in Arctic tundras tend to have large territories. Normally, two eggs are laid, being hatched after 23–28 days. Both parents incubate and rear the young, which become independent after 6–8 weeks. The number of rodents in the Arctic varies enormously between years, usually in a four-year cycle, and the birds relying on them breed successfully only during periods when rodents are abundant.

Inca Tern, immature *(Larosterna inca)*
Little Tern *(Sterna albifrons)*

Brown Noddy *(Anous stolidus)*
Inca Tern, adult *(Larosterna inca)*

Great Skua	*Catharacta skua*
	Ill. pp. 77, 130, 172, 188
McCormick's Skua	*Catharacta maccormicki*
	Ill. p. 17
Pomarine Skua	*Stercorarius pomarinus*
	Ill. pp. 39, 188
Arctic Skua	*Stercorarius parasiticus*
	Ill. pp. 14, 151, 189
Long-tailed Skua	*Stercorarius longicaudus*
	Ill. pp. 79, 162, 166, 189

Gulls

The large family *Laridae* contains around 45 species, as many as 38 of them belonging to the genus *Larus*, with six further genera. They are rather similar in general build, but vary somewhat in structure, colour, and size. Certain quite widespread species have become differentiated into particular forms, and a few of these are difficult to classify because of their geographical isolation and distinctiveness.

Often called "sea gulls", and familiar to most people, these birds are very common in harbours, rivers, and lakes, and along coasts. Their characteristics reflect an opportunistic nature which has made them adapted to such diverse situations. They walk well, with moderately long legs at the middle of the body. Their wings are sufficiently long and pointed for good gliding as well as for taking off and landing on the spot, and they can manoeuvre adeptly in the air. The tail is square in most species, and the bill is fairly long and slightly hooked. Gulls swim buoyantly. In colour, some are rather dark: many have mainly light underparts and darker upperparts, but others have a black mantle. Often the hood is black or dark brown in the breeding season, and most adults exhibit brightly coloured legs and bill. Immatures lack such bright colours, being generally more brownish and mottled, usually taking 2–4 years to acquire an adult plumage. Numerous species are quite similar, particularly regarding variations in plumage, but their identification is aided by differences in distribution where these exist.

Gulls occur in most geographical areas and all climatic zones, although none breed on the Antarctic pack-ice. More species live in the Northern than in the Southern Hemisphere, probably due to their evolutionary origin in the former. No breeding gull species are found in the central Pacific, reflecting the fact that gulls tend to prefer temperate waters and coastal habitats. Many also go inland to lakes, rivers, marshes, and estuaries, while the distribution of some species is centred on such freshwater areas. A number of these winter chiefly at coasts, and certain species prefer offshore waters, whereas only a few are truly oceanic. Their opportunism is illustrated by a remarkable adaptation to human activity: feeding on various types of offal around fishing vessels or other ships, in harbours or agricultural regions. Gulls use a great diversity of food, and many are scavengers, a habit that has enabled them to adapt to man. Some feed on eggs and chicks of other birds during breeding periods. Several are migratory—a few even crossing the equator—but many simply disperse from breeding grounds.

Most gulls breed in colonies, which are not very large except in a few cases, notably the oceanic Kittiwakes. Colony sites vary: small islands, cliffs, sand banks, marshes, or even trees are chosen, and the nests are usually built of such materials as grass, seaweed, or sticks. There are normally two or three eggs, incubated in 3–4 weeks. Both parents incubate and rear the young, which become independent after 4–6 weeks as a rule. Almost all gulls have an annual breeding cycle.

Dolphin Gull	*Leucophaeus scoresbii*
Ivory Gull	*Pagophila eburnea*
	Ill. p. 137
Pacific Gull	*Larus pacificus*
	Ill. p. 82
Lava Gull	*Larus fuliginosus*
	Ill. p. 19
Grey Gull	*Larus modestus*
	Ill. p. 35
Heermann's Gull	*Larus heermanni*
White-eyed Gull	*Larus leucophthalmus*
	Ill. p. 83
Sooty Gull	*Larus hemprichi*
	Ill. p. 82
Great Black-headed Gull	*Larus ichtyaetus*
Simeon Gull	*Larus belcheri*
	Ill. pp. 44, 219
Japanese Gull	*Larus crassirostris*
Great Black-backed Gull	*Larus marinus*
	Ill. p 122
Lesser Black-backed Gull	*Larus fuscus*
	Ill. pp. 18, 151, 184
Southern Black-backed Gull	*Larus dominicanus*
	Ill. pp. 15, 227
Slaty-backed Gull	*Larus schistisagus*
Western Gull	*Larus occidentalis*
Herring Gull	*Larus argentatus*
	Ill. pp. 18, 31, 161, 168–169, 173, 175, 189, 226, 227
California Gull	*Larus californicus*
Thayer's Gull	*Larus thayeri*
Glaucous-winged Gull	*Larus glaucescens*
	Ill. p. 230
Iceland Gull	*Larus glaucoides*
	Ill. p. 27
Glaucous Gull	*Larus hyperboreus*
	Ill. p. 215
Audouin's Gull	*Larus audouinii*
Ring-billed Gull	*Larus delawarensis*
	Ill. p. 83
Common Gull	*Larus canus*
	Ill. p. 206
Little Gull	*Larus minutus*
	Ill. p. 107
Relict Gull	*Larus relictus*
Laughing Gull	*Larus atricilla*
	Ill. pp. 17, 47, 146, 234
Franklin's Gull	*Larus pipixcan*
	Ill. p. 119
Mediterranean Gull	*Larus melanocephalus*
Bonaparte's Gull	*Larus philadelphia*
Chinese Black-headed Gull	*Larus saundersi*
Patagonian Black-headed Gull	*Larus maculipennis*
	Ill. p. 86
Andean Gull	*Larus serranus*
	Ill. p. 86
Northern Black-headed Gull	*Larus ridibundus*
	Ill. pp. 173, 219
Brown-headed Gull	*Larus brunnicephalus*
	Ill. p. 86
Grey-headed Gull	*Larus cirrocephalus*
	Ill. pp. 42, 222
Silver Gull	*Larus novaehollandiae*
	Ill. p. 87
Black-billed Gull	*Larus bulleri*
Slender-billed Gull	*Larus genei*

Ross's Gull	*Rhodostethia rosea*
	Ill. p. 137
Kittiwake	*Rissa tridactyla*
	Ill. pp. 114, 170, 190, 191,
	219, 226
Red-legged Kittiwake	*Rissa brevirostris*
	Ill. p. 214
Sabine's Gull	*Xema sabini*
	Ill. p. 107
Swallow-tailed Gull	*Creagrus furcatus*
	Ill. p. 127, 159, 183

Terns

The family *Sternidae* is a large one with around 42 species. It is sometimes treated as a subfamily *Sterninae* in the family *Laridae* of gulls, but otherwise it is given a separate status because of clear differences from gulls—as is normally the case with skuas, for example, which are much more similar to gulls. The terns are highly aerial birds and spend a great part of the day on the wing. The pelagic Sooty Tern probably does so for many weeks when not breeding, and its plumage is only slightly waterproof. Terns rarely rest on water, although they plunge-dive into it when feeding. Like the aerial frigate-birds, they have quite short legs which are unsuitable for swimming or walking. They move about on the ground to a very limited extent, yet often rest on small islands, sandbars, and floating objects.

Terns have long, pointed wings and often a long, deeply forked tail. Due to their forked tails and aerial habits, they are also known as "sea-swallows". The bill is long, rather slender, and slightly curved, and it is normally pointed downward when the tern flies around in search of food. Sizes vary according to ecological adaptations, from the very small Little Tern to the large Caspian Tern, but most species are relatively small. Many hover while looking for food, but they seldom dive far below the surface and they plunge from only a few metres above it. During breeding, the bill and legs are coloured yellow, orange, or red in most species, but black in some. Sexes are alike and there are usually seasonal differences in adults, whereas immatures tend to be more mottled.

Small fish are the chief food of terns, but some species also live on other small organisms such as insects and crustaceans. Most are coastal and feed in very shallow waters. Feeding inland in lakes, rivers, swamps, lagoons, and estuaries is done by many—all the year round in some species, and only during breeding in others. A few are pelagic. Terns occur primarily in rather warm waters, and those species inhabiting all latitudes visit the coolest ones only in summer. Most can be found in continental areas where fish fry are abundant. Many feed in fairly muddy waters, and the shallow waters off muddy or sandy shores often have great tern populations. Oceanic island areas have relatively few species, but the pelagic Sooty Tern occurs there in enormous numbers. Several species are migratory, in some cases travelling long distances across the equator. The Arctic Tern receives more sunlight per year than any other bird, as it rapidly crosses lower latitudes when moving between breeding grounds in the Arctic and wintering grounds in the Antarctic.

Being very sociable, terns often feed and rest in groups as well as normally breeding in colonies. Some of these are quite large and the nests are close together in a number of species. Few terns build nests, and the eggs are often laid in a hollow on sand or shingle, but frequently a nest is lined with plants, shells, or pebbles. Most breed on small low islands, and an entire colony may move to a new site if it is disturbed at the beginning of the breeding season. Only one egg is laid by some species, although two or three are the rule. Incubation takes around three weeks and, after about four more weeks, the young can usually fly. However, they are dependent on the parents for a long time afterward in certain species, and the young may accompany the adults during migration all the way to wintering areas.

Terns can be divided into three main groups: the black-capped species, the Inca Tern, and noddies. The first group is very large and will be separated here into five types, based on some external characteristics. To begin with, the marsh terns consist of three species in the genus *Chlidonias*. Small, chiefly dark in the breeding season, with a short forked tail, and feeding on tiny invertebrates, they breed in marsh areas and generally build a floating nest. Many of them winter far out at sea, others in offshore places, or in lagoons, estuaries, and swamps. In winter they look very similar and have mostly white underparts.

White-winged Black Tern	*Chlidonias leucopterus*
Black Tern	*Chlidonias nigra*
	Ill. p. 90
Whiskered Tern	*Chlidonias hybrida*
	Ill. p. 154

In the second group, large black-capped terns comprise three species in different genera—with a stout bill and a relatively short tail—as well as seven species of crested terns. The latter, once placed in a separate genus *Thalasseus* but now in the genus *Sterna*, are mainly white with light-grey upperparts, a black cap which ends with a crest at the nape, a medium-long forked tail, and a long slender bill; their forehead becomes white in winter.

Large-billed Tern	*Phaetusa simplex*
Gull-billed Tern	*Gelochelidon nilotica*
	Ill. p. 111
Caspian Tern	*Hydroprogne caspia*
	Ill. pp. 155, 197
Royal Tern	*Sterna maxima*
Crested Tern	*Sterna bergii*
	Ill. p. 91
Lesser Crested Tern	*Sterna bengalensis*
Chinese Crested Tern	*Sterna zimmermanni*
Elegant Tern	*Sterna elegans*
	Ill. p. 119
Sandwich Tern	*Sterna sandvicensis*
	Ill. p. 151
Cayenne Tern	*Sterna eurygnatha*

Medium-sized black-capped terns have a deeply forked tail. They are mainly greyish on upperparts and white on underparts, the front being white in non-breeding periods. Brightly coloured bills change to black, or chiefly black, during winter in most species.

Indian River Tern	*Sterna aurantia*
South American Tern	*Sterna hirundinacea*
	Ill. p. 31
Antarctic Tern	*Sterna vittata*
	Ill. p. 141
Kerguelen Tern	*Sterna virgata*
Common Tern	*Sterna hirundo*
	Ill. p. 91
Arctic Tern	*Sterna paradisaea*
	Ill. pp. 115, 181

Black Skimmer *(Rynchops nigra)*

Auks: Razorbill *(Alca torda)*,

Common Guillemot *(Uria aalge)*

Roseate Tern	*Sterna dougalli*
Forster's Tern	*Sterna forsteri*
Trudeau's Tern	*Sterna trudeaui*
White-fronted Tern	*Sterna striata*
White-cheeked Tern	*Sterna repressa*
Black-fronted Tern	*Sterna albostriata*
Black-naped Tern	*Sterna sumatrana*
	Ill. p. 81
Black-bellied Tern	*Sterna acuticauda*
Aleutian Tern	*Sterna aleutica*
	Ill. p. 215

Three oceanic species of the medium-sized type have a black cap, and black or very dark brownish or greyish upperparts, including the deeply forked tail. The forehead, underparts, and webs of the outer tail feathers, are white.

Spectacled Tern	*Sterna lunata*
	Ill. p. 81
Bridled Tern	*Sterna anaethetus*
	Ill. p. 147
Sooty Tern	*Sterna fuscata*
	Ill. pp. 81, 218

Very small black-capped terns have mainly greyish upperparts and white underparts. The forehead is always white in every species except the Damara Tern, being white only in non-breeding periods in the latter. Wing-beats are rapid and the forked tail is medium-long.

Fairy Tern	*Sterna nereis*
Amazon Tern	*Sterna superciliaris*
Damara Tern	*Sterna balaenarum*
Peruvian Tern	*Sterna lorata*
Little Tern	*Sterna albifrons*
	Ill. p. 94

The next main group of terns is a single distinctive species.

Inca Tern	*Larosterna inca*
	Ill. pp. 94, 95

In the last group, noddy terns, are three all-dark species with a lightish forehead, the Blue-grey Noddy, and the White Tern which has dark feathers only around the eye. They occur mainly at tropical and subtropical oceanic islands.

Brown Noddy	*Anous stolidus*
	Ill. pp. 95, 219
White-capped Noddy	*Anous minutus*
	Ill. p. 203
Lesser Noddy	*Anous tenuirostris*
Blue-grey Noddy	*Procelsterna albivitta*
	Ill. p. 17
White Tern	*Gygis alba*
	Ill. pp. 206, 235

Skimmers

The family *Rynchopidae* contains three species in one genus. They are somewhat tern-like with long, pointed wings, short legs, and a moderately forked tail. The upperparts are black or dark brown, while the forehead and underparts are white. The pupil is a vertical slit resembling that of a cat. The bill has a very peculiar shape, laterally compressed with the lower mandible much longer than the upper. This feature is an adaptation to the birds' extraordinary way of feeding, by "ploughing" the surface water with the lower mandible as they fly horizontally with steady, measured wingbeats. Whenever the lower mandible is struck by a small fish or other organism, the upper mandible snaps down to lock it fast. Their name, of course, originates from such feeding. Usually they eat in the early morning or late evening hours, or during the night. By day, they tend to rest in large groups on sand or mud-banks. They feed in lakes, lagoons, rivers, and shallow waters along coasts.

Most skimmers occur in tropical and subtropical areas. They breed colonially on coastal and river sand-banks, laying two to four eggs in a hollow. The chicks have mandibles of equal length at first, and the elongated lower mandible develops as the young mature.

Black Skimmer	*Rynchops nigra*
	Ill. pp. 98, 146
African Skimmer	*Rynchops flavirostris*
Indian Skimmer	*Rynchops albicollis*
	Ill. p. 17

Auks

The family *Alcidae* has 22 species of dovekies, razorbills, guillemots (or murres, tysties), murrelets, auklets, and puffins. Their name "auk" is of Scandinavian origin, and all are confined to the cold waters of the Northern Hemisphere, being replaced ecologically in the Southern by penguins and diving-petrels. Fossils seem to indicate that they had an evolutionary origin in the North Pacific Ocean—which now has 16 species, 12 of these endemic—and that they later spread to the North Atlantic via the Arctic Ocean, where six species still live and a seventh, the Great Auk, has become extinct.

The present-day auks are medium to small in size, with a stocky body, mainly black or dark-grey above and white below. Their wing surfaces are small, giving them a whirring flight, and the wings are also used for propulsion underwater. The tail is short and the legs are placed far back. Some species have ornamental head-plumes and colourful bills or feet during breeding. In winter, the adults lose such ornaments, and immatures are often duller or similar to them. Sizes and bill shapes differ according to ecological adaptations. Small fish, plankton, and crustaceans are the chief food, and auks eating plankton or crustaceans are generally smaller with shorter bills. Of these, six species have gular pouches for carrying large amounts of food to offspring. A few, primarily the small guillemots, feed over bottoms, but most do so in open waters. Some are rather pelagic, notably the puffins. All disperse far from breeding areas and the winter is spent entirely at sea. Closely related forms often differ in habitat preference, such as the Common Guillemot which occurs over warmer waters than does the Brünnich's Guillemot of the high Arctic.

As a rule, auks breed in colonies, which may be enormous and, in some species, comprise more than a million birds. A few species are rather dispersed when breeding: thus, the Kittlitz's Murrelet breeds in scattered pairs on mountain scree, several kilometres inland around the Bering Sea. Dovekie colonies, sometimes quite large, are occasionally located as far as 20 miles (30 km) from the nearest coast. Precipitous cliffs are often chosen, eggs being placed on ledges or in clefts. Other auks breed in natural holes or crevices in slopes. No nest, or at most a very small and imperfect one, is built. Breeding is annual, and one or two eggs are normally laid, both parents incubating. The young of many species leave the breeding site before they are fully able to fly, and their parents frequently accompany them at sea. In four species—the Xantus's, Craveri's, Ancient, and Crested Murrelets—the chicks leave the nest a few days after hatching, and can then soon feed themselves, although guarded by parents.

Auks are readily separable into seven groups as follows. The first consists of a single species, also called the Dovekie.

Little Auk   *Plautus alle*
                          Ill. p. 137

Secondly, there is a group of three large species in two genera. Black above and white below, with a rather long bill, they become white in winter and black in summer on the throat and foreneck. The last two species are also called, respectively, the Common Murre and Thick-billed Murre.

Razorbill   *Alca torda*
                          Ill. pp. 11, 34, 98
Common Guillemot   *Uria aalge*
                          Ill. pp. 38, 98, 207, 208, 223
Brünnich's Guillemot *Uria lomvia*
                          Ill. p. 142

Three species of guillemots (tysties) are mainly all-black in summer and white on the underparts in winter. Their colony sizes are relatively small.

Black Guillemot   *Cepphus grylle*
                          Ill. p. 127
Pigeon Guillemot   *Cepphus columba*
                          Ill. p. 215
Spectacled Guillemot *Cepphus carbo*

Two species are chiefly dark brownish, barred or scaly, in the summer, In winter, they become white on underparts and have a white stripe between the back and wings.

Marbled Murrelet   *Brachyramphus marmoratum*
                          Ill. p. 199
Kittlitz's Murrelet   *Brachyramphus brevirostre*

Four species of murrelets are small and chubby, with short bills, mainly dark above and white below.

Xantus's Murrelet   *Endomychura hypoleuca*
Craveri's Murrelet   *Endomychura craveri*
Ancient Murrelet   *Synthliboramphus antiquum*
                          Ill. p. 214
Crested Murrelet   *Synthliboramphus wumizusume*

The small auklets have ornamental plumes and short, stubby bills which are red or yellow except in the first species.

Cassin's Auklet   *Ptychoramphus aleuticus*
                          Ill. p. 214
Parakeet Auklet   *Cyclorrhynchus psittacula*
                          Ill. p. 214
Crested Auklet   *Aethia cristatella*
                          Ill. p. 215
Least Auklet   *Aethia pusilla*
                          Ill. p. 214
Whiskered Auklet   *Aethia pygmaea*
                          Ill. p. 17
Rhinoceros Auklet   *Cerorhinca monocerata*

Finally, the puffins are characterized by their white cheeks and by large, laterally compressed, triangular bills which have particularly bright colours during breeding.

Atlantic Puffin   *Fratercula arctica*
                          Ill. pp. 11, 27, 44, 224–225
Horned Puffin   *Fratercula corniculata*
                          Ill. p. 215
Tufted Puffin   *Lunda cirrhata*
                          Ill. p. 42

Having completed the roster of seabird species known today, we may proceed to a more detailed description and understanding of them through the subjects of the next chapters.

Chapter Four
SEABIRD MIGRATION

The free-ranging life of seabirds is part of a much wider perspective, for many also migrate over long distances. Such movements are undoubtedly expensive in terms of both energy and hazards: migrating birds often die because of environmental conditions, faulty navigation, and lack of food. Why birds fly so far is thus of great interest, and may be explained in three ways.

To begin with, the immediate causes of a specific migration must lie in some combination of environmental factors with others that are intrinsic to the birds themselves. The latter factors are determined by investigating the roles of genes and environment, particularly that of learning, in the development of individual birds. Further, we want to know how migratory habits evolved in bird species and became established in their populations.

Movements of seabirds

The places and times at which seabirds cross the oceans extensively are very diverse, as are the durations of their travels and of their residence in limited areas. But the species which clearly migrate do so during a period of non-breeding, and this usually has three stages: post-breeding migration, staying in a "target" area, and pre-breeding migration. Such directed movement is termed *true migration*. Its stages generally coincide with seasonal cycles, and can be described as autumn migration, wintering, and spring migration. However, in many species the immatures also migrate and tend to have a summering stage when the adults are breeding, while a few migratory species breed in winter.

Even during the breeding period, forays from a home base are common. Parents fly away to feed, or to obtain food for offspring, when not incubating eggs or protecting young—duties which are shared by both sexes in most species of seabirds. The relatively oceanic species may undertake very long foraging flights. Some tubenoses regularly range up to 600 miles (1,000 km) from the breeding site to feed, and frequently travel to target areas where feeding conditions are good. Yet in other cases we observe only dispersal in various directions around the breeding site. Foraging flights of varying lengths from temporary bases are also made, by some seabirds which remain fairly stationary after breeding not far away, and by the many coastal species which return to particular resting sites.

When not breeding, the most oceanic birds range over water for most or all of the time. Instead of true migration, many of them disperse widely and randomly from the breeding site, and may wander quite far away in search of food. This *nomadism* is much more common with seabirds than among birds of the land. A relatively limited kind of movement, which can occur anywhere, is an *eruptive dispersal* of seabirds that suddenly leave an area with unfavourable conditions such as lack of food. Likewise, storms and other disturbances are sometimes responsible for weather-induced movements or *wind-drifts* of seabirds, often consisting of a forward flight and return flight. During migration, too, seabirds taken off-course by wind-drifts normally compensate for these by a change in flying direction that brings them back to familiar areas.

All sorts of borderline cases can be found between the foregoing types of movement. Birds breeding close to a continent may disperse in every seaward direction but not towards land. Many species which breed at high latitudes slowly shift their distribution to lower latitudes during the winter, rather than truly migrating. Some species have migratory habits that vary among individuals or from one population to another. As for the nomadic species, they often make temporary stops in limited places. Since oceanic life is nomadic by nature, they generally move around a lot within their target areas when these do exist. In some species a *continuous migration* occurs, because they never stay long in particular target areas along a fixed route.

Migratory characteristics

Most of the migratory seabirds breed in latitudes with large seasonal variations in climate and food supply, so it is inevitable that many birds move to lower latitudes in winter. However, as similar climates and habitats occur in both hemispheres, each having abundant food during its summer season, some seabirds take advantage of both supplies by means of transoceanic and transequatorial migration. Quite a few species migrate from the Northern to the Southern Hemisphere and, in contrast to land-birds, there are numerous seabirds which do the opposite—notably some shearwaters, petrels, and storm-petrels.

Certain species breeding in rather high latitudes migrate to tropical or subtropical waters, thus showing a marked change in habitat preference between breeding and non-breeding periods: examples are the Black-bellied and Leach's Storm-petrels. Even more curious are those which breed inland and winter at sea—for instance phalaropes,

The ways in which seabirds travel are summarized below with symbols. Maps in this chapter include reference-signs with page numbers for the photographs that show the bird species concerned.

Nomadism: flying far and randomly while feeding.

Dispersal: leaving in various directions from a feeding area or breeding site.

Continuous migration: somewhat directed, without long stops except to breed.

True migration: directed to a target area of breeding or of non-breeding.

Rapid migration to a target area with no stops enroute for feeding.

Slow migration combined with feeding or resting along the way.

Transequatorial migration across the equator to and from breeding areas.

Latitude shift: a smaller change of distribution in breeding seasons.

Inland/seaward migration: between land and sea for breeding or wintering.

East–west migration: between breeding and wintering areas, or continuously.

Figure-of-eight route: exploiting wind directions during a migration cycle.

Circular route: a more frequent use of winds to save energy in migration.

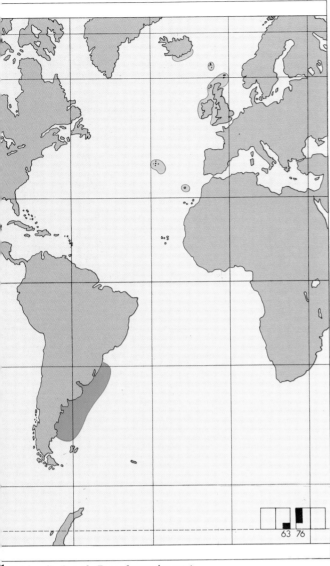

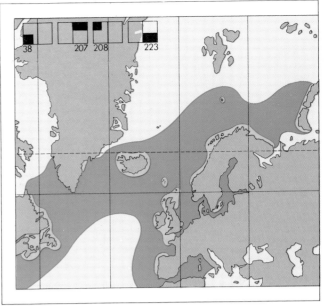

(Left) The Manx Shearwater illustrates a species with rapid, transequatorial migration to a target area. Its nominate race or subspecies, the Manx Shearwater proper, breeds in the eastern North Atlantic *(see pages 76–77)*, and crosses the tropics without much delay to spend the winter off southeastern South America. This is the only one of the several subspecies which undertakes a long directed migration.

(Above) The Common Guillemot also breeds in the North Atlantic,

but has no exclusive target area for wintering: it simply disperses in all directions.

(Below and opposite) Schlegel's Petrel leads a nomadic life in non-breeding seasons, wandering around over wide regions without a specific direction of flight. Shown here is a photograph of a bird in moult, taken off southern Brazil where the species is fairly common near the continental shelf in the southern autumn.

Breeding area
Wintering area

◀ Schlegel's Petrel *(Pterodroma incerta)*

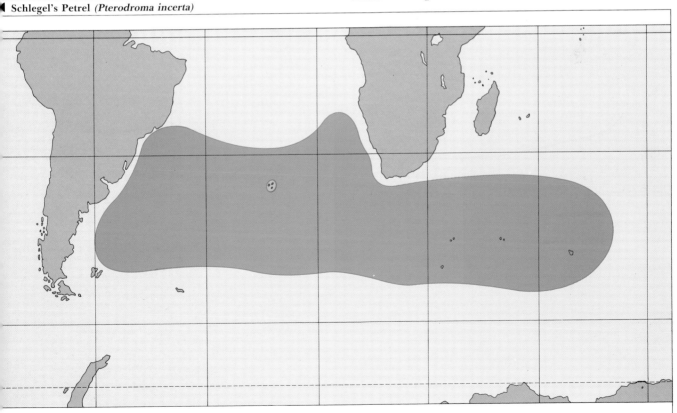

(Top right) The Arctic Skua is one of many seabird species which migrate between the hemispheres. Migration to and from breeding areas in the north may be rapid over regions unsuitable for feeding, but along continental coasts it is often slow and combined with feeding. Most individuals are found in the Southern Hemisphere during the northern winter.

⇒ Rapid migration
⇨ Slow migration

Wintering areas:
☐ common
☐ less common
▨ uncommon

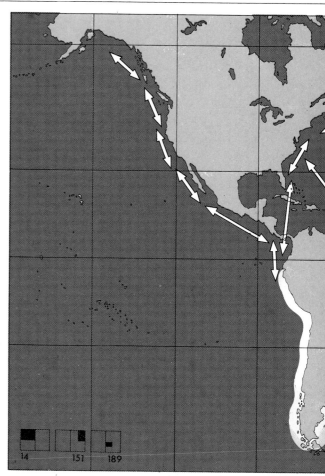

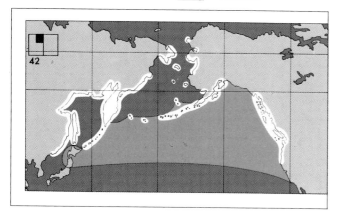

(Above) The Tufted Puffin slowly disperses southwards in the North Pacific Ocean during the winter. It is thus an example of a species with a slight latitude shift in distribution between the summer and winter periods.

☐ Breeding area
▨ Wintering area

(Below) The Wandering Albatross slowly drifts eastward with the strong westerly winds in the Subantarctic seas, exemplifying continuous migration. Individuals breed only every second year.

⇨ Migrating direction
☐ Breeding area
▨ Non-breeding distribution

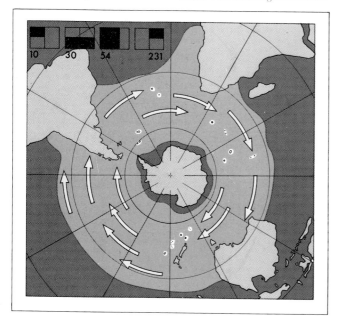

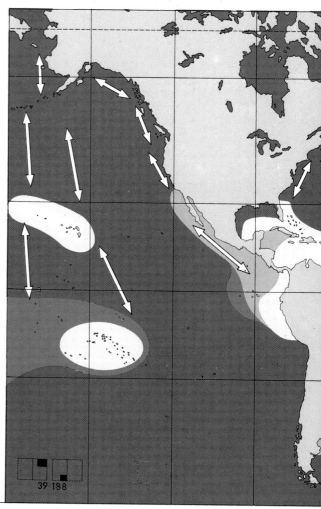

(Bottom right) The Pomarine Skua, like numerous other species, breeds inland and winters at sea. It winters chiefly in tropical and subtropical regions, experiencing a great difference in climate between the breeding and non-breeding periods. Though relying on rodents in the Arctic tundra during breeding, the birds have a varied winter diet with piratical feeding and free scavenging as well as fishing.

⇒ Rapid migration
⇨ Slow migration

Wintering areas:
☐ common
☐ less common
▨ uncommon
▨ rare

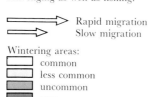

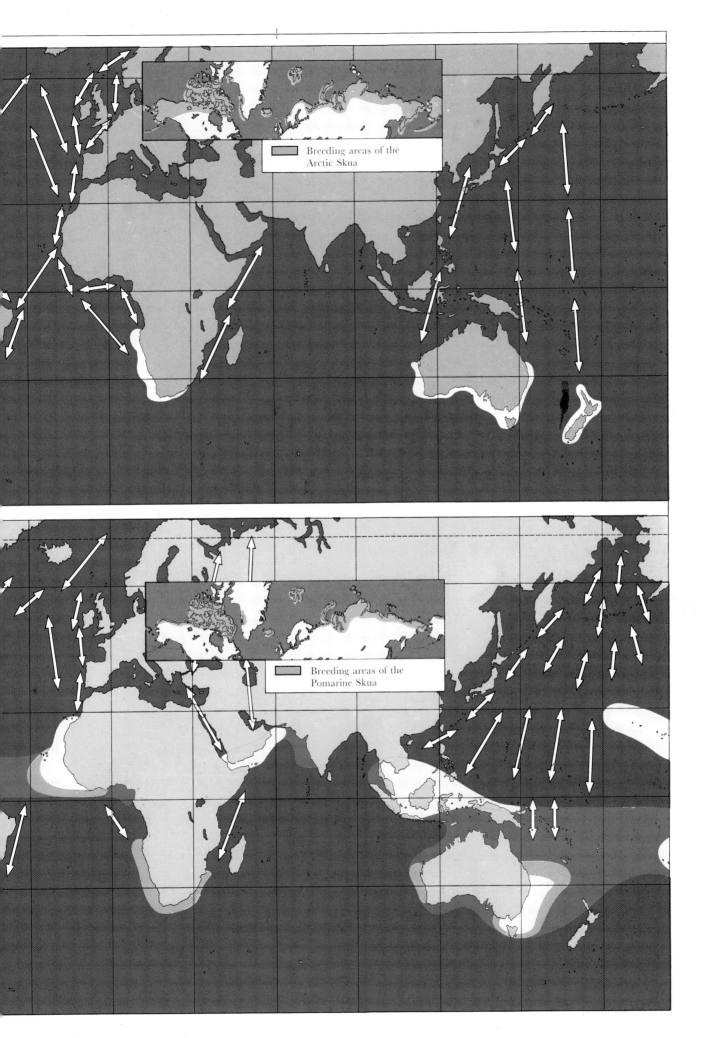

Breeding areas of the
Arctic Skua

Breeding areas of the
Pomarine Skua

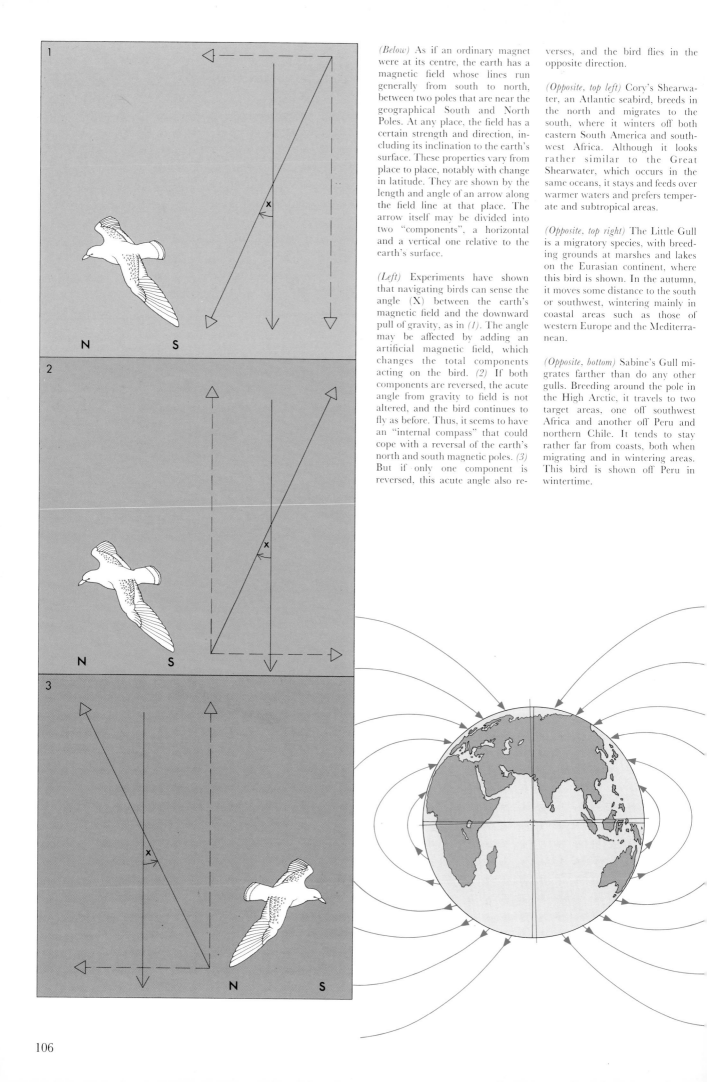

(Below) As if an ordinary magnet were at its centre, the earth has a magnetic field whose lines run generally from south to north, between two poles that are near the geographical South and North Poles. At any place, the field has a certain strength and direction, including its inclination to the earth's surface. These properties vary from place to place, notably with change in latitude. They are shown by the length and angle of an arrow along the field line at that place. The arrow itself may be divided into two "components", a horizontal and a vertical one relative to the earth's surface.

(Left) Experiments have shown that navigating birds can sense the angle (X) between the earth's magnetic field and the downward pull of gravity, as in *(1)*. The angle may be affected by adding an artificial magnetic field, which changes the total components acting on the bird. *(2)* If both components are reversed, the acute angle from gravity to field is not altered, and the bird continues to fly as before. Thus, it seems to have an "internal compass" that could cope with a reversal of the earth's north and south magnetic poles. *(3)* But if only one component is reversed, this acute angle also re-verses, and the bird flies in the opposite direction.

(Opposite, top left) Cory's Shearwater, an Atlantic seabird, breeds in the north and migrates to the south, where it winters off both eastern South America and southwest Africa. Although it looks rather similar to the Great Shearwater, which occurs in the same oceans, it stays and feeds over warmer waters and prefers temperate and subtropical areas.

(Opposite, top right) The Little Gull is a migratory species, with breeding grounds at marshes and lakes on the Eurasian continent, where this bird is shown. In the autumn, it moves some distance to the south or southwest, wintering mainly in coastal areas such as those of western Europe and the Mediterranean.

(Opposite, bottom) Sabine's Gull migrates farther than do any other gulls. Breeding around the pole in the High Arctic, it travels to two target areas, one off southwest Africa and another off Peru and northern Chile. It tends to stay rather far from coasts, both when migrating and in wintering areas. This bird is shown off Peru in wintertime.

Cory's Shearwater *(Calonectris diomedea)*

Little Gull *(Larus minutus)*

Sabine's Gull *(Xema sabini)*

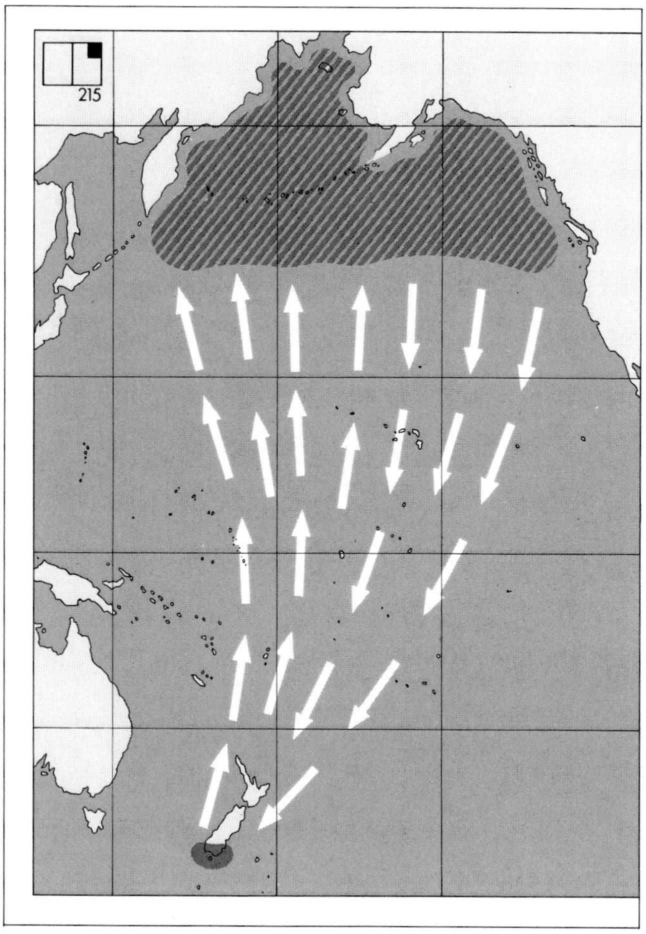

(Above) The Mottled Petrel is a further instance of tubenoses that migrate transequatorially. It follows a somewhat circular route over the Pacific by drifting with the winds, and spends the summer at rather high northern latitudes. Its breeding range formerly included both the north and south islands of New Zealand, but is now mainly restricted to a number of isles in the south.

Breeding areas
Wintering areas

(Below) The Shy Albatross is among a few seabird species that exhibit east-west migration. Breeding in the summertime on islands near southeastern Australia and southern New Zealand, it has been recorded in all southern seas during non-breeding seasons but is particularly common in two areas, near South Africa and western South America. This is a large bird, and the only albatrosses exceeding it in size are the Wandering and Royal species. Its name derives from the fact that, unlike many other albatrosses, it never follows ships.

Breeding areas
Wintering areas

(Opposite) The White-necked Petrel is separated into two subspecies, breeding respectively in the Kermadec and the Juan Fernandez Islands. All depart in winter, and birds from the latter area have been found far towards the west in the Pacific. Non-breeding birds occur in tropical and subtropical seas over almost the entire Pacific basin, although its central regions are probably favoured. Otherwise, we do not know exactly how the two populations migrate, and this is a frequent problem in the study of widespread seabird species.

Breeding areas
Wintering areas

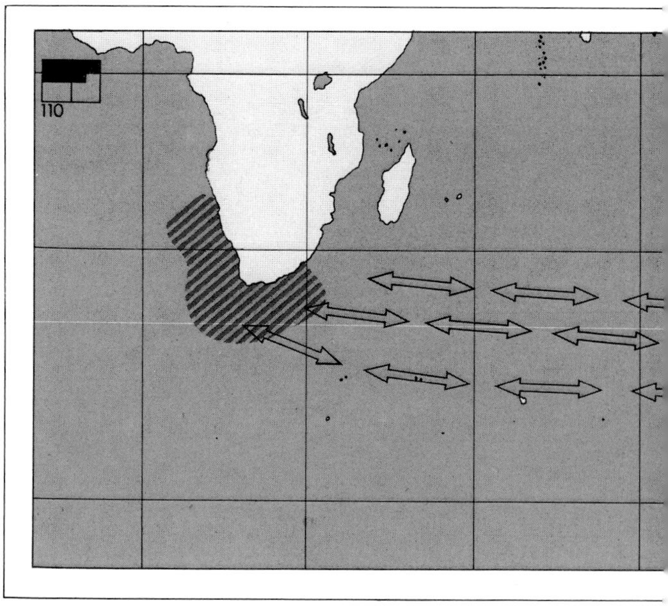

Pomarine and Long-tailed Skuas, and the Black Tern. We also find, strangely enough, a few seabirds breeding in winter in subtropical to temperate latitudes, some of them actually migrating across the equator afterward and experiencing winter in the opposite hemisphere as well. One such species is Solander's Petrel, breeding on Lord Howe Island near eastern Australia and migrating to the North Pacific. Still, non-breeders in these species stay in the opposite hemisphere during its summer period.

Seabirds also include several east–west migrators. Sooty Terns breeding in the West Indies migrate to the Gulf of Guinea, off the west coast of Africa. Shy Albatrosses, which breed off New Zealand and in southern Australia, partly disperse but have two definite target areas—one near South Africa and the other off Chile and southern Peru—thus migrating both west and east from the breeding grounds. Many seabirds in the southern oceans range around the whole Antarctic continent and drift with the strong westerly winds, exhibiting a continuous eastward nomadism. By contrast, birds breeding in the tropics often disperse widely and lack well-developed directional tendencies, although their nomadism may be more directed if they breed near a continent.

Flightless birds, too, have directed movements, and some penguin species migrate over great distances. Certain Magellan Penguins swim from the tip of South America all the way up to southern Brazil. Other birds that lose flying abilities during moult, and young auks that leave the breeding colony before they are able to fly, also swim far in particular directions. For instance, immature Brünnich's Guillemots swim together with their parents for more than 600 miles (1,000 km) in western Greenland.

Routes and timing

Many seabirds migrate over very broad zones, but some species pass along extraordinarily narrow ones. These lanes are frequently found off a peninsula or land mass, which has to be rounded and therefore concentrates the birds, as happens near northwest Spain in autumn. But the Short-tailed and Great Shearwaters migrating to the Northern Hemisphere follow quite narrow paths even far out at sea, showing considerable skills of navigation.

Why a species has come to adopt a certain route is an interesting question. In some cases the species' area of distribution has been extended in a manner which seems to have involved a given migratory route. Yet the chosen

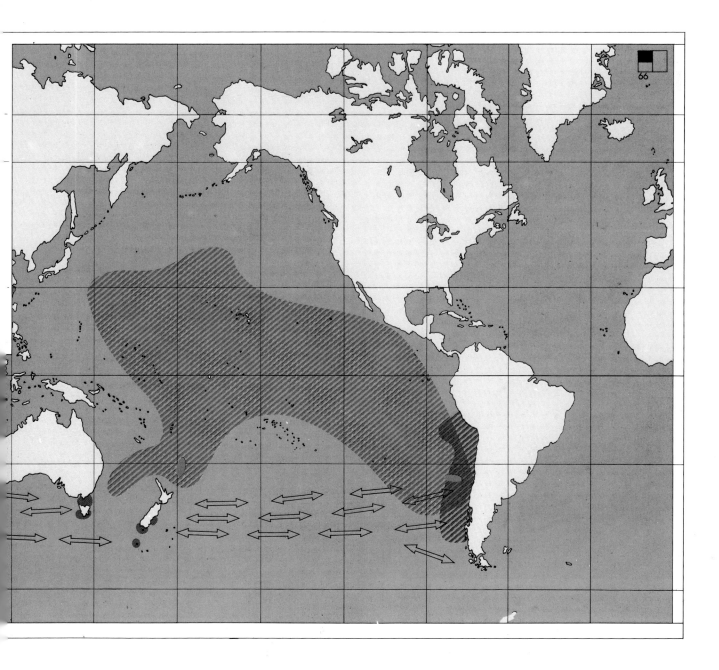

path is usually the most "economical" one, and this is not always the shortest in geographical terms. Winds often make a longer route more convenient, commonly tracing a circle or, sometimes, a figure-of-eight pattern over the oceans. The lane, and the extent of temporary stops, may differ somewhat from year to year, depending on variations in winds or food supplies. Innate control of a bird's route is relatively strong in particular species—and it tends to be associated with innately controlled timing.

There are fascinating contrasts between species as regards the timing of migration. Those with strong innate factors influencing their migration have very regular times of arrival and departure, even if external conditions change radically. Other species are frequently much affected by severe winters at high latitudes. The speed of continuous migration is comparatively great in some species. A fast passage may occur over certain waters or land areas, giving way to limited nomadic life elsewhere. Residence in a wintering area can be long, as with phalaropes, or rather short as in the case of some tubenoses with extended breeding cycles.

If the breeding area has few good nest sites, it may be of value for one or both parents to guard the site for a time before egg-laying begins. In such species, the male often arrives earlier than the female and defends the site, but in phalaropes the female arrives first. Gannets are partial migrants, since the adults—and particularly males—stay near the breeding colony all the year round, whereas the immatures make a long trip to West Africa. Numerous instances of immatures migrating longer distances than adults can be found among seabirds. In high-latitude breeders, the immatures frequently migrate or disperse farther towards low latitudes in winter than do adults, and return in summer to their place of birth even if they are not yet old enough to breed; they usually reach the summering area much later than the adults.

Performance

Detailed knowledge of how seabirds carry out migration has come to light. Many are very sociable and gather in large groups when resting on water or land, or when feeding. Some also migrate in groups, but the groups are normally small, and solitary migration is common. The navigating skills of numerous tubenoses are shown by their solitary migration over vast distances. Species such as the Sooty, Short-tailed, and Great Shearwaters, while conspicuous for

Shy Albatross *(Diomedea cauta)*

Short-tailed Shearwater *(Puffinus tenuirostris)*

Pale-footed Shearwater *(Puffinus carneipes)*

Gull-billed Tern *(Gelochelidon nilotica)*
Magellan Penguin *(Spheniscus magellanicus)*

(Above) These Shy Albatrosses are shown off South Africa, one of the two wintering areas to which they migrate *(see page 108)*.

(Left) Short-tailed Shearwaters form a "raft" near the Aleutian Islands. This extremely abundant species breeds in southeastern Australia and around Tasmania, and migrates along a figure-of-eight route far across the Pacific.

(Top right) The Pale-footed Shearwater, here photographed off southeast Arabia, breeds in Australia and on islands in the south Indian Ocean. It migrates to the Arabian Sea over a circular route, as well as travelling to the North Pacific.

(Centre right) This Gull-billed Tern is shown in an estuary in India. It winters in rather low latitudes, but many birds of the species breed in temperate areas.

(Bottom right) An immature Magellan Penguin is seen off southern Brazil, having migrated by swimming from a breeding area farther south.

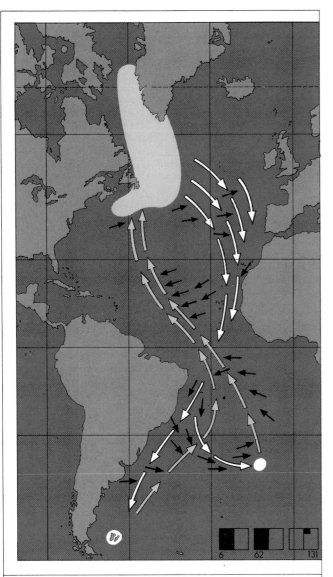

moving in big groups within limited areas, often fly singly or in small groups during rapid long-distance migration.

More nomadic birds tend to wander alone, as do many gadfly petrels, albatrosses, and storm-petrels. Birds in the order *Pelecaniformes*, however, may fly rather far in energy-saving V-formations. A peculiarity of some tern species is that individuals seldom migrate singly. Arctic Terns almost always migrate in small groups, and the Sooty Tern—which leads a nomadic life in tropical oceans—usually travels in fairly large groups.

Over the water, seabirds generally migrate at low altitudes, notably the tubenoses that take advantage of variable winds above the waves. Only when crossing over land on their way to breeding grounds may they gain great altitudes. It is quite common for some birds, such as gulls, to fly rather high when migrating in the same direction as the wind, but low over the water when migrating against it.

Average speeds through the air tend to be 25–45 mph (40–70 km/h) for the larger migratory seabirds. Speed relative to the ground depends on the strength and direction of the wind. A number of species migrate in different directions during autumn and spring, so as to avoid unfavourable head-winds. Partly for this reason, some amazingly rapid flights over long distances have been recorded. One ringed Manx Shearwater made a trip from the British Isles to Brazil in sixteen days, an average of 460 miles (740 km) per day. Nearly as impressive was a Laysan Albatross which, in a homing experiment, travelled 3,200 miles (5,150 km) back to its breeding site in ten days.

The total distance covered during a migration is also surprisingly great in some species. Short-tailed Shearwaters normally make a trip of 10,000 miles (16,000 km) from Tasmania to the Bering Sea every year, and one ringed bird did it in six weeks. Arctic Terns annually shift in latitude from 82° N to 74° S, a span of more than 10,600 miles (17,000 km). The tiny Wilson's Storm-petrel migrates over 6,800 miles (11,000 km) each way between the North and the South Atlantic.

Evolution of migration

The fact that all seabirds are adapted to certain habitats and ecological niches may seem inconsistent with their often lengthy migrations, which involve differences in climatic zones and even in ecological relationships to other animals. Why do some seabirds that winter in the tropics breed in high latitudes, instead of staying in the tropics all year and breeding there? What leads some others to breed inland after wintering entirely at sea? These illustrate the fundamental questions which evolutionary theory tries to answer about the migratory habits of seabirds.

It should be recalled that the genes of individuals, if they enhance survival and reproduction, can become more abundant in a population even when parents lower their own survival chances by reproducing. Some of the migratory habits of seabirds may have evolved because they make breeding more successful although the parents' survival chances have thereby diminished. Migration can also be the best way of surviving, as is shown by many non-breeding immatures which migrate, and in some species it is actually the immatures that travel the longest migratory distances.

The role of food and breeding sites

Seabirds not only need to find land for breeding, and means of protecting their eggs and offspring from predation or bad weather. They require an adequate feeding area near the

---

Breeding areas
(southern summer)

Post-breeding migration
(southern autumn, northern spring)

Wintering area
(northern summer)

Pre-breeding migration
(northern autumn, southern spring)

Prevalent wind directions

Figure-of-eight migration
The Great Shearwater starts breeding in November. On the islands of Tristan da Cunha and Gough, it is estimated to form populations of around three million birds. Few seem to breed in the Falkland Islands, but their numbers may grow in future, as the species is abundant near Argentina. The birds migrate northwards over unproductive warmer waters in late April and May to spend the summer in the northwest Atlantic. In early autumn, they migrate through the eastern North Atlantic, and (according to observations by this author) pass Brazil nearer to the coast than on their northward journey. This figure-of-eight route allows them to migrate most economically, because they benefit from tail-winds, avoid flying directly against prevalent head-winds, and can make use of side-winds for energy-saving dynamic flight above the ocean waves.

breeding site, and cannot reproduce if their foraging flights are too long. Suitable places for breeding, or natural sites for nests, are frequently scarce to begin with—and large parts of the oceans lack good breeding islands although food is plentiful there. Consequently, an alternating distribution of seabirds, from good feeding areas in non-breeding periods to good sites for breeding, has probably given some species the best reproductive success in the long run. This may be particularly true for those breeding in lower latitudes.

Food production in high latitudes is greatest during the summer, and for a short period the Arctic and Antarctic seas are enormously fruitful. The long summer days in such regions also allow more time for foraging by seabirds which need daylight to find prey. But the relatively dark, harsh, barren winters render survival quite difficult. Migration to these areas only in the summer for breeding, therefore, is likely to have been of value for both the reproduction and survival of many species. On the other hand, it is very doubtful whether a tropical species today would suddenly begin to breed at high latitudes, where it would be poorly adapted. Habits of migration seem to have evolved extremely slowly in such cases, combining navigational skills, ecological adaptations, and further properties.

Changes in distribution

While the present value of the migratory habits shown by a species is often easy to understand, problems can arise when we try to explain how they gradually evolved from less complicated habits. Could there once have been any value at all in a simpler manner of migration than what is required now? Skill in navigation, for instance, must have been indispensable from the very beginning of seabird evolution. However, the particular characteristics of migration in a species may be related to its history of distribution. The species might, for example, have shifted its breeding range from an original area, where it no longer breeds but to which it continues to return by migrating.

We now know that processes such as continental drift caused gigantic alterations in the earth's geography, and seabirds have presumably changed their distribution accordingly. Likewise, long-term climatic trends could have enabled migratory habits to evolve slowly, and it is certain that world climate has been greatly transformed since the ice ages were replaced by warmer periods. The exact migratory routes of different populations in a few species apparently reveal how they spread after the last ice age. Thus, the two oceanic phalaropes, the three smaller species of skuas, and Sabine's Gull breed around the North Pole, but parts of their populations migrate to separate regions, probably reflecting the ways in which their breeding distributions shifted when the last ice withdrew. Some species, too, may have simply retained their breeding areas as their migratory habits became more pronounced during a climatic change.

Other examples of seabird distributions seem to indicate the sudden establishment of a species in a new area very far from an old one. The Great Skua evidently spread to the extreme south from the Northern Hemisphere, and the White-faced Storm-petrel to the North Atlantic from the Southern Hemisphere. Whether distant migrations away from a breeding area may have been established abruptly through genetic changes is hard to determine, but the possibility cannot be ruled out. A mutant gene could, for instance, give a new direction to an individual in a species which already migrates far, and the new gene could establish itself if that direction enhances survival.

Far-ranging migrations between high latitudes of the two hemispheres, in cold-water species like the Great and Sooty Shearwaters, are also difficult to explain by gradual adaptation, since feeding conditions in the tropics must always have been too poor to serve as an earlier habitat. Perhaps these species were originally more nomadic, and eventually acquired mutant genes controlling directions and distances of migration. Several nomadic cold-water species from the Southern Hemisphere, including the Cape Pigeon and the Black-browed Albatross, have been encountered in the Northern Hemisphere occasionally, and a few of them possibly find their way back as well. If such deviations enhance survival, associated genes may spread and finally make such journeys normal.

Orientation and navigation

Ascertaining a position or route between places in known surroundings is termed orientation, and following a route between places without known landmarks is navigation. In contrast to most plants, animals have powers of movement, not only in the relation of their body parts but usually also through space. Hence they encounter problems of both orientation and navigation, requiring a nervous system to process clues from the environment, besides motor organs to direct movement. Migrating seabirds raise a number of questions as to which organs and senses they employ, how their nervous system works, and what environmental clues they react to. The answers may prove awesomely complex, for there must be factors determining their directions, distances, speeds, destinations, and times of travel.

Such factors can be divided into two main groups. The internal, or endogenous, ones are properties of the nervous system, hormonal levels and gland activity, conditions of the reproductive organs, and inherent daily or annual rhythms within the organism. The external, or exogenous, factors stimulate activity of the organism, as in hormonal production, the autonomous nervous system, or direct actions. External factors include light, climate, temperature, barometric pressure, food supply, and social communication. These may affect the internal factors, as when a state of readiness or unrest is slowly built up and ultimately contributes to the start of a long migration, either to a wintering area or back to a breeding site. Although our descriptions of such factors are often at the end of long causal chains which remain obscure, our understanding must begin somewhere and the little we do know today is intriguing.

Further issues must also be resolved, particularly as regards how good the navigating abilities of seabirds are. Homing experiments have frequently been conducted by taking birds from an area—generally their breeding site—and by releasing them at different distances and directions from that area, so as to study their success in returning. Sooty Terns and Brown Noddies, breeding at Dry Tortugas in the Gulf of Mexico, were tested as early as 1915 and, from up to 800 miles (1,300 km) away, flew home in a few days. Thorough investigation, notably of the Laysan Albatross and Manx Shearwater, has revealed an astonishing ability to return across a whole ocean. The birds were found to have headed in the right direction from the very beginning, rather than wandering randomly.

Some such released birds are observed to head for home after a brief initial circling. One Manx Shearwater brought to Venice, from a breeding colony at Skokholm in the Irish Sea, circled into the air after its release and then flew

Kittiwake *(Rissa tridactyla)*

directly towards home over land, being captured at its nest fourteen days later, while other birds of the same species returned from Switzerland. Releases in areas which the birds could never have previously visited prove that they know their location relative to the breeding colony without learning a "map" of the new surroundings.

It has been suggested that such birds learn the route by which they are transported, and extrapolate backward to find their way home. But "detour" experiments show that the birds fly directly home even when taken over a much longer indirect path, and in other cases they succeed when transported in revolving drums. Thus, true navigation without the help of learned features in the surroundings has been demonstrated in birds. This is equally clear from the abilities of immatures, especially among tubenoses, to migrate to a wintering area unaccompanied by adults.

That seabirds sometimes navigate incorrectly should be pointed out as well. To the delight of many bird-lovers, individuals of numerous species are occasionally found quite far from their normal range. According to certain records, such stray birds never find their way back home. Some albatrosses observed in the North Atlantic have stayed there without returning to the Southern Hemisphere, a famous example being the Black-browed Albatross that remained around Mykines in the Faeroe Islands from 1860 to 1894. Birds released in homing experiments often fail to come back, perhaps due in part to accidents along the route, but doubtless also because these birds get lost. Cases in which birds become disoriented under particular conditions are of great interest, yielding hints about the environmental information that birds need in navigating. Disorientation in fog or heavy overcast occurs with some species, indicating that the birds depend on seeing the sky. However, such conditions do not seem to

(Above) The Kittiwake, a common pelagic species, occurs in both the North Atlantic and North Pacific Oceans. Shown here is an immature, and such young seabirds frequently migrate farther away from breeding areas than do adults. This could be due to a large, normal variation among offspring in a species which reproduces sexually—but clear differences in migration between adults and immatures are also firmly established in some seabird species.

(Opposite) The Arctic Tern is an example of a species with circular migration. Many of those reaching the Antarctic travel around this entire continent during the southern summer *(top)*. The birds later migrate rather rapidly through the tropics, to breed around the pole in the Arctic. They are thus generally reckoned to be the bird species which experiences most sunlight per year.

Migratory directions
Wintering areas

Arctic Tern *(Sterna paradisaea)*

impair the orientation of other species, and the method of navigation evidently varies among species.

Sensing in seabirds

Traditionally, the five main types of senses with which animals obtain knowledge of their surroundings are vision, hearing, smell, taste, and touch. In fact animals employ additional senses, as of temperature, pain, kinesthesis (relative movement of body parts), and equilibrium (movement of the body relative to surroundings, sensed in the inner ear by birds). Their clues come through receptors to the central nervous system, and there may be some more direct influence on the latter, like the effect of changes in lunar gravitation on certain animals.

Visual, auditory, and olfactory senses are the three which have generally been considered most important for orientation. All these are used by seabirds, although the olfactory sense is probably significant only in the tubenoses. Through vision, animals learn the structure of the environment, being imprinted with some kind of spatial "map" of landmarks or celestial objects. Further maps can involve awareness of relations between sounds, as of waves at coasts and reefs—or between the smells of particular waters, adjoining land, and bird colonies. Such maps from different senses need not be independent of each other, but are presumably combined to give the seabird a consistent image of its surroundings.

A new sense, discovered recently, is employed in both orientation and true navigation: the ability to sense the earth's magnetic field. Several kinds of animals possess this faculty, and among seabirds it has been found in penguins. Ring-billed Gulls are also shown to be affected by magnetic clues, and most seabirds seem likely to share the ability. Exactly how it functions is not yet known. Magnetic material, chiefly the mineral magnetite, occurs in the nervous system of many animals, and is concentrated in some of them at a small part of the brain, which thus appears to serve as a receptor. In others, magnetite is widely dispersed within the brain, its role remaining unclear.

Experiments with land-birds have given interesting results on the properties of this magnetic sense. Birds are affected by the inclination of the earth's magnetic field relative to the horizontal. As it varies with latitude, the birds could thereby determine north-south distances as well as compass directions. Whether they actually do so is unknown, but this sense responds to very small changes in strength or direction of the earth's magnetic field. Animals that can normally orient by such means become disoriented in magnetic storms during solar eruptions, or over geographical areas with local magnetic anomalies. The earth's field varies in strength with the latitude, being less than half as strong at the equator as at the poles, and birds have been disoriented by artificial magnetic variations of comparable size—yet migration is slow enough for birds to adjust to the variation with latitude. It has even been suggested that animals can orient in their normal range by learning a magnetic "map" of local anomalies.

Magnetite in the nervous system could be of use in further ways. There is a daily rhythm in the magnetic field of the earth, as it expands and contracts due to heating and cooling of the atmosphere. Such variations might affect organisms by, for example, regulating their internal time-dependent activities. This branch of research is new, and few species have been studied, so that differences among them in regard to magnetic sensing are some of the possible discoveries to be expected.

Methods of navigating

Whether vision, hearing, and smell are as valuable for true navigation as they are for orientation has been much investigated. The olfactory sense may play a role in areas with regular wind directions, and some experiments seem to show that even birds such as carrier pigeons—which have a poorer sense of smell than do tubenoses—can use it to an extent. True navigation by both the sun and stars has been demonstrated for some bird species, proving that they use vision, which is very keen in birds. Still, how the nervous system processes visual clues in such navigation is not clear.

Two distinct methods of true navigation are employed by birds. In fairly simple *unidirectional navigation*, the bird flies along one compass direction for some distance and, if wind-drifted, it continues without compensating for the displacement. This has typically been found in immatures of certain land-birds, migrating for the first time in their lives. Adults from the same breeding area do compensate for drift and head towards a goal, although they might be exhibiting orientation after having learned features of the nearby environment.

In a more complex *goal-directed navigation*, the bird finds its way towards a target area. This has been demonstrated in some homing experiments with seabirds. To cross a two-dimensional space, such as the surface of the earth, a bird must use at least two environmental factors which vary regularly with changes in location. For instance, the Pole Star's height above the northern horizon varies gradually with latitude, allowing birds to determine compass directions and latitudes. A second factor, however, is difficult to identify. Other celestial objects vary in position with daily and annual cycles as well as latitude, and a bird would apparently need both a knowledge of these variations and an accurate physiological chronometer in order to make use of them. This seems to demand too much from the nervous system of a bird, although the fact that birds do possess such a chronometer has been proven by laboratory experiments when the sun and stars are employed in migratory navigation. Thus, we still do not know precisely how birds steer by the skies, and perhaps only very approximate positions or directions toward goal areas are obtained in this way by seabirds.

Many seabird species probably migrate in the simpler unidirectional manner during their first year of life, while learning enough about the surroundings to aid them later—using features of the nearby waters and coasts, if not also "star maps" and characteristic movements in the sky. Then they may adopt goal-directed migration to follow the seasons. A period of "imprinting" early in life, when star maps are learned for use in determining compass directions, has been demonstrated in Indigo Buntings (*Passerina cyanea*). Some other land-birds are confused by summer or winter maps of stars, but find correct directions when shown spring or autumn maps.

The abilities and properties of tested birds make it plausible that seabirds can orientate toward a final goal by viewing and hearing and smelling familiar surroundings, after having navigated into a known area. Most species probably do not rely on a single sensory system for navigation, but can combine celestial and magnetic and olfactory clues, disregarding one source if it conflicts with the others. Errors during a given day may be counteracted by those of the next, so that mistakes become small in the long run.

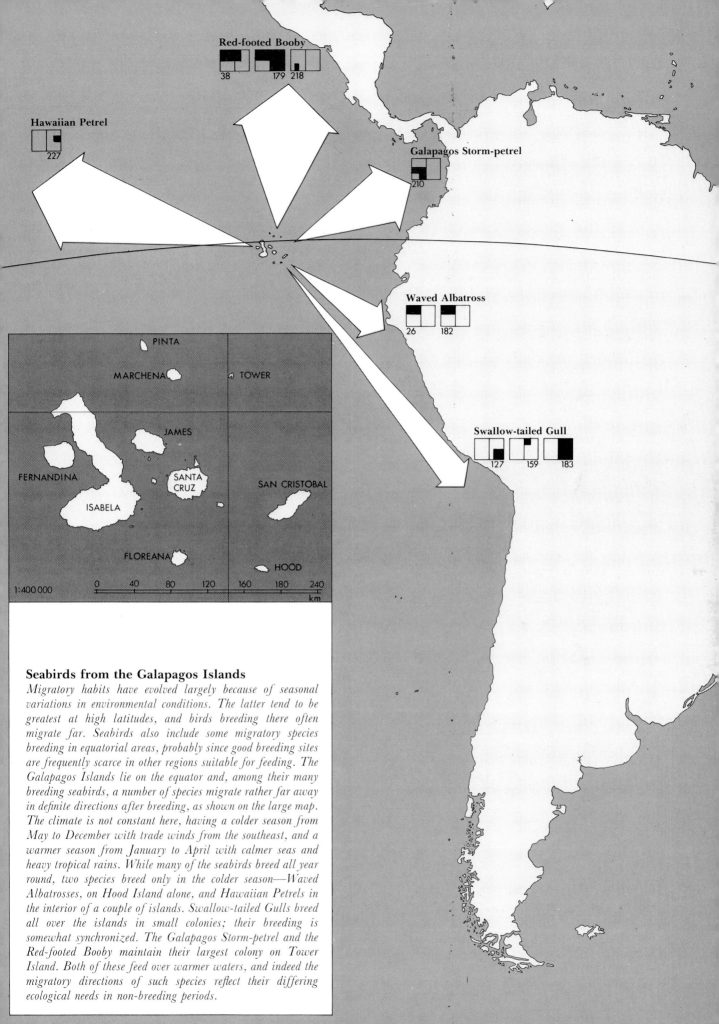

Red-footed Booby

38 179 218

Hawaiian Petrel

227

Galapagos Storm-petrel

210

Waved Albatross

26 182

Swallow-tailed Gull

127 159 183

PINTA

MARCHENA   TOWER

JAMES

FERNANDINA

SANTA
CRUZ

SAN CRISTOBAL

ISABELA

FLOREANA

HOOD

1:400 000

0   40   80   120   160   180   240
km

Seabirds from the Galapagos Islands

*Migratory habits have evolved largely because of seasonal
variations in environmental conditions. The latter tend to be
greatest at high latitudes, and birds breeding there often
migrate far. Seabirds also include some migratory species
breeding in equatorial areas, probably since good breeding sites
are frequently scarce in other regions suitable for feeding. The
Galapagos Islands lie on the equator and, among their many
breeding seabirds, a number of species migrate rather far away
in definite directions after breeding, as shown on the large map.
The climate is not constant here, having a colder season from
May to December with trade winds from the southeast, and a
warmer season from January to April with calmer seas and
heavy tropical rains. While many of the seabirds breed all year
round, two species breed only in the colder season—Waved
Albatrosses, on Hood Island alone, and Hawaiian Petrels in
the interior of a couple of islands. Swallow-tailed Gulls breed
all over the islands in small colonies; their breeding is
somewhat synchronized. The Galapagos Storm-petrel and the
Red-footed Booby maintain their largest colony on Tower
Island. Both of these feed over warmer waters, and indeed the
migratory directions of such species reflect their differing
ecological needs in non-breeding periods.*

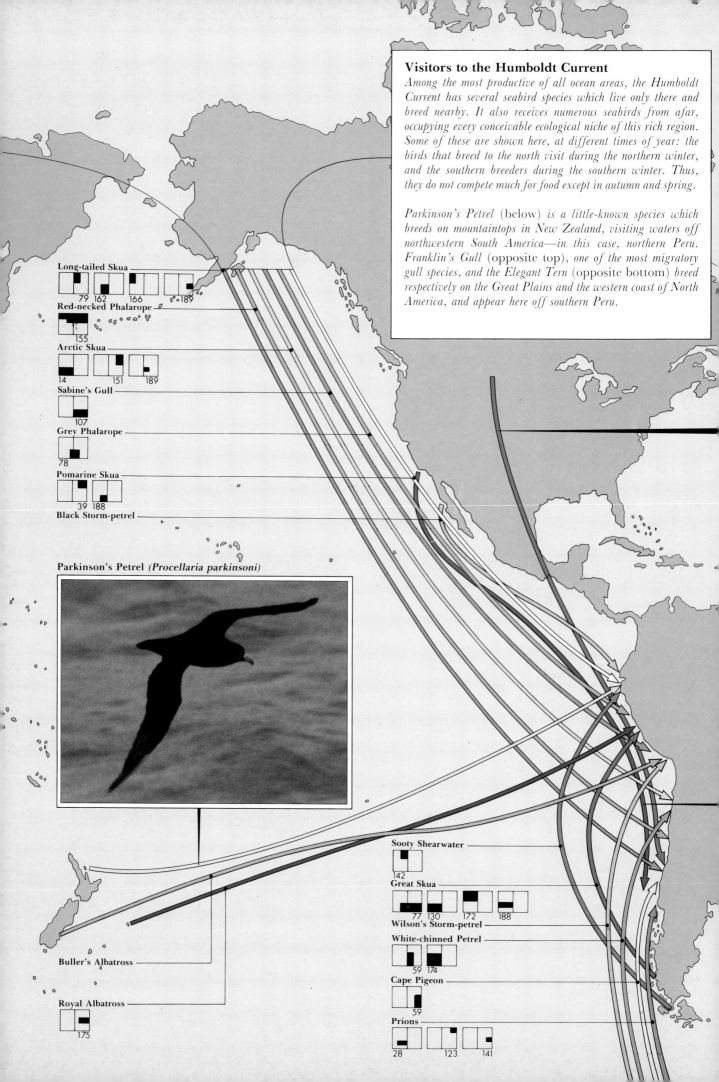

Long-tailed Skua
79 162 166 189

Red-necked Phalarope
155

Arctic Skua
14 151 189

Sabine's Gull
107

Grey Phalarope
78

Pomarine Skua
39 188

Black Storm-petrel

Parkinson's Petrel *(Procellaria parkinsoni)*

Buller's Albatross

Royal Albatross
175

Sooty Shearwater
142

Great Skua
77 130 172 188

Wilson's Storm-petrel

White-chinned Petrel
59 174

Cape Pigeon
59

Prions
28 123 141

Franklin's Gull *(Larus pipixcan)*
Elegant Tern *(Sterna elegans)*

Individual development

Until now, we have primarily discussed two types of explanations for seabird migration: immediate causation, taking into account the internal and external factors of orientation and navigation, and evolutionary processes. The third type assesses the importance of both genes and learning when an individual acquires its present properties during development from the fertilized egg to the migratory situation.

Genes are clearly necessary for the development of certain properties that help a bird to carry out its migration. For example, many seabirds put on a reserve layer of fat before beginning to migrate. Immatures in some species navigate correctly to a distant wintering area without the aid of adults. Navigation itself is made possible by the structure of the nervous system. Birds commonly start a long migration when neither hunger nor bad weather are forcing them to do so, and stop at particular places along their route. It seems that genes have conditioned the nervous system in a way which makes environmental phenomena—such as amounts of light—release hormonal production and other activities that contribute to starting or stopping a migration.

Seabirds differ as much in genetic constitution as in migratory habits and navigational powers. If genes are dominant in one species, learning may be essential for another. In some cases it is known that immatures learn migratory routes and wintering areas from parents, which teach by example and can be imitated. This is true, for instance, of immature Sandwich Terns that follow their parents all the way from Europe to Southwest Africa. There are further species whose immatures probably adopt routes and wintering areas by trial-and-error, their degree of success influencing subsequent migration. Trial-and-error learning is also likely to be important for the more nomadic species which choose approximate areas with the best feeding conditions as they grow older.

Individual differences in migration that depend on learning can be seen even in seabirds with relatively similar genes. Banding or ringing experiments on birds have given diverse results here. Of several Arctic Skuas ringed in Finland, one was recaptured in Egypt, although others were found migrating towards West and Southwest Africa. Most Common Terns ringed in Britain migrate towards Southwest Africa, but some have been recovered in Brazil. Birds from more or less the same breeding area are often observed by such means to migrate quite differently.

Thus, while there may be a genetic variation affecting migratory habits within a single population, it is possible that genes at times determine only very approximate migratory directions. However, the majority of seabirds are ultimately faithful to breeding areas, and their homeward migration shows the importance of a goal that has been learned through former acquaintance.

Chapter Five
SEABIRD ECOLOGY

Some of the basic concepts in the science of ecology—the housekeeping of nature—have been mentioned in Chapters 1 and 2, but must now be outlined more closely. We shall examine the positions of seabirds in ecosystems, the roles they play as predators and as food in their relations to other organisms, their importance in various marine ecosystems, and how energy and nutrients flow through the ecosystems of which seabirds are a part. Towards an understanding of these details of seabird life, a few general facts about ecological systems will be discussed first.

Marine ecology

An ecosystem consists of a *community* of organisms, with the total *populations* of interrelating species, and a *physical* environment. It therefore has both *biotic* (living) and *abiotic* (non-living) components. The former can be divided chiefly into primary producers (plants), macroconsumers (animals), and microconsumers (mainly bacteria and fungi). The abiotic ingredients making up the environment are essentially its inorganic substances, organic compounds, and climate.

Ecosystems and communities

With the distinction between producers and consumers, we also meet the differences in levels of nourishment. Such *trophic levels* belong to the *food-chains* (or webs) in ecosystems. These interrelate *herbivores* (or phytophages) living on plants and *carnivores* (or zoophages) living on other animals. Primary producers assimilate light energy from the sun, and take in nutrients and further necessary materials from the physical environment. Thus, they are called *autotrophic* (self-nourished), whereas the consumers depend on the *primary production* of plants—a kind of energy storage—and are called *heterotrophic* (other-nourished). Since consumers, like primary producers, reproduce and grow, the increase in biomass of consumer populations is known as *secondary production*, a storage of energy that has been assimilated through consumption and partly spent.

Organisms are killed and consumed by animals. Dead organisms are sometimes consumed by scavengers, but they also disappear in other ways, being decomposed by microconsumers. The roles of organisms, therefore, may involve a process of *decomposition* as well as production and consumption. Parts of dead organisms, together with decomposers, can form a detritus which is eaten by consumers termed *detritivores*. Similarly, excrement can become food for *coprophages*.

There are generally many trophic levels making up long and complex food-chains in marine ecosystems. Very tiny one-celled algae are consumed by marine herbivores, which in turn are usually quite small. Diminutive carnivores often eat these, living at a third trophic level, and are subsequently devoured by somewhat bigger ones. However, it is mostly at the lower trophic levels that carnivores are specialized for feeding on a single level. Carnivores at high "heterotrophic" levels may feed on many kinds of animals at different trophic levels.

Some species of unicellular algae are relatively large, and often occur clumped into sizeable particles. They can thus be consumed by rather big herbivores—for example, by fish as large as anchovy, or by krill. Feeding on the latter are numerous seabird species, at a third trophic level. Among these are fairly large birds like certain penguins, as well as smaller species like phalaropes, plankton-feeding storm-petrels, and filter-feeding prions. Otherwise, most seabirds feed on marine animals at higher trophic levels and, as a result, belong to more elaborate food-chains.

Detritivores and herbivores also concern two very different ways of nourishment in ecosystems, a detritus food-chain and a grazing food-chain. Many detritivores tend to get their energy from bacteria that decomposes detritus, but those which feed on decomposing parts of organisms may still be relatively large in size—like some fish and snails—and they may be eaten by birds. Although the vast majority of seabirds undoubtedly feeds on animals in the grazing food-chain, detritus-eating animals can to some extent be included in seabird diets, particularly in certain coastal areas. For instance, while few animals feed directly on mangroves, these regions have been found to be enormously productive, and the energy they store is of great importance for their animal populations, due to consumption of decomposing plant material by detritivores. The same applies to estuaries and salt marshes, where many birds eat marine animals in detritus food-chains. Such areas are often key spawning-grounds for marine animals as well as feeding-grounds for numerous coastal seabirds.

The community in an ecosystem is defined by its species populations. However, no ecosystem is totally isolated. There is always some interchange between ecosystems that blend into each other, and the whole earth is thus integrated as an ecological entity. The transition zones between habitats or ecosystems are of considerable interest. In such border areas, sometimes named *ecotones*, the conditions often change rather abruptly—for example, in marine ecosystems, between the continental shelf waters

(Left) The Great Black-backed Gull, *Larus marinus*, normally stays along the North Atlantic coasts, scavenging on refuse and on larger animals at higher trophic levels—and, in summer, taking eggs and young of seabirds and coastal birds. Due to this diet, it is never as abundant as many other gull species in the same areas.

(Opposite top) In contrast are prions, of the genus *Pachyptila*, which feed on small animals—often by filtering the sea water for herbivorous plankton—in short food-chains of the open ocean in the Southern Hemisphere. Thus, they belong only to a third trophic level, and frequently reach enormous population sizes.

Pterodroma sp.?

and deep oceanic waters, or within convergence zones between two oceanic water masses. Quite frequently, these areas are more productive than the surrounding seas, and seabirds can be seen in great numbers here. Another kind of border area, the *tension zone*, exists where a river flows out into the ocean. The conditions and ecology of river waters differ greatly from marine waters, notably in regard to salinity—and the position of the zone itself may vary, especially in an area with strong tides. Aquatic organisms naturally have difficulty in adapting to such variations, but a more stable environment commonly occurs at some distance from the river mouth, and this region may be highly productive because materials that are scarce in the sea are added by river waters.

Many seabird species differ ecologically through being adapted to distinct habitats and ecosystems: tropical or arctic, coastal or oceanic, and so on. Yet a given ecosystem also contains a number of species in different *ecological niches* with corresponding roles. Feeding-niche differences may occur in three main ways, according to the time and place of feeding, or to the kind of food. First, two species may take the same food during different periods of the day or night, requiring distinctive adaptations. For instance, tropic-birds often eat large squid in twilight, and their plunge-diving method is unsuitable at night when other birds, like the Swallow-tailed Gulls and some gadfly petrels, take similar food. Second, we find cases such as a tropical island in the Pacific, where Brown Noddies and Sooty Terns have been seen to feed on remarkably similar food, but the noddies were generally feeding closer to shore than the terns. Third, differences in kind of food may occur between species or between sizes within a species, the latter arising particularly in marine ecosystems since many aquatic animals grow more or less continuously throughout their lives.

The "competitive exclusion principle", mentioned in Chapter 1, states that complete competitors cannot coexist. By "complete" is meant that they live in one ecological niche—with exactly the same time, place, and kind of feeding—and that the food resource in question limits the size of the population. If populations are limited by other

Where sea meets land, conditions vary greatly between different parts of the world. Some coasts are low with wide beaches, while others are rocky and pounded by strong waves. But even the latter may be very productive areas, as waves help to mix substances in the water. Larger algae can grow on steady rocks, and attached animals such as molluscs or barnacles have better access to tiny organisms and particles in the flow of water past them. Reefs often also have rich communities which include food for coastal seabirds. As illustrated here, the generalist gulls roam the coastal zone over most of the globe, taking advantage of its infinitely adaptable forms of life.

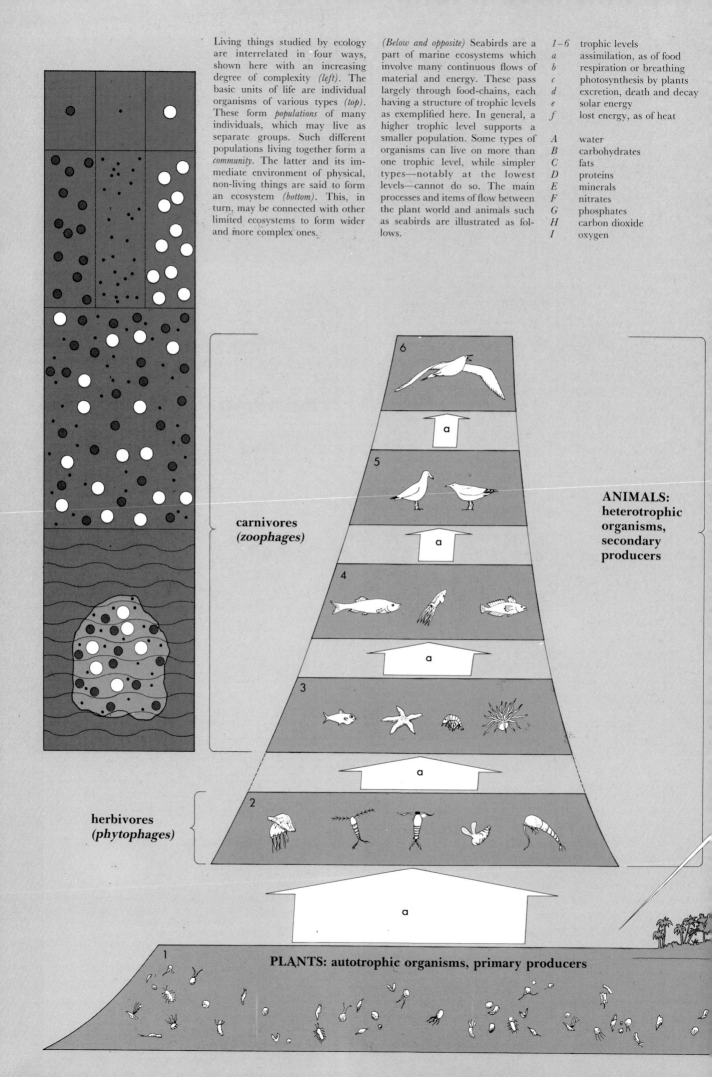

Living things studied by ecology are interrelated in four ways, shown here with an increasing degree of complexity *(left)*. The basic units of life are individual organisms of various types *(top)*. These form *populations* of many individuals, which may live as separate groups. Such different populations living together form a *community*. The latter and its immediate environment of physical, non-living things are said to form an ecosystem *(bottom)*. This, in turn, may be connected with other limited ecosystems to form wider and more complex ones.

(Below and opposite) Seabirds are a part of marine ecosystems which involve many continuous flows of material and energy. These pass largely through food-chains, each having a structure of trophic levels as exemplified here. In general, a higher trophic level supports a smaller population. Some types of organisms can live on more than one trophic level, while simpler types—notably at the lowest levels—cannot do so. The main processes and items of flow between the plant world and animals such as seabirds are illustrated as follows.

1–6	trophic levels
a	assimilation, as of food
b	respiration or breathing
c	photosynthesis by plants
d	excretion, death and decay
e	solar energy
f	lost energy, as of heat
A	water
B	carbohydrates
C	fats
D	proteins
E	minerals
F	nitrates
G	phosphates
H	carbon dioxide
I	oxygen

ANIMALS: heterotrophic organisms, secondary producers

carnivores (zoophages)

herbivores (phytophages)

6

5

4

3

2

PLANTS: autotrophic organisms, primary producers

1

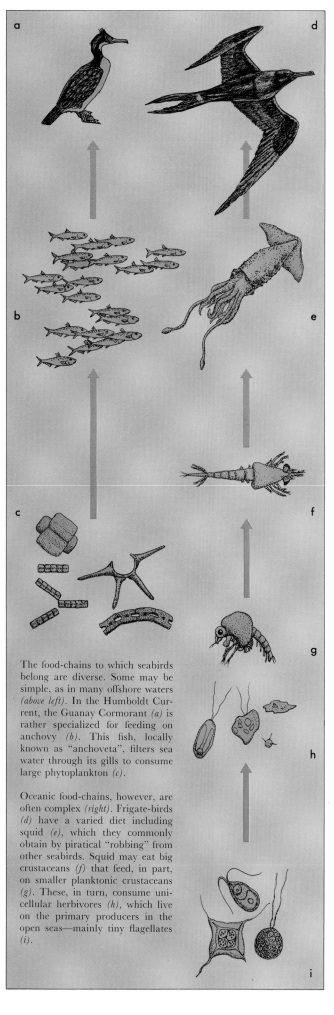

The food-chains to which seabirds belong are diverse. Some may be simple, as in many offshore waters *(above left)*. In the Humboldt Current, the Guanay Cormorant *(a)* is rather specialized for feeding on anchovy *(b)*. This fish, locally known as "anchoveta", filters sea water through its gills to consume large phytoplankton *(c)*.

Oceanic food-chains, however, are often complex *(right)*. Frigate-birds *(d)* have a varied diet including squid *(e)*, which they commonly obtain by piratical "robbing" from other seabirds. Squid may eat big crustaceans *(f)* that feed, in part, on smaller planktonic crustaceans *(g)*. These, in turn, consume unicellular herbivores *(h)*, which live on the primary producers in the open seas—mainly tiny flagellates *(i)*.

By specializing in ecological niches, different seabird species can live together, forming a community with other organisms. *(Above)* The Black Guillemot is a rather coastal bird, often diving to feed over the sea bottom. It thus uses a spatial niche which is inaccessible to non-diving birds, and its types of prey differ from what other birds in the same areas catch. It coexists with further species of alcids, which tend to feed in more open waters.

(Right) The Swallow-tailed Gull is the only species of gull which is specialized for feeding on squid. Its large eyes are an adaptation for hunting at night. Hence, around the Galapagos Islands where it breeds, it does not compete with the Red-billed Tropic-bird, which feeds on such prey chiefly during twilight.

Even closely related species of seabirds may coexist in the same breeding habitat by occupying different ecological niches. These diagrams show the food choices of some fairly similar terns and noddies on Christmas Island in the Pacific Ocean. Measured vertically on each graph are the percentages of prey with various sizes.

The Sooty Tern and Brown Noddy eat much the same food, in spite of breeding on the same island. But they are ecologically separated in space, as the former generally feeds farther from land than does the latter.

The Lesser Noddy looks quite like the Brown Noddy, yet is smaller and has a slender, more pointed bill. It eats more fish and, on the average, smaller ones. Here we notice the usual rule that smaller seabirds feed on smaller prey.

The Lesser Noddy and Blue-grey Noddy differ in both the kind and size of main foods. Indeed, the little Blue-grey Noddy eats the smallest items of all, including unexpected prey such as marine water-striders.

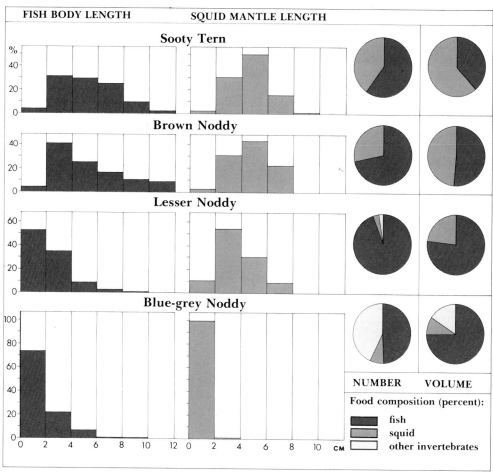

factors than food, two species may continue to occupy the same niche in an ecosystem. Predators are such a factor, as they often tend to take animals of certain kinds most easily, so that these animals may not be able to compete much with other species in the same niche. The removal of predators may influence a community profoundly. In some ecological experiments where predators have been removed artificially, the species diversity decreased, and a few species that had once suffered from predation began to dominate while others disappeared. Species within communities have frequently evolved together over millions of years, establishing mutual adaptations, so that a rapid change like the extermination of certain species by man may have great effects on a whole ecosystem.

Niche occupancy makes it clear that animal species are specialized in their feeding, but they may vary in the degree of specialization: some are highly selective, and others more generalized or opportunistic in nature. We can thus distinguish *niche breadths* with regard to the variety of resources exploited. To the extent that species exploit the same kind of food, or feed at the same time or place, a *niche overlap* can also be observed. Feeding traditions sometimes prevail, particularly in opportunist species which may prefer to consume a locally abundant type of food or at a certain convenient place. Such animals often adapt easily to changes in these conditions, showing that ecological relations are not always strictly or genetically fixed. This is illustrated among seabirds by the many gull populations which have adapted to new conditions resulting from human activity, with novel kinds of food available to those species that are sufficiently adaptable.

Environmental factors

Several conditions in the environment must be fulfilled by an organism which survives and reproduces. There are conditions for the existence, size, and properties of individuals, as well as for species populations and entire communities. During the course of evolution, species have become adapted to particular habitats with their own conditions, and some organisms even manipulate the environment to make it suitable. Adaptations concern not only physical factors but also other organisms: predators and prey. While seabird adaptations have already been discussed in Chapter 2, a full ecological treatment demands a look at the environmental conditions too.

Physical factors often involve ecological minima and maxima, or *limits of tolerance*, for the existence of an organism. Its survival may be impossible under extremes of temperature, salinity, or supply of materials. In some cases, there is a *minimum requirement* such as the amount of food needed by an individual consumer. Often, however, a corresponding maximum level is hard to specify, as with the amount of oxygen in the air.

Just as populations have characteristics like size, density, and birth rate, communities are characterized by their species diversity, relative population sizes, and other features. Environmental conditions can influence such characteristics, and those which determine population size are of particular interest. In addition to the limits of tolerance for individuals, there are *regulatory factors* for the growth of individuals, as well as for the growth, production, and size of populations. Thus, the amounts of light, heat, and certain materials may be regulatory factors of primary production. As individuals grow and as populations become larger, the organisms may use up some of the materials in the environment, so that population growth will eventually stop. Since many of these factors involve minimum requirements, one of them may be the *limiting factor* for production and population size. This is not easy to identify in a complex situation. For example, the Sargasso Sea is known to be very unproductive, and might at first seem limited by an important nutrient like phosphate or nitrate, but close examination in one place has proved the deficiency to be of iron. When iron was added, production increased, yet available nutrients were scarce and soon became depleted, leading to a new equilibrium with another material as the limiting factor.

The population size of consumers like seabirds, and secondary production, are dependent on environmental physical factors as well. But primary production and the availability of food are generally most important in regulating them. The biomass of consumers is always related to the energy stored by primary producers, even though secondary production will always be much less than primary production because the consumers spend a lot of energy, dispersing it into the environment. However, many other factors may be limiting: some seabird species have a large population size, and some a small one, in the same area, at times depending on the character of their niche occupancy. Normally there is a great number of factors regulating a consumer population, and it is frequently very difficult to find out why a certain seabird species has the population size that we observe.

More exactly, the size of a population reflects the difference between its natality (birth rate) and mortality (death rate). Both are regulated by various environmental and internal factors, and by the nature of population interactions. Two interacting populations often influence each other in such a way that their birth and death rates are mutually dependent. For example, a population under predatory pressure may have a high birth rate but, if the predators disappear, the population increase may use up resources so that the birth rate falls. Ecosystems commonly contain many populations involved in very intricate interactions. In order to clarify the effects on population size, three main types of factors are generally distinguished, as follows.

First, *density-independent* factors occasionally control the mortality in seabird populations. Severe storms sometimes wreak havoc on seabirds, and the percentage of a population killed by adverse weather may bear no relation to the population size or density. Second, *density-dependent* factors control both mortality and natality. An increase in population density may raise the mortality by attracting more predators, by making the spread of disease easier, or by entailing greater competition for a limited resource like the number of good nesting holes. It may also force some birds to breed in sub-optimal sites, where the natality is lowered due to greater predation or to lack of protection against heat or cold. Indeed, increased density may affect a factor in the environment, such as the food supply. Although the total biomass of food often seems unlikely to go down significantly through consumption by seabirds, the concentration of prey at the surface—where seabirds feed—may well be reduced as a result of their feeding, so that they must spend more energy in search of food. This may be particularly important around a seabird breeding colony, where natality may therefore be density-dependent. Some research on tropical seabirds apparently indicates that their population sizes are limited in such a way by reproductive rates.

Third, sometimes the population size seems to be limited by a lowering of natality through *self-limiting mechanisms*. However, there are serious doubts among biologists that any such mechanisms could have evolved for "the good of the species". Individuals which deliberately lower the birth rate in competition with others which do not would be at a disadvantage, and genes causing a lower birth rate would be unable to spread. Observations indicate that the lowering only begins to occur when there is already a lack of some resource, implying that the self-regulating factor is a secondary effect of density-dependent factors. In any case, such mechanisms operate by various means: the birds may become more aggressive, population pressure may induce emigration, broods may be reduced, adults may refrain from breeding altogether in certain years, or maturity may be deferred. For example, the Long-tailed Skua, which is dependent on highly fluctuating populations of rodents for breeding, only breeds successfully every fourth year, and very few birds even lay eggs in other years. On the whole, self-limiting mechanisms always seem to be released by density-dependent factors, and all empirical investigations tend to show that seabirds try to bring as many offspring into the world as they possibly can.

Many seabirds have, as a rule, a comparatively low birth rate. In some of the species studied, few of the eggs laid have resulted in fledged immatures, as in Abbott's Booby where breeding success is less than 10%. Others have rather great success, but few of the immatures survive their first year, as in the Northern Gannet, so that relatively few birds are added to the adult population each year. Yet many well-known seabirds are remarkably stable in population size. The adults often live for a rather long time, and their mortality rates are frequently small—for example, as low as 3% for the Royal Albatross. However, temporary conditions occasionally strike hard: the severe winters during World War II killed a great part of the Finnish population of Razorbills, and the warm "El Niño" current sometimes causes a very high mortality among the guano-producing seabirds in Peru.

Some seabird populations exhibit a steady change in size. The Northern Gannet has shown a more or less constant 3% annual increase since the last century, probably due to an end to persecution by man, and it is hard to say when this increase will level off. Many penguins are also increasing rapidly in numbers today. But various seabird populations—such as auks in the North Atlantic—reveal a steady decrease in size. Breeding success is alarmingly low in many species, so we are obviously witnessing a disequilibrium in the regulation of their populations.

Energy and productivity

Food not only supplies seabirds with necessary materials but is also required as an energy source. We have already outlined principles of energy flow and the importance of cost/benefit relations. These will now be explained further, and the nature of energy flows in marine ecosystems to which seabirds belong will be examined.

Light energy from the sun is assimilated, through photosynthesis by autotrophic organisms, in a *euphotic zone*: the upper layers of ocean waters into which sunlight reaches. Some of the energy is used up, but some is stored in primary producers—mainly algae—at a rate that we call the *primary productivity*. The rate is often limited by low availability of light, as at high latitudes in winter seasons, or at greater depths under the sea surface. Primary producers, in turn, are food for consumer populations which grow, and whose rate · of energy storage is known as *secondary productivity*. In order to determine the productivity of a particular population during a given time period, one must measure both its total change in weight, or *biomass*, and its loss through consumption by other organisms during that time.

Energy use by seabirds

Bioenergetics, the study of how organisms use energy, is valuable in understanding seabird ecology. This simplified picture shows the relative amounts of the four main uses for energy obtained from food, on an annual average in two seabird populations. The total energy needed depends on many factors, including the bird's size. Here, one bird is compared with two others which are closely similar to it, and weigh as much together, but are not as big. The smaller birds need more energy because their metabolism, or "burning" of energy in the body for all uses, is faster. They also use relatively more energy for heat, as they lose more heat to the environment, since their body surface area is comparatively greater. In general, among very similar types of animals, those living in colder climates tend to be somewhat larger, and this is known as Bergmann's rule. They also tend to have shorter protruding parts such as the bill in birds; this is called Allen's rule. However, a larger bird's greater individual weight makes its movements harder, especially on land, requiring a larger proportion of energy for that use.

Cost/benefit relations of energy use are important, too, in regard to the food eaten by seabirds. Normally, there is an "optimal" size of a predator for a certain size of prey. Feeding abilities are also influenced by physical properties. But even if a big predator is able to catch tiny prey, it may not do so because of the great energy cost in feeding, since such prey contain little energy. Thus, we usually find upper and lower limits to the size of food that a predator lives on. In a predator food-chain, each predator tends to be larger than the prey at a lower trophic level, unlike a parasite food-chain in which the organisms at successively higher levels are smaller.

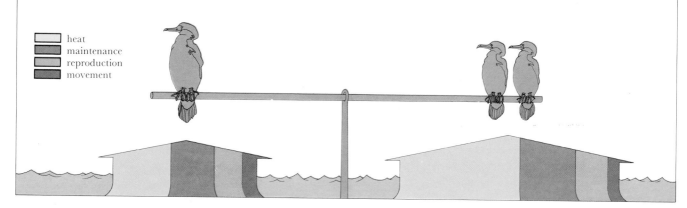

heat
maintenance
reproduction
movement

Great Skua (Catharacta skua)

Great Shearwater *(Puffinus gravis)*

Guanay Cormorant *(Phalacrocorax bougainvillii)*

Indian Cormorant *(Phalacrocorax fuscicollis)*

(Above) Oceanic productivity varies enormously with location. The azure-blue Sargasso Sea *(top left)* has almost no phytoplankton. Its feeding conditions are too poor for this Great Shearwater, migrating from the South Atlantic to richer northern seas. But the nutrient-laden upwelling waters of the Humboldt Current *(top right)* are optimal for plankton growth, which makes them deep-green. Most of the plentiful seabirds shown here are Guanay Cormorants.

Seabirds often connect the sea and land ecologically. Gulls break mussels by dropping them from a height onto particular rocks, where their shells may enrich the soil *(centre left)*. The birds use certain rocks as resting places and, by excreting, may aid the growth of lichens *(centre right)*. But excretion can become a kind of environmental pollution, killing trees on which the birds rest and nest. Shown here are mainly Indian Cormorants *(bottom right)*.

(Opposite) The Great Skua avoids chasing tiny birds, as it would probably use more energy than they provide. Instead, smaller skua species (jaegers) of the same family occupy this feeding niche.

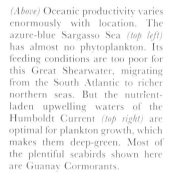

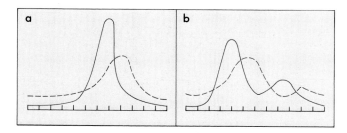

(*Above*) The biomass of plankton in the sea varies with the month and the region. This annual cycle, from January to December, is shown for phytoplankton (solid curves) and zooplankton (broken curves), in (*a*) the Arctic and (*b*) the temperate North Atlantic.

(*Below*) Trophic levels such as phytoplankton, zooplankton, fish, and seabirds (from lowest to highest in this example) differ in (*c*) biomass at a given time, and (*d*) productivity (increase of biomass over a period of time), measured horizontally here.

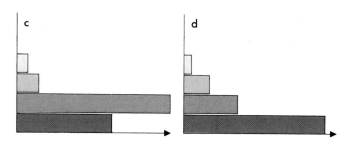

Primary and secondary production

Oceanic plant life needs sunlight, nutrients, and further substances, whose availability changes with the seasons. Populations of marine animals vary in related ways, and it is these which supply most of the prey for seabirds. Migration and reproduction among seabirds are adjusted to such periodic fluctuations, making optimal use of food resources. A main feature of this cycle is the difference in amounts of the smallest marine plants and animals, or plankton, as illustrated at left. During winter at high latitudes, the faint sunlight allows very little primary production of new plants, although old ones are consumed or decomposed to release nutrients which become widely mixed in the sea due to rather equal water temperatures. With the warmth of the polar summer or temperate spring, plant production rises in an "algal bloom", but falls when nutrients are used up—and when the temperate summer heats up the surface waters so that they cannot obtain nutrients from deeper layers. Secondary production of tiny animals is correspondingly increased or decreased, yet their mass often exceeds that of plant food because they are larger organisms, can live on stored reserves, and have a slower metabolism and population turnover.

Organisms need energy for diverse purposes: growth, storage of reserves, maintenance, respiration, and reproduction. But highly evolved, warm-blooded, homeothermal (constant-temperature) vertebrates—like birds—grow only during the juvenile period of their lives, and their storage of reserves is seasonally variable. Thus, their net secondary productivity occurs chiefly during reproductive periods, when new individuals are added to the population. At other times, a lot of energy may flow through the population without any secondary productivity at all, while consumption may allow many nutrients to flow through and be excreted into the environment with no change of biomass. If this is not taken into account, the ecological importance of seabirds in comparison to large cold-blooded aquatic animals will easily be underestimated.

Another essential fact concerns the rate at which an organism uses energy. A large organism, of course, has a greater total energy use than a small one. Yet small organisms need more energy per weight unit, having a higher metabolic rate, than do large organisms. Thus, a population of small organisms uses energy faster than does a population of large ones with equal biomass. A result of overlooking this difference is that the ecological importance of small animals has often been underestimated while the role of large ones has been exaggerated.

The average length of life varies greatly between kinds of organisms. Many of the primary producers in the sea have short lives, since they are rapidly consumed. This frequently prevents their total biomass from increasing much when the primary production itself is rising because of more favourable conditions. Consequently, their biomass may be far less, at a particular time, than that of the "standing crop" of herbivores. Even if the seas look rather blue and clear, with little algae apparent to the human eye, the primary production can be substantial and animal populations in the area may turn out to be surprisingly large.

Consumers, even in periods of growth, spend most of their energy in various activities, so only a small part of the energy contents of consumed organisms is stored as secondary production. As mentioned already, seabird populations may have no secondary production at all in non-reproductive periods. Growth efficiency, and the rate of energy storage, differ widely among types of animals, depending on a number of factors. An animal may get barely enough food for survival, but abundant food allows as much as 20–30% of the consumed energy to be stored, and 10% is generally taken as the average for all kinds of animals. Thus, to produce an animal of a certain weight, ten times that weight of food will have been consumed. To maintain a population's size or to increase it, great amounts of food may be required, and some types of animals consume as much per day as they weigh. Seabird parents often have difficulty in finding food over long foraging distances, and they occasionally bring just enough food for maintenance. In some species, the rearing of young takes much time and, partly for maintenance during such long fledging periods, considerable food is required. In sum, a lot of energy is lost and dispersed to the environment at each trophic level of the food-chains, usually making the biomass of populations progressively smaller at higher levels.

Food-chains from tiny unicellular primary producers to seabirds may be very long, particularly in oceanic waters: for example, via small zooplankton, larger zooplankton, small planktivorous fish, and bigger fish-eating fish, to birds at a sixth trophic level. In such cases, seabird populations cannot be large. But seabirds feeding on herbivorous marine animals are at only a third trophic level, so their populations may be enormous. For instance, the Guanay Cormorant in the Humboldt Current—mainly consuming anchoveta, a filter-feeding herbivorous fish with a rapid growth and up to three spawning periods per year—has at times reached a population of tens of millions of birds. Likewise, some penguin species feeding on herbivorous krill have colonies numbering in millions. Certain smaller seabirds also feed on herbivorous plankton and, although their populations are not as great in biomass because of the high metabolic rate in such small birds, there may be a quite high flow of energy through them. Some plankton-

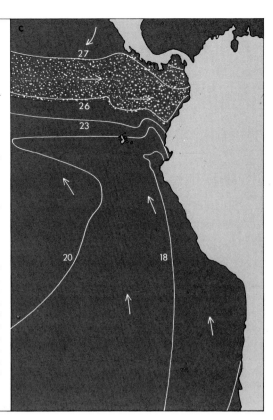

Ocean currents profoundly affect life at sea, as both nutrients and very small organisms drift with the water. The directions and stability of water movements thus give each ocean area a particular degree of productivity.

(a) An island in the course of a major current causes turbulence, bringing colder waters and their rich nutrients to the surface. (b) Giant eddies are sometimes formed in mid-ocean, for example when bends become separated from the meandering flow of the Gulf Stream in the North Atlantic. Large masses of water are thereby isolated from surrounding seas. (c) Upwelling, nutrient-laden water, as in the Humboldt Current off western South America, gives the best conditions for primary production. Its outward flow from land makes the sea unusually cold even at great distances. Shown here are the directions of flow, water temperatures in Centigrade, and the relatively warm oceanic zone near Central America.

feeding storm-petrels are exceedingly common, and the Wilson's Storm-petrel probably numbers in hundreds of millions.

Energy in ecosystems has important aspects other than its flow through organisms. An example is heat energy: life can exist only within limits of tolerance in a narrow temperature range, and most organisms are adapted to particular ideal temperatures. Although environmental heat may add needed energy to organisms, excessive heat or cold requires them to spend energy for cooling or heating. Temperature levels also affect the diffusion rates and solubility of gases in water. These factors may decrease rapidly in warmer waters, as with oxygen—presenting great difficulties for species with high oxygen demands, like salmon, while the available oxygen may be used up by large animal communities or by much decaying material in the water. On the other hand, cold waters can have an equally adverse effect on organisms, since biochemical reactions become slower at low temperatures. Another example of energy lies in the movement of water itself, as when tidal currents add energy to an ecosystem and increase the transport or mixture of nutrients: such currents may be very significant for the productivity of areas like estuaries and mangrove swamps.

Nutrient cycling

Of the diverse materials which all organisms need in addition to energy, some are in good supply and do not limit population size or productivity. Others, however, are scarce and a few of them, very important for primary production, occur in quite limited amounts within most ocean areas. Nutrients exhibit a circular flow from the physical environment, through organisms, and back again, the main cycles being those of phosphorus, nitrogen, and sulphur. It is especially the amounts in the first two cycles which often limit productivity in marine ecosystems.

Primary producers grow in the euphotic zone where enough light exists, but nutrients must also be there if any growth and reproduction are to take place. Nutrients are released into the environment by various means, and this does not always happen in the productive zone for assimilation by primary producers. Indeed, nutrients are regularly returned to other parts of the environment, as in deep waters or on land, and they must be brought back to the euphotic zone somehow in order to rejoin the chain of organisms in oceanic ecosystems. For an understanding of marine life and the primary productivity of different areas in all seasons, insight into the nature of nutrient flows is an absolute necessity.

Nutrients in food, rather than being entirely assimilated by the consumers, are largely released into the environment through excretion. Consumers often excrete in places away from the euphotic zone. Particularly in deep oceanic waters, many animals migrate vertically—down into dark areas during the daytime, and up to the productive surface layers for feeding at twilight and during the night—thus carrying nutrients from the feeding zone to be excreted in deep unproductive layers. The opposite kind of transference is done by most seabirds, which excrete at the surface. But sometimes seabirds, as well as shore-dwelling animals that eat the produce of the seas, bring nutrients onto the land. Certain guano-producing seabirds deliberately retain excrement to be used as nest-building material in the breeding colony on land. Fortunately, through precipitation on land, nutrients are partly returned to the seas by flowing water, chiefly in places where rivers join the marine waters.

Besides the consumption of organisms by macroconsumers, their decomposition by microconsumers can release nutrients. This occurs at the very place of decomposition, yet it often does not happen in the productive surface waters. Gravity makes dead matter sink, frequently to the bottom, and recirculation of nutrients to the surface depends on water currents. A knowledge of water flows in the ocean is thus essential to any explanation of high and low primary productions in different places. Vertical water movements and degrees of turbulence, as well as conditions which prevent them and induce stability, are especially important here.

Conditions in the world's oceans affect seabirds not only because they all eat marine food, but since many of them live mainly in the water rather than on the wing. These conditions may vary greatly between regions and seasons, as do those of atmospheric climate *(see pages 22–23)*. The two patterns are closely related in some ways, as when ocean currents are driven by winds, or when a climate zone has boundaries with constant water temperatures. This combination of environmental differences, and its influence on other forms of life, is reflected in the adaptations of both localized and widespread species of seabirds. Yet seabird communities, like marine organisms which they exploit, depend far more strongly on water conditions than on general climate.

Shown here are surface conditions on an average throughout the year. Water temperature is a fundamental factor, but the fact that it does not exactly follow latitudes is due to the circulation of water in currents and upwelling areas. The latter, as well as the principal convergence areas, are extremely productive and feed vast numbers of seabirds. Cold water is usually associated with richer conditions than is warm water, although parts of the tropics are often fairly productive. A further factor, the salt content of sea water, varies slightly with warmth and the influx of fresh water, and tends to be highest in subtropical zones.

(a) Alaska Current
(b) North Pacific Drift
(c) California Current
(d) equatorial currents
(e) equatorial countercurrents
(f) Humboldt (Peru) Current
(g) West Wind Drift
(h) Labrador Current
(i) Gulf Stream
(j) Canary Current
(k) Caribbean Current
(l) Brazil Current
(m) Falkland Current
(n) Benguela Current
(o) Agulhas/Mozambique Current
(p) Monsoon Drift
(q) West Australia Current
(r) East Australia Current
(s) Kuro Shio (Japan Current)
(t) Oya Shio (Kamchatka Current)

Latitude *(degrees* north or south) is shown at left on the map. Isothermal water temperature (**degrees** Centigrade) is at right.

convergences:
A Antarctic
S Subtropical

upwelling areas
warmer currents
colder currents

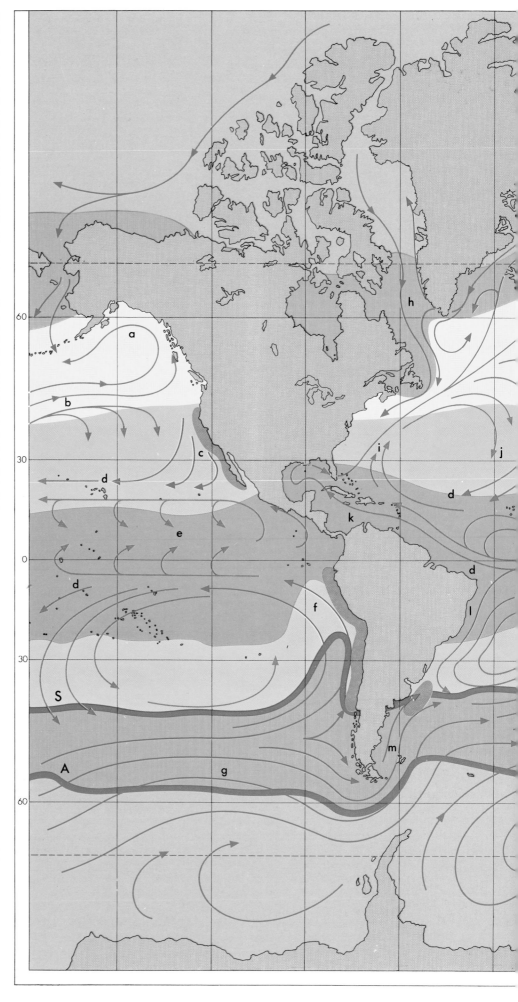

134

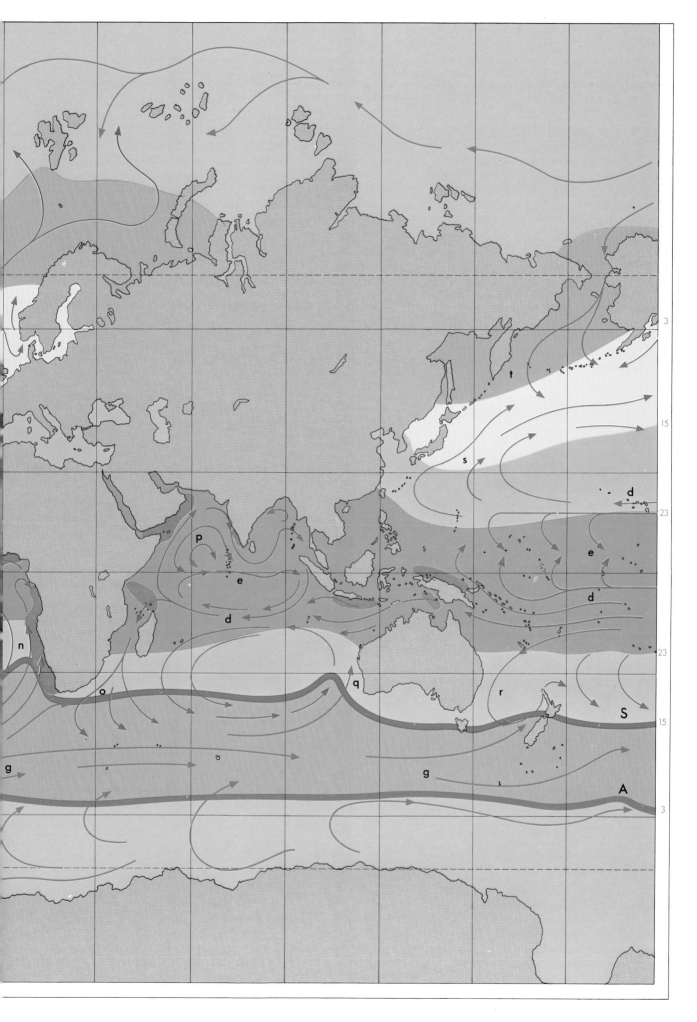

Numerous forces create movements in oceanic waters: tidal effects of the moon, wind friction, the earth's rotation, and gravity are main examples. Gravity makes water flow from land into seas, and also makes water masses of different density move vertically within the seas. When two such masses are near each other, the lighter water may rise while the heavier water sinks, bringing nutrients back from the depths to the surface layers. Differences in sea-water density normally depend on a contrast in temperature or salinity. The causes of salinity are variable—low precipitation and high evaporation can increase it in some areas, and fresh water from rivers or melting icebergs can decrease it in others. Once the water movements are induced, their direction is often greatly affected by land masses and islands. Islands in the course of principal ocean currents cause turbulence, and land masses contribute much to the effects of tides on water turbulence.

As for temperature, strong vertical differences frequently impose a stable layering of surface waters. Thermocline boundaries develop between the warm surface water, heated by sunlight, and the cool deeper water, so that these masses become mutually isolated and nutrients cannot flow back to the productive surface. A thin, warm surface layer often develops at higher latitudes in the summertime, while it is permanent and deeper in the tropics. But water masses of equal temperature and salinity mix more freely, yielding great primary production, as is commonly the case at high latitudes.

Horizontal separations, too, exist between water masses. The characteristics of sea water may be relatively uniform over a vast area, with a clear border zone or *convergence* where it meets another such area. At the sides of the convergence, the water often flows in different directions, with turbulence and, sometimes, one water mass sinking beneath the other. This mixing can bring nutrients up to the surface, and can allow one side to add a material which may be limited on the other side, so that productivity becomes very great. Certain convergences have comparatively permanent positions, like the Antarctic convergence, or a zone near eastern North America where the Labrador Current and the Gulf Stream meet. In further instances, the horizontal convergence may be only occasional, as when due to tidal currents back and forth in a coastal area, or to local wind-induced surface currents. It has also been found that giant eddies of uniform water masses are sometimes formed in the oceans, becoming isolated from surrounding seas during long periods. These eddies may drift across an entire ocean, as from Gibraltar to the West Indies—or they may be formed by water from coastal areas off eastern North America in the Gulf Stream and drift eastward. Physical conditions and communities of organisms often remain intact for a considerable time within such water masses.

Winds play a prominent role in oceanic life. Their friction against the water, by increasing wave motion, helps both the diffusion of atmospheric gases into the water and also the mixing of water which aids the spread of nutrients. Similarly, winds induce water currents and many large-scale ocean currents are thus driven. The wind direction relative to a land mass has important effects on primary production in the coastal waters: if it blows landward, impoverished surface water may flow that way and sink at the coast, pushing down the richer water, whereas the latter may instead well up at the coast if surface water flows out with a seaward wind. The main upwelling areas occur off coasts with strong trade winds continuously blowing seaward, and these are among the most productive marine regions, yielding about half of all the fish caught in the world. The sizes of seabird populations vary accordingly, with enormous numbers in some rather limited places and comparatively few over large parts of the oceans.

Seabird habitats

From the basic environmental conditions which influence primary producers and consumers, we now turn to specific habitats and their significance for seabird life. While some seabirds are very widespread, none range over all the possible habitats, and many are confined to a particular kind of habitat. The preferences shown by diverse seabird types, as described in Chapter 3, can be explained in greater detail as follows. Two environmental factors are most useful in distinguishing between habitats, a coastal and pelagic (ocean-water) variable and a climatic variable, with associated differences in food for seabirds. The oceans may be divided naturally into zones by means of these variables, and the majority of seabird species are confined to one zone or to a couple of adjoining zones, although some migratory species alternate between zones during the course of seasons.

The coastal/pelagic variable

Bordering all the seas where they meet the land is a fairly narrow *littoral or inshore zone*. Farther out, the land masses are surrounded by continental shelves, up to some 650 feet (200 metres) deep, with generally abrupt edges sloping into greater depths: this is the *neritic or offshore zone*. The deepest ocean areas constitute a *pelagic or oceanic zone*. Thus, sea waters can be divided into neritic waters over the shelves and oceanic waters in the deep oceans.

Numerous seabird species inhabit only one or two of these zones. Coastal birds, feeding in the inshore zone, often depend on the land for resting, and commonly feed along shores or near the bottom. Offshore birds are more or less independent of land, and they feed on organisms characteristic of neritic waters. Pelagic birds are totally independent of land except for breeding—they feed in oceanic waters, and many species rarely visit neritic waters as they tend to breed on oceanic islands.

Within these main zones are the more distinctive habitats to which seabirds have adapted. For example, coasts vary widely in character, some being rocky with steep slopes, while others are low-lying with sandy or muddy shores and with a broad area of shallow waters. Some coasts have an extensive region of mangroves, and in other places there are great estuaries, deep fjords, or broad archipelagos, the extent of tides causing further differences. The continental shelf bordering neritic waters may also be irregular and, in oceanic waters, the tropical coral reefs are a notable instance of complex habitats although their high productivity supports relatively few seabirds.

Among the preferences of seabirds, we find that gulls and terns are mainly coastal in habits—the latter favouring shallow waters—as are species like the Arctic Skua and the Black Guillemot, but none of the tubenoses. Both coastal and offshore zones include the majority of cormorants, when at sea, as well as the only species of exclusively marine pelicans, the Brown and the Chilean. Attracted chiefly to offshore waters are the Royal Albatross and various species of skuas, shearwaters, and diving-petrels. Many birds of the last two types range in both the offshore and oceanic zones, along with penguins, fulmars, small albatrosses, storm-petrels, most boobies, gannets, frigate-birds, the two marine phalaropes—largely in upwelling areas—and several of the alcids. Oceanic waters appeal particularly to the Kittiwakes, Sooty Terns, Long-tailed Skuas, most albatrosses, gadfly petrels, certain species of storm-petrels, tropic-birds, Red-footed Boobies and, in non-breeding periods, puffins and some of the smaller plankton-feeding alcids.

The climatic variable

The oceans are divided naturally into climatic zones, especially because of the existence of intervening convergences. From south to north, these zones are: the Antarctic, the Subantarctic (Antiboreal or South Temperate), the South Subtropic, the Tropic, the North Subtropic, the Subarctic (North Boreal or North Temperate), and the Arctic (which is separated into a Low Arctic and a High Arctic zone). A large proportion of seabirds is confined to one or two zones, or migrates between corresponding zones in the Northern and Southern Hemispheres. A few seabird groups are limited to only one hemisphere, such as the penguins, prions, and diving-petrels to the south, and auks to the north.

The southernmost zones

Due to major ocean currents, the borders between zones do not follow latitudes exactly. But two fairly clear convergences stretch round the globe in the Southern Hemisphere, bordering the Subantarctic zone. One is the Antarctic convergence, extending more or less along the 50° parallel in the Atlantic and Indian Oceans, and 10° further south in the Pacific, with marked differences in water temperature and salinity between its sides. The other, a subtropical convergence, varies somewhat seasonally in position. In these convergences, the euphotic layer is rather shallow,

often only some 30–50 feet (10–15 metres) deep, because of the great plankton density which absorbs light at the surface. Both areas are enormously productive in summertime, supporting vast populations of seabirds as well as other marine animals.

Within the Antarctic and Subantarctic zones are the majority of penguins, the tubenoses being also well represented by species of all their main groups. In the order *Pelecaniformes*, only some species of cormorants and the Australian Gannet live there. The order *Charadriiformes* is rather poorly represented, for example by the two larger species of skuas when breeding, and by the three smaller species (jaegers) as regular visitors in the northerly areas. Few gull species are found, although the Southern Black-backed Gull is numerous. Tern species are few, yet numbers are great in some places, and one instance is the migratory Arctic Tern from the far north.

The middle zones

Conditions in the lower latitudes differ markedly from those of higher latitudes. There are smaller seasonal variations, hotter temperatures, weaker winds, and generally a more stable layering of the surface waters due to their warmth. The depth of the euphotic zone varies with the degree of plankton richness. Since there is often little plankton, the sunlight may reach down to some 330 feet (100 metres), but the layering is still too stable for nutrients from the cool deep water to reach so far upward. The most impoverished seas of all are mid-ocean areas of the Subtropic zones, with a climate characterized by permanently high barometric pressures, weak winds, and weak ocean currents. These areas are deserts of the seas, with sparse marine life and tiny seabird populations.

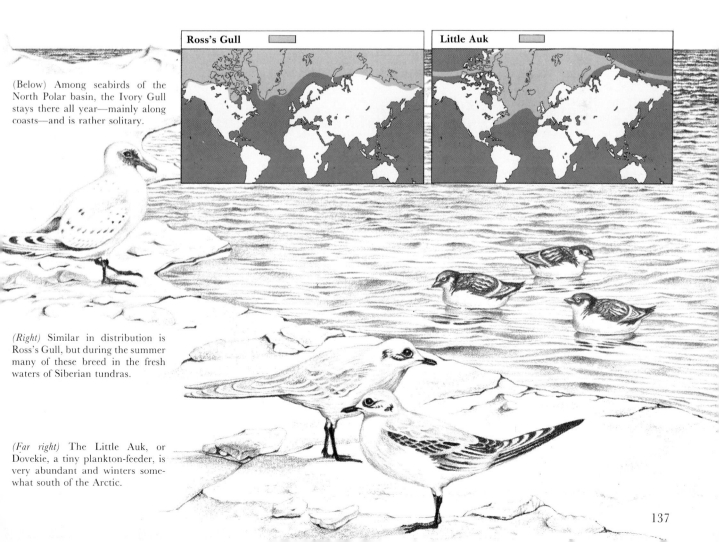

(Below) Among seabirds of the North Polar basin, the Ivory Gull stays there all year—mainly along coasts—and is rather solitary.

Ross's Gull

Little Auk

(Right) Similar in distribution is Ross's Gull, but during the summer many of these breed in the fresh waters of Siberian tundras.

(Far right) The Little Auk, or Dovekie, a tiny plankton-feeder, is very abundant and winters somewhat south of the Arctic.

137

Habitats in the seas depend on two main variables: climate, ranging from tropical to polar, and distance from the coast. Thus, latitude and the extent of the world's oceans at each latitude influence populations of seabirds. *(1)* Shown approximately here, as proportions of a circle's width, are the relative areas of *(a)* land, *(b)* continental shelves off coasts, and *(c)* deep oceans at different latitudes. The coastal zone itself is very narrow, while both land and offshore waters are least extensive in the south. *(2)* The density of seabirds in coastal waters at each latitude, measured in birds/km², is given here as a yearly average. *(3)* Similar measurements for oceanic waters indicate a greater dispersal of seabirds, and a larger proportion of them in tropical regions.

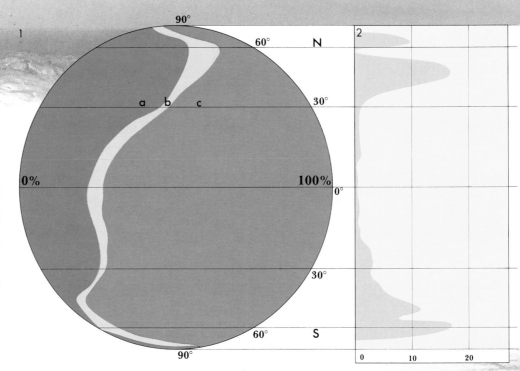

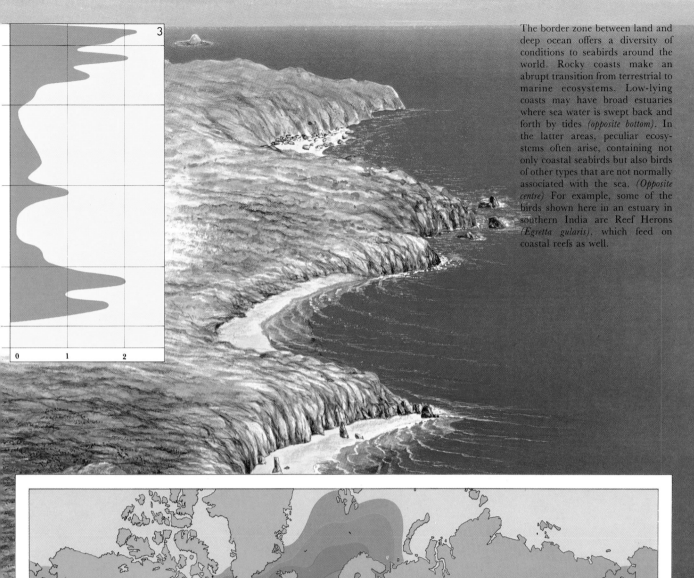

3

The border zone between land and deep ocean offers a diversity of conditions to seabirds around the world. Rocky coasts make an abrupt transition from terrestrial to marine ecosystems. Low-lying coasts may have broad estuaries where sea water is swept back and forth by tides *(opposite bottom)*. In the latter areas, peculiar ecosystems often arise, containing not only coastal seabirds but also birds of other types that are not normally associated with the sea. *(Opposite centre)* For example, some of the birds shown here in an estuary in southern India are Reef Herons *(Egretta gularis)*, which feed on coastal reefs as well.

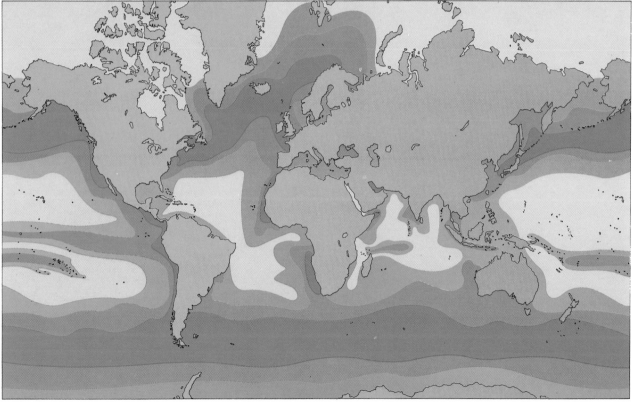

(Above) Primary production in the oceans has a strong effect on the numbers of seabirds in each area. *(Right)* Production is aided by circulation of water at uniform temperatures, which is greater in cold seas than in the layered water of very sunny regions.

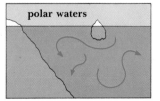

polar waters

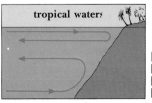

tropical waters

Annual fixation of carbon in the sea's organic substances due to photosynthesis, as shown above:

- 0–50 grams/square metre
- 50–100 grams/square metre
- 100–200 grams/square metre
- over 200 grams/square metre

Seabird communities of the Antarctic

The southern seas are quite well-endowed with seabirds and have a particular variety of penguins and tubenoses. Many species are limited in distribution, and fewer live in the pack-ice zone than in the somewhat warmer waters beyond the Antarctic convergence—although some seabirds disperse widely, notably in the winter. Portrayed here are several species which occur rather commonly to the north of the Antarctic coast proper. The Blue-eyed Cormorant and the Antarctic Tern belong to seabird orders that are otherwise seldom represented in that region. The tubenoses, except when visiting their breeding grounds, generally range far from land, where squid is an important food for many of the albatrosses and petrels. Prions and the Grey-backed Storm-petrel are plankton-feeders, while the three species of penguins shown here eat substantial amounts of krill.

(1)   Adélie Penguin
(2)   Chinstrap Penguin
(3)   Macaroni Penguin
(4)   White-headed Petrel
(5)   Kerguelen Petrel
(6)   Antarctic Petrel
(7)   Southern Giant Petrel
       (light phase)
(8)   Southern Fulmar
(9)   Brown Petrel
(10) Antarctic Tern
(11) Grey-headed Albatross
(12) Sooty Albatross
(13) Snow Petrel
(14) Broad-billed Prion
(15) Grey-backed Storm-petrel
(16) Blue Petrel
(17) Blue-eyed Cormorant

Great-winged Petrel *(Pterodroma macroptera)*
Brünnich's Guillemot *(Uria lomvia)*

Sooty Shearwater *(Puffinus griseus)*

(Above) These two seabird species are of similar size and colour, and belong to roughly the same climatic zone, but they differ in regard to food and to regions of water. The Great-winged Petrel *(left)* is a winter breeder of the Subantarctic, feeding mainly in oceanic waters. Although the Sooty Shearwater *(right)* breeds in the south, it feeds largely in offshore waters, and migrates to the North Pacific and North Atlantic in the northern summer.

(Left) Brünnich's Guillemot is quite like the Common Guillemot, but the two tend to be separated in climate, the former occurring chiefly in cold Arctic waters and the latter in Subarctic ones.

(Opposite) A widespread bird in the southern Atlantic and Indian Oceans is the Yellow-nosed Albatross. Its distribution is centred in warmer waters than are other, similar albatrosses of these seas, and a few records of it exist from the North Atlantic.

Yellow-nosed Albatross
(*Diomedea chlororhynchos*)

Yet, near terrestrial deserts in the same latitudes, winds blow rather constantly from the continents, resulting in rich upwelling conditions off the coasts. All major upwelling areas of the seas occur in the Subtropic zones. The borders between Tropic and Subtropic zones are to some extent arbitrary, as there are no clear convergences. But the subtropical seas have a more definite stratification of the surface waters in summertime, while the seasonal change of stratification in the Tropic zone—where water temperatures remain above 23°C (73°F) at the surface all the year round—is minimal.

In the tropics, conditions differ sharply between belts of strong trade winds and the tropical doldrums with weak winds and heavy rains near the equator. The regular easterly ocean currents in the trade-wind belt are replaced by countercurrents closer to the equator. Particularly in the Pacific, rather permanent convergences separate these oppositely flowing waters—although in the Indian Ocean, the surface currents are more irregular due to the influence of monsoons. In general, the extensive vertical mixing of water in its convergences makes the Tropic zone more productive than the high-pressure areas of the Subtropic zones, despite great variations between the conditions of its different regions.

The seabird communities of the Tropic and Subtropic zones are often similar. Many species of tubenoses, and most of the order *Pelecaniformes*, are examples. In the oceanic waters, gadfly petrels are characteristic. The upwelling areas frequently attract a particular group of species, and some species are even endemic to certain such areas, like the Humboldt Current. A few penguin species, prions, and diving-petrels occur in the South Subtropic zone, chiefly in upwelling or offshore areas. Some of the albatrosses are also regular in the Subtropic zones, although avoiding the impoverished high-pressure regions. In the order *Charadriiformes*, phalaropes are abundant in winter in upwelling areas—and skuas of all species occur, while only the Pomarine Skua favours these warm-water areas in non-breeding periods. Gulls of many species live close to the continents, and terns are plentiful as well.

The northernmost zones

Borders between the North Subtropic and Subarctic zones are clearly defined only in the western parts of the Atlantic and Pacific Oceans, where southward-flowing cold water meets northeastward-flowing warm subtropical water. However, it has been seen that the isotherm of 19°C (68°F) for the warmest month is a suitable continuation of these natural borders. The Subarctic zone, like its equivalent in the Southern Hemisphere, is characterized by regular and very strong westerly winds, with an extensive vertical mixing of water. Borders between the Subarctic and Low Arctic zones are more arbitrarily defined, according to temperatures and to areas where Subarctic oceanic waters mix with typical Arctic waters. The Arctic zone covers the entire polar basin, and the presence of ice naturally delimits the High Arctic from the Low Arctic zone.

Tubenoses of all groups except prions and diving-petrels are widespread, though the order is not as prominent as in the Southern Hemisphere. Skuas occur particularly in summertime, and the gull family is a typical Northern Hemisphere group with many representatives in these cold zones. Terns are also frequent, apart from the highest latitudes where, however, the Arctic Tern is numerous in summer. Auks are very characteristic of these zones and do not occur elsewhere.

Seabird food

The relationship between primary production and seabird populations is not always so simple that, at a particular place and time, a high or low primary production leads to a proportionately large or small population size. Certainly the herbivorous aquatic animals must feed where the primary producers are, but animals may be long-lived. They commonly move away from feeding areas, either actively or by drifting passively in water currents, while subsisting on stored reserves. Primary production is highly seasonal in some areas and, between its peak periods, many animals subsist on stored fat for a considerable time. In order to understand seabird ecology, we must examine the availability of the organisms that seabirds feed on, as well as where and when these are consumed.

Availability of food

Physical laws and cost/benefit relations not only fix the limits of seabird sizes, but also determine the size range of animals eaten by seabirds. The degree of concentration of prey is equally important. If organisms are too patchily distributed, the cost of finding and catching them is often greater than the benefits, so that no individual can subsist on them. Thus, a seabird population may not simply be smaller in size if a resource becomes scarcer: the conditions for existence of the population may disappear altogether, a crucial fact to remember in terms of conservation. On the other hand, if prey are normally very concentrated, there is a possibility of feeding on them collectively instead of one by one. Some seabirds have evolved in this direction, such as tubenoses that filter the sea water through lamellae on the bill, or pelicans which occasionally use their big pouches to catch rather small fish in dense shoals.

Various conditions can make seabird prey more concentrated. Herbivorous animals occur at times in great density because a high primary productivity has caused a local population growth at consumer levels. Many animals normally live in shoals or other groups for diverse reasons. One of these may be avoidance of predators, since a large dense group will confuse a predator which catches prey individually. Further, predatory fish—notably tuna and mackerel—often drive small prey to the surface in groups, making it available for seabirds. Although erratic movements of the prey at the surface render it difficult for seabirds to catch, the absence of such preying fish would probably leave very few fish at the surface available to seabirds in some areas, particularly in warmer seas.

Upwelling water is important for primary production, but there is often little food for seabirds at the very place and time of upwelling. It takes a while for herbivorous animals to increase population sizes when a high primary production begins, and the number of animals may be greater at some distance from the spot of upwelling if the flow of water is too strong for zooplankton. On the other hand, an area of sinking water without much primary production can have a relatively enormous concentration of animals. This important phenomenon occurs because herbivorous plankton drift towards such an area after growing elsewhere. If the zooplankton are able to compensate for the downward flow of water by their buoyancy or active movements, they gradually increase in numbers, and a succession of animals at ever higher levels in the food-chain is attracted.

For example, long convergence fronts—where two water masses meet and one or both of them sink—sometimes

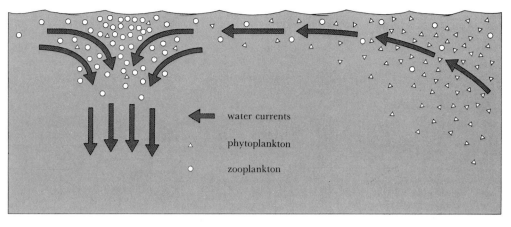

Oceanic life is often influenced by convergence zones with currents that differ in direction or in strength. One such zone is a "front" where two surface currents meet and the water sinks. If these conditions persist, all kinds of floating matter and drifting organisms may be gathered there in large amounts. Even if the front has little primary production of phytoplankton, its concentration of zooplankton can become great enough to attract carnivores like seabirds on higher trophic levels.

water currents

△ phytoplankton

○ zooplankton

persist over long periods, and the zooplankton concentration may become so great as to form a thick "soup". More mobile carnivorous animals including seabirds often come there in abundance, even though the required primary production is limited to other areas at the sides of the front. Phalaropes are a case in which the most numerous birds occur somewhat out at sea, where water sinks locally within the major upwelling areas of the oceans. Such fronts are rarest in stable water with uniform wind directions or weak winds, but are common in places with variable currents, near main convergence zones, in equatorial areas with changing currents, and temporarily along coasts with strong tides. Variable wind directions can develop local wind-induced surface currents with frontal conditions where water sinks. In the Sargasso Sea, weeds occasionally drift into a front, forming long and thick rafts. Where currents flow towards the land, water frequently sinks off the coast, allowing concentrations of zooplankton and other animals to increase at times in spite of low primary productivity.

Seabirds have one important advantage over animals in the water: their great mobility across long distances with rather low energy use. This is especially valuable at sea where the conditions often vary greatly between seasons and years. However, a disadvantage of seabirds is their restriction to a fairly shallow surface layer for feeding. Some dive and swim more deeply, and the Emperor Penguin has even been found to feed as far as about 825 feet (250 metres) down, but most species are surface-dwellers by comparison. Fortunately, they are aided by the fact that primary production occurs in an upper zone and herbivorous animals must come to the surface for feeding.

Main types of seabird food

Of the very many animal species living in the oceans, only a limited number is significant as food for seabirds. Apart from scavenging seabirds, which feed on large dead animals that happen to float up to the surface or onto beaches, there is also a limitation to the size of food. Most aquatic animals have larval stages, often beginning as plankton even if they become bottom-dwelling at a later stage, and they may grow by degrees throughout their lives. In some part of their life cycles, they may be food for seabirds. Plankton itself, a collective name for the great variety of organisms that drift or float passively, is eaten by some small seabirds. The eggs of many aquatic animals, after hatching, yield larvae which are frequently rather immobile, although particularly fish fry soon increase in mobility with age. Relatively large individuals in the class *Crustacea*, too, move slowly over modest distances, and numerous species of these are important as seabird food. Besides crustaceans,

squid and fish are the main diet of seabirds, preference being given in each group to certain species and sizes.

Invertebrate foods

Among the crustaceans in the phylum *Arthropoda*, the primitive planktonic *Calanus* is valuable as food, both for seabirds and for other animals which they eat. The abundant euphausiids occur as krill in Arctic and Antarctic zones, and diverse seabirds feed on them as well as on larger animals like squid which do so. One species, *Euphasia superba*, is particularly prominent in the Antarctic, and further species are plentiful in waters around Australia and New Zealand. The latter area also has seabirds eating the hyperiid amphipod *Euthemisto australis*, but otherwise the Subantarctic zone does not seem so rich in euphausiids. Instead, the lobster-krill *Munida gregaria* often occurs in enormous swarms, notably off southern South America. There are reports of feeding by prions on hyperiid amphipods in many areas. In addition to decapods, copepods are important as crustacean food for seabirds. Floating seaweed contains crustaceans which seabirds feed on, and coastal seabirds take weed-dwelling or bottom-dwelling crustaceans.

Another class of arthropods, the insects, is not normally associated with the sea, but some species are taken by seabirds feeding at sea. Terns and gulls often eat insects blown to sea, and marine water-striders have been shown to be rather important around tropical islands, as food of the Blue-grey Noddy. An equally odd invertebrate diet consists of primitive jellyfish, sometimes eaten by seabirds like fulmars and frigate-birds, while great albatrosses have even been observed to feed on the formidable *Physalia*, or Portuguese man-of-war, although they probably obtain little energy from it. Certain kinds of worms also offer food, especially for coastal seabirds such as gulls.

Molluscs include a number of types which are commonly eaten by seabirds. In the class *Cephalopoda*, for instance, many of the 700 species of squid have tremendous value for pelagic seabirds. Squid are abundant in oceanic waters and occur in big schools, often living only for a few years. The small individuals may be eaten by lesser seabirds like small petrels and Sooty Terns, whereas large ones serve the bigger petrels and some shearwaters, penguins, and albatrosses. The latter frequently feed on *Amplisepia*, and the family *Ommastrepidae* is particularly important in the tropics. Certain squid species seem to die in great numbers after spawning and then become available to seabirds. Sizeable dead squid may float up to the surface and be picked apart by scavenging seabirds such as fulmars and larger petrels.

Among other molluscs of value to seabirds are the pelagic and coastal snails, pteropods, and some mussels. Gulls can

(Right) Among the many methods of feeding used by seabirds is that exhibited by these Laughing Gulls. While flying, they "surface-dip" by picking small organisms or particles from the water. Their webbed feet are normally employed when pushing off from the water to gain speed, or when hovering as they feed.

(Below) Skimmers are named for a method similar to "ploughing" the water surface. They fly along it with regular wing-beats and, when something is hit by their lower mandible, the upper one instantly locks the food fast.

(Opposite bottom) The Bridled Tern is seen here feeding over a school of small tuna, which has driven tiny fish to the surface. Like many other seabirds, terns are thus aided indirectly by aquatic predators that use the sea surface as a barrier to trap prey against. Increased concentration of prey makes it easier to catch, but it reacts with erratic swimming and may make the surface "boil" so that individuals are difficult for seabirds to capture. However, fish jumping clear of the water to escape tuna are sometimes caught in the air by these terns.

Laughing Gull *(Larus atricilla)*

Black Skimmer *(Rynchops nigra)*

learn to break the hard shells by flying up in the air and dropping the animals to the ground. This is also done occasionally with sea-urchins in yet another phylum, *Echinodermata*. The shells of mussels are crushed by the strongly muscled stomachs of eiders, and of Long-tailed Ducks which—for example—winter by the millions in the Baltic region while feeding mainly on mussels.

Vertebrate foods

Fish are eaten in all seabird habitats, but they are particularly important in neritic waters and upwelling areas. The variety of herring-fishes in the family *Clupeidae* is taken in notably large quantities, such as the herring proper in Subarctic and Low Arctic waters, and the Antarctic herring in the far south. To these are added sardines in many parts of the world, sprat in the eastern North Atlantic, and pilchards here as well as in the Benguela and Humboldt Currents. The Humboldt Current itself has anchoveta, among the numerous anchovy fishes eaten in widespread regions. Capelins, and sand-eels among the family *Ammodytidae*, are valuable at high latitudes in the Northern Hemisphere, along with smelt and—mainly in their younger stages—codfish of the family *Gadidae*. In tropical oceanic waters, flying fishes and halfbeaks are important as food, taken mostly when driven to the surface by tuna. An equal role is assumed by Antarctic cods of the family *Nototheniidae*. Smaller mackerel are eaten chiefly by gannets, and the fry of many species by terns in shallow waters. Less common species nourish certain types of seabirds, such as the cormorants, Shags, and Black Guillemots which take many bottom-dwelling fish of no economic value.

Some seabirds have a diet of more evolved vertebrates. The scavenging species feed on seabirds and migrating land-birds which die at sea, as well as dead marine mammals of all kinds, and they even eat their placentae when giving birth. Giant petrels, frigate-birds, skuas, and some large gulls are remarkable as predators on seabird chicks in breeding colonies, and also take many seabird eggs. Frigate-birds catch significant numbers of young turtles on beaches when these hatch from eggs.

Feeding methods

The ecological differences between seabirds include both place and time. Unless the first factor involves simply living in distinct ecosystems, it means that seabirds in one ecosystem may have diverse locations, as well as hours and types of prey, for feeding. Corresponding differences are found in the methods and physical adaptations of seabirds—as when they must dive into the ocean to take prey that occur below the surface, or must be quick to catch agile animals. A study of feeding, therefore, provides a good view of ecological niche separations among seabirds, and helps to explain the coexistence of species within a single ecosystem.

Surface feeding in flight

Catching food at the surface while flying is a method evolved by certain species for food which is normally dispersed, occasional in its occurrence, or composed of rather mobile animals, and small enough to be swallowed whole. The birds fly around in search of food and take what they find without settling. Examples are some small petrels, storm-petrels, terns, and skimmers, as well as frigate-birds, skuas, and gulls. Variations of the method can be noticed: certain birds pick or snatch food without using their feet, and others employ their feet to oppose the wind or to take off and gain speed. Frigate-birds and terns never use their feet while "surface-dipping", but gulls sometimes do so. The southern storm-petrels have long legs and are specifically adapted for a continuous pattering of the water as they pick up or suck in small particles or plankton. Numerous seabirds pursue and catch flying fishes in the air, particularly the frigate-birds, some boobies, and Sooty Terns. The skimmers have a very peculiar technique of skimming the water surface while flying back and forth. Antarctic prions "hydroplane" at times, filtering the water with the bill as they paddle with wings outstretched.

Bridled Tern (Sterna anaethetus)

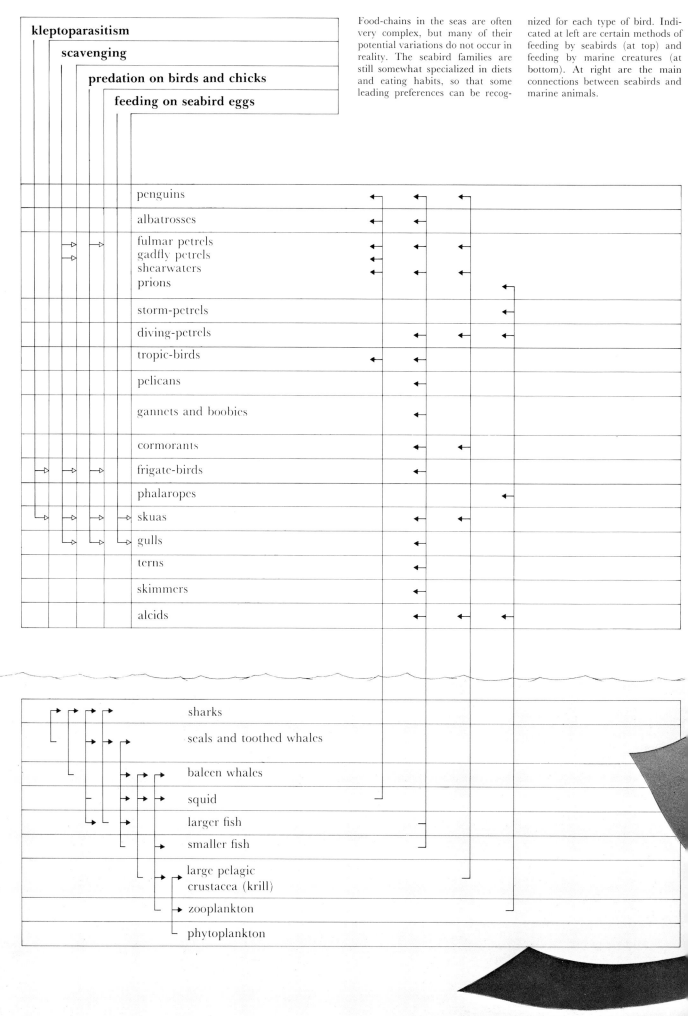

kleptoparasitism

scavenging

predation on birds and chicks

feeding on seabird eggs

Food-chains in the seas are often very complex, but many of their potential variations do not occur in reality. The seabird families are still somewhat specialized in diets and eating habits, so that some leading preferences can be recog- nized for each type of bird. Indi- cated at left are certain methods of feeding by seabirds (at top) and feeding by marine creatures (at bottom). At right are the main connections between seabirds and marine animals.

penguins

albatrosses

fulmar petrels
gadfly petrels
shearwaters
prions

storm-petrels

diving-petrels

tropic-birds

pelicans

gannets and boobies

cormorants

frigate-birds

phalaropes

skuas

gulls

terns

skimmers

alcids

sharks

seals and toothed whales

baleen whales

squid

larger fish

smaller fish

large pelagic
crustacea (krill)

zooplankton

phytoplankton

Surface feeding while swimming

Another method is used for prey that is not very mobile and cannot escape from swimming birds. The food must be fairly concentrated if this approach is to offer advantages. But seabirds often fly around until finding sparser food, then settle on the water and swim up to the prey, particularly when it is relatively large in size—and scavenging seabirds frequently feed in the same way. Many seabirds that are unable to dive can reach downwards, or force themselves slightly into the water as they swim. Prions and fulmar petrels with lamellae on their beaks filter-feed plankton while swimming. Otherwise, the method is commonly employed by albatrosses, fulmars, larger petrels and gadfly petrels, many shearwaters, pelicans, phalaropes, skuas, and gulls.

Surface diving and pursuit

Aquatic animals that are especially adapted to life in the surface waters can sometimes escape from aquatic predators by flying or tail-walking, but they remain available to seabirds as food. A greater vertical niche of feeding, however, exists for diving birds. Some of these eat types of animals that do not occur on the surface at all, such as bottom-dwelling ones. Diving birds that can fly must be adapted to physical conditions in both the air and water, despite the large differences between those environments.

Even the deep-diving penguins do not seem to suffer any ill effects from the fact that water pressure increases with depth. As for mobility, a compromise between speed of flying and rapid movement in the water is difficult to achieve, and only the non-flying penguins are very fast in water. Generally, propulsion with wings—as by penguins, shearwaters, diving-petrels, and auks—gives a higher speed than do feet. Yet cormorants, swimming mainly with their feet, may take mobile prey by sneaking up to it in water with poor visibility and quickly shooting out their long necks toward it. The energy requirements for their movement are much greater in water than in air, so a larger concentration of food is needed by divers than by many surface-feeding birds, and underwater swimmers are found only in the richer parts of the oceans.

Of the various kinds of food taken by this method, fish, squid, and crustaceans are most important. The two principal techniques used are mid-water feeding and bottom-feeding, with correspondingly distinct species of prey. Some penguins employ only the former technique, but others use both. Shearwaters that dive, diving-petrels, and most auks are mid-water feeders, while the Black Guillemot is a bottom-feeder. Cormorants like the Shag can use either technique, and many others feed mainly at or near the bottom, whereas marine species—particularly in the Southern Hemisphere—tend to be mid-water feeders.

Plunge-diving

Birds that dive from the air far down into the water can take advantage of layers deeper beneath the surface, as do underwater swimmers. Their rapid approach enables them to take prey which seabirds with other feeding methods find difficult to catch. Thus, they occupy a separate ecological niche in terms of both the place and kind of food. By flying, they are also able to seek prey in a less energy-demanding way than do many underwater swimmers with reduced wing-areas, and they can make use of food types which are relatively scattered. The plunge-diving tropic-birds, taking rather large but scattered prey, even manage to subsist in highly impoverished subtropical seas.

Plunge-divers are, in part, ecologically separated by their sizes, which correspond to differences in prey size, and by

In addition to the upward flow of nutrients and energy through the food-chains illustrated here, all the animals contribute to a flow of nutrients back into the environment by their excretion and decomposition. These nourish the lowly phytoplankton, completing the whole cycle of elements. For primary production, phytoplankton can grow only in surface waters where such nutrients are deposited or are transferred by sea currents. Moreover, bigger phytoplankton (like diatoms and dinoflagellates) in offshore waters allow shorter and more efficient food-chains between them and fish, than do those (like microflagellates) in the deep oceans.

Audubon's Shearwater *(Puffinus l'herminieri)*
Red-legged Cormorant *(Phalacrocorax gaimardi)*

Sandwich Tern *(Sterna sandvicensis)*

(Opposite top) With plentiful food in the surface waters, an Audubon's Shearwater may feed while swimming forward along the surface, using its wings occasionally for more rapid movement. If the water is fairly clear, the bird often looks down to find food and may dive and swim underwater to catch prey.

(Opposite bottom) The Red-legged Cormorant is one of two typical cormorant species in the Humboldt Current, the other being the more numerous Guanay. It is relatively coastal, while the Guanay feeds in open waters. Both hunt by diving and swimming rather deeply.

(Above) The Sandwich Tern is among many seabirds that hunt by plunge-diving. Here it lifts off, after an unsuccessful dive.

(Right) The Arctic Skua, also known as the Parasitic Jaeger in North America, is shown here in winter quarters. It lives to a great extent by "kleptoparasitic" chasing of other seabirds until they regurgitate any food carried in their crops.

(Below) The death of a seabird may lead to its being largely consumed by scavenging seabirds before it decomposes. This carcass is that of a Lesser Black-backed Gull.

Arctic Skua *(Stercorarius parasiticus)*

Lesser Black-backed Gull *(Larus fuscus)*

(1) It is not hard to demonstrate that many seabird species can coexist in the same habitat by occupying different ecological niches. This often happens when similar and closely related species utilize the available resources in somewhat distinct ways. The example at right, from Farne Island off northeast England, concerns two species of terns and two species of alcids: *(a)* Arctic Tern, *(b)* Sandwich Tern, *(c)* Atlantic Puffin, *(d)* Common Guillemot. In each pair, the same general places and times of day are employed for feeding, with the same methods—the terns plunge-dive near shore and the alcids pursue their prey by swimming underwater at sea. Yet the species differ in regard to the sizes of a type of prey which are taken.

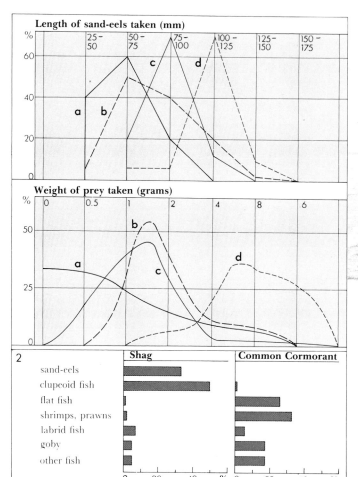

Surface feeding while flying

Shown above and opposite are the main feeding methods of seabirds.

The above feeding technique is especially common among the frigate-birds, skimmers, some storm-petrels, and gulls. They fly around without settling on the water, now and then snatching prey from the surface. Certain birds, such as frigate-birds, boobies, and Sooty Terns, may even take fish in the air as these jump from the water.

(2) Ecological separation by feeding on different types of prey is seen in two cormorant species which coexist in the same general habitat in the British Isles. The Shag feeds largely in open waters, and the Common Cormorant feeds closer to littoral areas with access to bottom-dwelling fish.

their abilities to dive deep. Gannets and boobies can plunge-dive deepest, gannets perhaps even down to 30 feet (10 metres) occasionally. Terns tend to dive more shallowly, often feeding in rather muddy waters, although some species do not plunge-dive at all. Many terns combine their plunging with hovering for detection of prey. Gulls and skuas plunge-dive at times, while imperfectly and from relatively low heights. Brown and Chilean Pelicans plunge, though shallowly. A variant is shown by certain tubenoses, particularly albatrosses and large petrels: they fly around rapidly and, when suddenly noticing prey near the surface, plunge obliquely forwards with a splash. Sometimes the same technique is used by gulls and boobies. One of the tubenoses, the Brown Petrel (or Pediunker), also plunge-dives from fairly great heights. There are underwater swimmers, too, which fly about in search of food and splash down into the water when they find something, complemented by active swimming afterwards, an example being many shearwaters. As the plunging method is used mainly for taking mobile prey, it is mostly fish and squid which are caught in this way.

Predation on higher vertebrates

Seabirds include no outright predator on mammals or birds, but in some cases their diet is supplemented by feeding on higher vertebrates, as mentioned already. The main prey is probably limited to exhausted or disabled birds at sea, whether or not these come from land. Giant petrels, fulmars, large skuas, and certain large petrels and gulls engage in such predation occasionally as well. The same kinds of seabirds obtain much of their food by

scavenging, especially in non-breeding seasons. There is little difference between taking an exhausted bird and eating one which is dead, although the capacity to kill varies greatly among the scavenging seabirds. Some birds with a powerful hooked bill also scavenge on large carcasses, like those of fish, squid, marine mammals, and birds, by tearing away pieces of flesh that can be swallowed. Otherwise, all kinds of refuse, fish offal, dead animals, and even whale dung are taken.

Kleptoparasitic, or piratical, birds may be said to "rob" food which other animals have caught. A few species are more or less adapted to this type of feeding, but other opportunist species also indulge in it sometimes. Gulls may simply snatch fish from the bill of a feeding pelican, and cormorants have been observed to feed in the mouths of foraging baleen whales. Borderline cases exist in resource competition, when two birds struggle for a piece of food by dragging it from one another's bills. More clear kleptoparasitism is seen frequently around seabird colonies, where parents arrive with food for their offspring. Many gulls, and even some terns, feed here by robbing food from the bills of incoming birds. It is a common habit for animals to empty themselves of both carried food and excrement when they want to increase their manoeuvrability and chances of escape by becoming lighter. An attacking bird may therefore feed on regurgitated food, as is normal with the more specialized kleptoparasitic seabirds, the frigate-birds and the skuas. This type of feeding is of basic importance for the Arctic Skua. The manoeuvring skills and force of these specialists are really impressive, and place them not far short of a capacity for direct predation on highly evolved animals like other birds.

Feeding while swimming

This method is used for food that is not very mobile and occurs in surface waters. Various kinds of seabirds feed in such a way and, understandably, it is most common among scavengers.

Diving and underwater pursuit

Certain seabirds are particularly adapted to this feeding method. They include the penguins, diving-petrels, cormorants, and alcids, while some shearwaters use it less successfully.

Plunge-diving

Highly mobile prey, such as fish at moderate depths, are best caught by this method. Among the experts in its use are gannets and boobies, tropic-birds, terns, and the Brown and Chilean Pelicans.

Miscellaneous feeding

Opportunists like gulls and skuas succeed in obtaining diverse food resources. Scavengers, including large fulmars and other petrels, may kill birds. Seabird chicks are often taken by these as well as by frigate-birds. The latter commonly exemplify piratical feeding, even in the air. Seabird eggs are eaten by some species more occasionally.

Cooperation during feeding

Cooperation is of great importance for the feeding success of some seabirds, particularly in certain species of the order *Pelecaniformes*. For example, many pelicans feed in groups, swimming in a line and driving the prey ahead, while sometimes reaching down to take fish simultaneously. Some cormorants also drive prey while they swim and dive in lines. Simultaneous plunge-diving is often done by groups of gannets and boobies, and in the latter case it may be initiated by one individual giving a short whistle. Such diving probably increases the degree of success, as fish cannot then escape so easily. In other seabird orders, cooperation is less clear, although many birds in addition to cormorants that feed by swimming under water—like penguins—frequently feed in groups and this may well enhance their success.

The cycle of life and death

Natural regularities and hardships impose a number of variations on the survival of seabirds, and consequently on their ecological roles. First, as with all organisms, there is an entire life cycle from the fertilized egg to the adult's death. Not unusually, seabird food differs according to age in this cycle. The young are given food in abundance during the breeding period, which may be unlike the normal diet of independent birds in non-breeding periods, due to seasonal changes in prey and to the fact that most seabirds breed seasonally. A few investigated species have even been shown to feed chicks with somewhat different types of food during various stages of their growth. Newly fledged immatures often cannot find food easily, the required skills

being learned gradually with age. It has been shown that the immatures of certain gulls lead a rather shore-dwelling life, taking prey with little mobility that is readily caught, while adults pursue more agile prey demanding great skill. In resource competition, the adults have an advantage over less experienced immatures, which are also more vulnerable to particular kinds of predators.

Even if ecological differences occur in the entire life cycle of an organism, they are not as prominent as those exhibited by many species in the annual cycle. Seabirds have a relatively short period of growth, followed by a rather long life with stable characteristics and ecological tendencies—yet the annual influences on them are often very significant. Most conspicuously, in higher latitudes where the seasonal changes are great, some clear distinctions in ecology exist between the summer and winter. The summer is the chief spawning period for numerous aquatic animals, whose smaller individuals such as fry are thus abundantly available at that time. The breeding of most seabird species is adjusted to this food supply, with corresponding patterns of distribution and migration. The latter also leads seabirds to take up roles in different communities during the year, resulting in a spatial shift of ecology and, frequently, in some change of diet. Since aquatic animals often migrate as well, notably in connection with their own reproduction, there may be large variations in the community composition of a certain area during an annual cycle.

Reproduction in the summertime means that the younger stages of both seabirds and their prey organisms are added to ecosystems mainly during this season. Some of the most formidable enemies of seabird chicks occur among

Red-necked Phalarope *(Lobipes lobatus)*

Whiskered Tern *(Chlidonias hybrida)*

Interesting connections between oceanic and terrestrial ecosystems are illustrated on these pages.

(Top left) The Red-necked Phalarope acquires a beautiful plumage when breeding in Arctic fresh waters, but it is more drab when wintering at sea *(above)*. The Whiskered Tern also changes its plumage markedly between the times of breeding in marsh areas *(centre left)* and wintering in marine waters *(bottom left)*. Both of these species undergo a great seasonal shift in ecology.

(Opposite bottom) A curious kind of link between the ecosystems of land and sea is shown by immature Brahminy Kites *(Haliastur indus)* giving piratical chase to a Caspian Tern.

Caspian Tern *(Hydroprogne caspia)*

seabirds themselves. Predation on seabird colonies by giant petrels, larger gulls, and skuas is normally impossible in the winter, however, implying a definite shift of ecology. These birds also scavenge widely, an activity with further seasonal variations in food. Disabled young and exhausted adults become available in seabird colonies, and some aquatic animals—like salmon in rivers—die in large numbers after spawning and provide a resource for seabirds. Stillborn young and placentae are offered by the seasonal migration and breeding of many marine mammals. Kleptoparasitic feeding, too, is most profitable around seabird colonies, and is adopted by gulls which do not normally employ it in the winter, while even many skuas and frigate-birds find it more valuable there than at sea.

Spectacular seasonal differences occur among bird species that breed inland but, during the winter, take up positions in oceanic ecosystems. Some pelicans and cormorants are more marine in winter than when breeding. Many gulls and terns exhibit remarkable shifts between freshwater breeding areas and wintering in marine waters, and the so-called "marsh terns" are frequently pelagic seabirds in winter. Phalaropes stay mainly at sea, yet breed on the Arctic tundra in summer with insect larvae as the chief diet. Smaller skuas (jaegers) become terrestrial predators on the summer tundra, mostly eating rodents and young birds. The tropics, although renowned for relatively constant conditions, have certain seasonal variations in ecology as well. Some seabirds breed annually there, and frigate-birds depend partly on food from seabird colonies. One investigation of a tropical island in the Pacific has shown the diet of the White Tern to contain a fish proportion of 93% in August but only 10% in February.

An additional factor is that the food of seabirds may change somewhat from year to year. Conditions at sea often vary significantly, and spawning can be quite successful for a particular organism in one year but not the next. Due to its fluctuating population size, a species of fish may become more or less important to seabirds with each year, and several species must be studied over a number of years in order to get a complete view of seabird ecology. The populations of such a species can also exhibit certain ecological differences due to local conditions.

The causes of death among seabirds are similarly variable. In the life cycle, some individuals die while young and others live to old age, with great differences even in the same species. Seabirds frequently assume distinct ecological roles through their death at different ages. For example, chicks are normally killed and consumed by other kinds of animals than are adults. Chicks and inexperienced immatures often have a high mortality, because of starvation or their vulnerability to predators. Terrestrial predators tend to cause death only in breeding areas, and predation on seabirds by other seabirds is not a prominent cause of death in adults. When adults die, there are commonly other causes such as starvation, adverse weather, or old age.

Among the diverse birds of prey and mammals which threaten seabirds, man is of course the most dangerous. Human activities also indirectly kill many seabirds at times, with oil spills and other pollution. Some seabirds are taken by aquatic predators, such as sharks, and those that dive are particularly vulnerable. The leopard seal is a terrible enemy of penguins. Certain aquatic animals, including sharks, eat seabirds which have already died, although it is hard to know whether this was the case with fish whose stomachs are occasionally found to contain rings that were put on seabirds. Probably other fish do take some seabirds, and the fact that most birds feeding over tuna shoals do not dive into the water has been explained as an adaptation to avoid being killed by the furiously feeding tuna.

Seasonal variations occur in seabird diseases, which spread more easily in colonies with close contacts between many birds. Epidemics, and starvation, sometimes kill large numbers of seabirds. So do storms and severe colds, taking the greatest toll in autumn and winter. It is not unusual for seabirds to die in areas they traverse during migration, and where they do not actually feed. External and internal parasites are further enemies which may weaken them. Even poisonous conditions at sea can affect them, for example during dinoflagellate blooms. The ecological niches of seabirds often shift according to such causes of death. But the dead seabirds remain a part of the environment, and may be simply decomposed as food for microconsumers, bringing nutrients back into circulation within the world's ecosystem.

Chapter Six
SEABIRD BEHAVIOUR

How ocean birds adapt to, and interact with, the physical environment and organisms of other species are aspects of behaviour discussed elsewhere in this book. We shall now pay much closer attention to interactions between organisms of the same species, and to the fundamental principles of the behavioural sciences in connection with seabirds. This involves not only describing the diverse types of behaviour and establishing when and where they occur, but also explaining them. The three basic kinds of explanation noted in the preceding chapter are applicable here as well: immediate causes of behaviour, individual development through inheritance and learning, and the evolution of genes in populations.

As long as an organism is alive, it maintains innumerable activities. There are continuous physiological processes in its body, electromagnetic ones in the nervous system, exchanges of gases and liquids and heat with the environment, tactile interactions, visible movements, and others. Many of them cannot be directly observed, or are involuntary phenomena like breathing and effects of the autonomous nervous system. These are not generally regarded as behaviour, although we find various borderline cases. Activity guided more or less by reflexes normally has little voluntary control, yet may often be modified by learning. While pupil reflexes and blushing of skin are examples of what is not considered behaviour as a rule, they may have important communicatory functions. In addition to the chief behavioural phenomena of visible movements under voluntary nervous control, some apparent non-actions such as sleeping, resting, and sitting are also treated as types of behaviour.

All branches of zoology are interested in behaviour, but it has given rise to special fields of study. The latter, as pursued by psychologists, have long made use of animals for experimentation and are sometimes termed "animal psychology". Among the leading questions in such research is the extent to which behaviour is learned or innate. Two schools of thought, working on both the descriptive and explanatory levels, are firmly established in this respect. "Behaviourism" is particularly concerned with learning and modification of behaviour, whereas "ethology" concentrates mainly upon innate sources of behaviour. Insofar as these sources have been discovered, evolutionary theorists try to explain how the genes conditioning them have acquired a permanent role in populations.

Innate behaviour

Since all the physical properties needed for behaviour of an organism are conditioned by both genes and the environment, it is not easy to isolate the innate aspects of behaviour which depend on genes alone. Regular ways of behaving in a population might suggest, but hardly prove by themselves, innate control through inheritance. Many bird species, for instance, sing in a stereotyped manner, and experiments have shown that song patterns are often learned—in some cases forming "traditions" which every individual follows. However, such learning requires a nervous system and other characteristics with a genetic basis. If we notice exactly what is learned and why, as well as varying degrees of difficulty that organisms experience in learning, we can frequently identify innate factors of a less direct kind.

Each bird is born with a particular physical constitution, including its nervous system and sensory apparatus, in a distinctive habitat. Consequently, there are limitations to its possible types of behaviour, and the young can learn some types more readily than others. A gull may attempt different methods of feeding, but will never be as successful as terns in plunge-diving because its properties are less suitable for this method. Thus, even when birds learn by trial-and-error, the manifold influence of genes should not be overlooked.

Inheritance often has a still stronger effect upon learning. Guillemots and many terns learn to recognize both eggs and chicks, while some terns can even recognize their eggs when these are placed in another bird's nest. Gulls never learn to recognize eggs, but do recognize chicks shortly after these hatch. Gannets cannot learn to recognize either eggs or chicks, and will adopt others' chicks that are placed in their nests, although they do attack the young from other nests that walk into their territories. Evidently there are inherited properties of the central nervous system that facilitate recognition by certain means according to the species concerned. This is also true of hearing, as in many gulls which recognize their mates by sound. A gull may stand sleeping in a colony where hundreds are calling, and suddenly be awakened by the call of its mate returning from a foraging trip. Similarly, young penguins and their parents in enormous crèches find each other partly through calls.

A striking example of genetically controlled learning is

(Right) A Magnificent Frigate-bird fills his enormous throat-pouch with air while waiting on a breeding site for a female. Whether his unusual appearance and the blushing of naked skin should be described as "behaviour" is, however, questionable. There are many such cases among seabirds, in which the terminology needed for a scientific study of their actions is not as clear as it may seem.

(Below) An opposite problem for the behavioural scientist often arises when, like this Masked Booby, a seabird appears to be doing nothing at all. Inactivity or passivity, including resting or sleeping as well as sitting on a "look-out", may nevertheless be at least partly voluntary and is certainly observable. Therefore, it must be regarded as a kind of behaviour.

Magnificent Frigate-bird *(Fregata magnificens)*
Masked Booby *(Sula dactylatra)*

Swallow-tailed Gull *(Creagrus furcatus)*

Pied and Black-faced Cormorants
(Phalacrocorax varius, fuscescens)

Behaviour is described largely in terms of its purpose or function, for example when calling it a "threat" or an "appeasement". But the function of an activity in seabirds may be hard to determine.

(Top left) A Swallow-tailed Gull is apparently taking a look at its feet, whose webs are torn in this indi-vidual. Such "toe-pointing" be-haviour, though, is commonly shown by gulls of many species for no obvious reason, and there may be a more general explanation.

(Top right) A Pied Cormorant is yawning in the company of a Black-faced Cormorant. Whether yawning serves any useful purpose is not certain, but it may be related to the circulation of body fluids.

(Below) One often sees cormorants standing with outstretched wings, as in one individual among these Double-crested Cormorants. This behaviour undoubtedly enables the bird to dry out its wings, but additional functions are possible.

Vitamin D may be formed in the feathers during sun-bathing. It has also been suggested that a bird can signify ownership of a resting site with outstretched wings, and this action may serve to increase the space between that bird and its companions.

Double-crested Cormorant *(Phalacrocorax auritus)*

the phenomenon of *imprinting*. Some things are learned only during one period of life—which may be very short—and cannot be learned afterward even if the appropriate stimuli are given. In contrast here are two kinds of chicks: "nidifugous" or "precocial" ones that leave the nest soon after hatching, and "nidicolous" or "altricial" ones that stay in the nest. Among seabirds, the chicks of skuas, gulls, and terns are generally precocial, while the young of some auks also leave the breeding site before they are fully fledged, and in some penguins and pelicans the young form crèches. Precocial chicks, on the whole, learn to recognize their parents a short time after hatching. If they are not in sensory contact with the right parent during this period, no such learning will occur later. Various additional types of imprinting take place, as in learning to identify species or sex, and bird songs may be imprinted. Thus, innate factors often determine the time and possibility of learning behaviour.

Signalling behaviour

Signs are important in the regulation and coordination of organisms' activity. Besides environmental phenomena which animals commonly regard as signs, communication involves signs that are transmitted by other animals. In ethology, these are known as "sign stimuli", "trigger stimuli", or "releasers" as they give rise to particular activities in the animals receiving such signs. The activities may be overt behaviour, or processes like hormonal production and moods which are harder to observe but can influence subsequent behaviour. The understanding of many signs, notably those used for communication between species, is learned. By trial and error, for instance, animals may learn suitable reactions to threats from other species, by being attacked at first when not reacting properly.

Ethology, though, has proved that the understanding of some signs has a strong innate basis. An example is the ability of Herring Gull chicks to interpret adults' warning

A typical example of seabird behaviour is illustrated here. In scientific terms, a stimulus from the environment acts through the bird's sensory apparatus on the *innate releasing mechanisms* with which it is born. A mechanical picture of this process is often suggested by ethologists.

(a) The stimulus is like a key which has to fit a lock. If the stimulus were not suited to the properties of the bird, as if the key could not turn in the lock, there would be no response. This can happen when birds receive signals from individuals of other species.

(b) The turning key releases the bird's innate mechanism, which will react if it has been "set".

(c) What sets the mechanism is a mood or *action-specific energy*, like a spring if this has been coiled to produce tension.

(d) The result will be a particular response, such as wing movements in a *fixed action pattern*.

calls even before the eggs are hatched and learning occurs. Another is understanding of the displays given by birds when breeding, clearly essential for inhibiting hybridization between species of birds. It has been assumed that an *innate releasing mechanism* exists and causes the response of understanding such signs.

The releasing activity, or sign, is frequently an inherited form of stereotyped behaviour, a short sequence of movements which ethology calls a *fixed action pattern*. It usually has an all-or-none character, occurring in only a single way. Many displays by seabirds are of this innately fixed type and have the function of sign stimuli as described above. The sign may, in turn, release another fixed action pattern in the bird receiving it. Exchanges of stimuli between animals belong to the subject of "feedback" which will be discussed later.

Fixed action patterns are not always released by an appropriate stimulus. They may happen when a stimulus is very weak and unsuitable, or with almost no stimulation. Their occurrence often depends on inner motivations, or moods, termed *action-specific energy* in ethology. Such are the motivations influenced by hormonal levels in birds, according to the weather and increasing daylight in springtime. A readiness to act can also be built up through social stimulation in colonies and communication between mates. More temporary "drives" to act may arise as well, for instance in behaving aggressively. Inner motivations occasionally lead to *appetitive behaviour*, in which the animal seems to be looking for something that might release further activity when it is found.

In certain cases, an animal reacts more strongly to a stimulus which exaggerates what is normal for the species. Such *supernormal stimuli* have been particularly well studied in seabirds. Thus, under experimental conditions, a hungry gull chick may peck more frequently at the tip of an artificial bill, whose appearance is more contrasting than that of a gull

(Right) Birds may respond more strongly to a *supernormal stimulus* that overemphasizes the characteristics of a normal one. For example, the Herring Gull has been found to prefer an artificial gigantic egg to its own egg of normal size, if it is allowed to choose between the two in an experiment. It tries to sit on the bigger egg even though it is physically unable to do so.

(Left) Herring Gulls may engage in wing-pulling when they dispute the borders of their neighbouring territories. But if one bird feels a conflict between the drive to attack and the urge to escape, it frequently does neither, and begins to pull at the grass as if this were its opponent. Such a substitute form of aggression is an instance of a *redirected response*. Generally, animals in conflict situations sometimes behave in a way which is totally irrelevant and inadequate to the circumstances then involved. These reactions are called *displacement activities* by ethologists. Thus, cormorants that face a dispute occasionally exhibit false incubation, and Common Terns often react by preening their feathers.

161

Magnificent Frigate-bird *(Fregata magnificens)*
Long-tailed Skua *(Stercorarius longicaudus)*

(Above) In the initial stages of pair formation, several actions are shown by a male Magnificent Frigate-bird as he waits on a site and tries to attract a female. He vibrates his wings, exhibits his scarlet inflated throat-pouch while bending his neck backwards, and clatters his bill when an interested female flies past. The female's selection of a partner is crucial for pair formation, and a very large throat-pouch may lead her to respond more strongly than does a small one. This would be an example of a supernormal stimulus, and such a sexual selection may help to explain its evolution.

(Right) This Long-tailed Skua chick, rather recently hatched, is a nidifugous bird which leaves the nest shortly after hatching. In such cases, there is usually a brief period of *imprinting* early in life. The chick then learns to recognize its parents, enabling it to respond properly to them as well as to enemies.

162

Peruvian Booby *(Sula variegata)*
Brown Pelican *(Pelecanus occidentalis)*

(Top right) Plunge-diving birds such as Peruvian Boobies may, through their feeding activities, announce the presence of food to both conspecifics and birds of other species. They may thus attract other birds from great distances, which have learned to connect this behaviour with the availability of food—an example of *associative learning.*

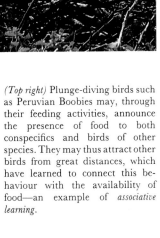

(Right) The Brown Pelican is normally rather shy of man, but its fear can be gradually removed if it is fed regularly in certain places. Such modification of behaviour is common among all kinds of animals, and is called *habituation* by scientists.

parent's bill. A similar explanation is given for the evolution of gaudy structures and colours in the males of some species, where the females have so many possible mates that their choices can influence the conspicuous properties evolved by males. This is probably true of frigate-birds, the males being free to breed more often than females, which give prolonged post-fledging care to the young. Mate choice is an important selective force, and such "sexual selection" with its competitive aspects has doubtless been prominent in the evolution of advertising traits and reproductive behaviour.

Learning and conditioning

Genetically programmed behaviour patterns enable seabirds to master many of the biologically crucial situations in their lives. But as genetic evolution is a slow process, innate behaviour can be of value only in those situations which occur normally. It may prove totally inadequate when the environmental circumstances are rapidly changing, and an ability to adapt to new situations by modifying behaviour is highly advantageous. Finding food, avoiding dangers, and acquiring skills are typical activities with learning. Such individual adaptation of seabirds, to the prevailing conditions in areas where they usually stay, allows them to exploit resources more efficiently and to increase their chances of survival considerably.

Ways of learning, or gaining knowledge, involve different degrees of general experience and actual practice. By *observational learning*, animals can identify and interpret diverse objects and natural phenomena. Details of the surroundings for navigation, as well as migratory routes and wintering areas in the case of some seabirds, are recognized—as are enemies, prey, and places of feeding.

Behaviour involves many possible connections between *(1)* a stimulus and *(2)* a response. An animal receives information from the environment and may respond to it in various ways. This enables us to show how behaviour is learned.

Associative learning takes place when stimuli are connected to responses by particular means that become established in an animal's nervous system. For example, a new stimulus may be associated with an old one which has already been connected to a response, until the new stimulus produces the old effect: such a response is then known as a *conditioned reflex*. Another example, illustrated here, occurs when a reward or punishment is associated with a new stimulus and response,

strengthening or weakening their connection: this is *instrumental conditioning*. Seabirds that follow ships to eat their refuse are a good instance.

(a) A passing ship stimulates a bird, which responds by following it and—if rewarded by pieces of fish— learns to do so regularly.

(b) Such a reward may disappear, or be denied as a punishment.
(c) A bird may then learn to stop following ships, and to become habituated to their passage.
(d) A different reward of pieces of bread can be introduced so that the bird associates it with ships.
(e) This "trial-and-error" process can teach the bird to respond to ships regularly as before.

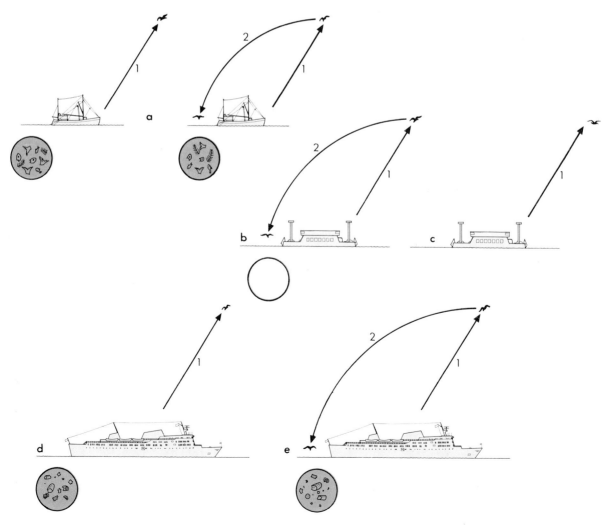

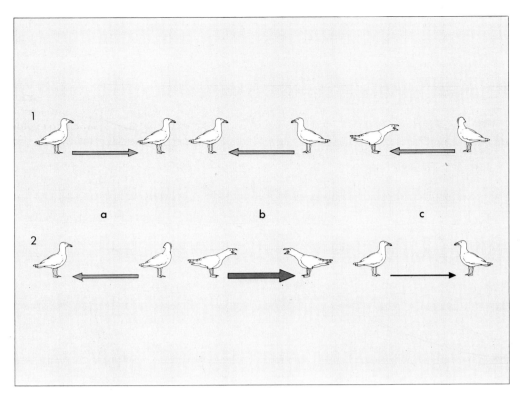

(Left) In communicative behaviour, (1) a stimulus by one bird causes (2) a response by another bird. This often involves feedback, in which (a) the response then acts as a stimulus on the former bird. For example, one bird approaching another can see its reaction. (b) If the feedback is positive, the second stimulus is called "excitatory" and will make the former bird respond by an increase in the manner of behaving. Thus, an approaching gull may react to the upright, aggressive stance of another by proceeding to attack. (c) If the feedback is negative, the second stimulus is called "inhibitory" and the former bird will decrease such behaviour. A gull may stop attacking if it sees another "head-flagging" as a kind of appeasement.

Investigations show that birds, when feeding, are often guided by some kind of "search image" which is learned. They develop specific feeding habits, and frequently fail to find rare food because no search image has been acquired for it.

Avoidance of enemies is dependent on an animal's use of proper "escape reactions" when it perceives dangerous predators. This release of certain responses to certain stimuli is an illustration of *associative learning*, which often establishes a connection between external stimuli and the responses that regularly follow them. While the nervous system commonly produces a chain of events from the stimulus to the response, learning can modify links in the chain. The stimulus may first arouse inner drives or action-specific energies, whose interrelationships are affected by learning. As a result, old "motor programs" in a bird's behaviour may be released by new stimuli, or no longer released—and even replaced with new ones to be released—by old stimuli.

Very simple associations are found with genetically programmed reflexes, which release responses to stimuli in a rather direct way. How learning can modify them is exemplified by what we call a *conditioned reflex*: if some new stimulus regularly occurs at the same time as the usual stimulus, or slightly before it, the reflex will be changed so that the same response is released by the new stimulus alone. In other words, the animal learns to expect that the usual stimulus follows the new one, and eventually reacts whether this happens or not.

Certain stimuli, however, must be followed by others in order to release any response. Animals are normally aroused by sudden and unfamiliar sensations—but they may cease to react if these are not regularly followed by significant events. Such *habituation* takes place, for example, with phenomena which at first cause reactions of alarm and escape, yet are accepted when they prove not to be dangerous. The "escape distance" that a bird keeps between itself and humans will often become very small if the bird is not molested. Gulls are frequently wary of man, but approach closely where fish offal is constantly thrown out.

Another important process is what we ordinarily call *trial-and-error learning*. Variations in behaviour may occur randomly, then become established if they have positive effects, or are extinguished if they have negative effects. For the behaviour which is thus tried out, there are varying degrees of success, with rewards and punishments. These depend partly on an innate mechanism which allows such positive or negative "reinforcement", leading to a permanent change in features of the animal's nervous system.

Scientifically, this kind of learning is known as *instrumental (operant) conditioning*, and it occurs in numerous situations. Birds may exhibit it in acquiring methods or strategies of feeding—notably opportunistic species like gulls, which can learn to break mussels by dropping them to the ground from some height. Commonly, instrumental conditioning forms a connection between two activities that were originally separate, where one is essential for attaining the other as a reward. Whole chains of activities may be established in such a way.

Interactions among species

Some of the activities of seabirds in relation to other kinds of animals deserve particular attention as regards behaviour. While cooperation by different species for mutual benefit can occur, competition between them is at least as frequent. Resource competition need not involve direct behavioural interaction of one species with another. But interference competition does so, and is often caused indirectly by competition over a resource—such as food, resting places, or nest sites. The resultant aggressive acts may be actual physical attacks or threats of attack.

Violent behaviour is also used in defence against predators or kleptoparasites. Birds defend themselves by pecking or biting when attacked. Seabirds like gulls and terns, collectively attacking predators over colonies, employ "harassing" or "mobbing" behaviour to defend their young. Even non-fledged immatures, notably after having grown in strength, lunge and bite at intruders. Both the adults and

Northern Fulmar *(Fulmarus glacialis)*

(Left) The Long-tailed Skua commonly shows "mobbing" behaviour towards man or other intruders in a territory, particularly if these come too near eggs or chicks.

(Above) The Northern Fulmar, like most other tubenoses, communicates vocally to a great extent during breeding, often jointly on the nest site as shown here.

(Below) Wing-stretching by the Blue-footed Booby is probably not a kind of signalling. To be sure of this, a long study may be needed to look for possible responses by receiving birds.

(Opposite top) The red eye-rings of a female Great Frigate-bird differ from the blue ones in Magnificent Frigate-birds, enabling males to avoid pairing with females of the wrong species.

(Opposite bottom) Aggressive behaviour and threats sometimes occur even between different species of seabirds, as in this case between *(left)* a Pied and *(right)* a Black-faced Cormorant.

Long-tailed Skua *(Stercorarius longicaudus)*
Blue-footed Booby *(Sula nebouxii)*

Great Frigate-bird *(Fregata minor)*
Pied and Black-faced Cormorants *(Phalacrocorax varius, fuscescens)*

Analog communication

During conflicts between animals, communicative behaviour normally evokes the drive to attack or to escape, as well as the balance which may be reached between these drives. There may be a continuous variation in ways of expressing the possible strengths of a drive, rather than a number of clearly different expressions. The communication is then called analog rather than digital, and some examples are shown here with Herring Gulls. In conflict situations, they often stand with their necks in an upright position. (1) Anxiety is announced by a long thin neck, with the bill held upward. (2) If drives to attack and to escape are fairly balanced, uncertainty is announced by holding the bill horizontally. (3) When the drive to attack is predominant, the bill is held slightly downward as though ready to peck at opponents. With such a mild threat, the wings are still in pockets. (4–6) Ever stronger threats can be expressed by degrees to which the wings are held outward and the bill is pointed downward.

young of many tubenoses, particularly fulmars, spit oil as a defence.

The opposite type of protective behaviour is escape, which tends to be less costly and dangerous than aggressive defence. It therefore has a higher adaptive value in general, although exceptional situations arise—as with cornered animals that cannot escape, or a good food resource that is worth competition. Most seabirds have clear "escape distances", but these vary enormously from one species to another, and normally even differ according to the kind of animal that approaches.

For dangerous predators such as eagles and humans, the seabirds which have suffered heavily from them may have a very large escape distance. It can be several miles (km) in the case of some cormorants. With certain species, it depends on the locality. Coastal seabirds, in areas where these have not been persecuted by mammals, are often closely approachable by people. While escape distances are innately based in part, traditions also play a role, and habituation is occasionally involved. Numerous seabirds are renowned for their fearlessness, particularly in regions like the Galapagos Islands or the Antarctic, with no terrestrial mammalian predators and a rather recent arrival of man.

Other kinds of nonaggressive, protective behaviour include evasive manoeuvres such as zigzagging and sharp turning, common in all seabirds when under attack. The smaller species can manoeuvre more easily than large ones and are frequently able to avoid them. Some seabirds, like phalaropes and skuas, protect offspring by luring away nearby predators, feigning injury with a kind of *distraction display*.

Gulls and terns, if attacked by aerial predators or even kleptoparasites, sometimes form dense flocks making joint evasive manoeuvres. They evidently benefit because the attacker cannot easily single out any individual for attack. How genes conditioning such behaviour could have spread is understandable. Although one bird with these genes would not possess any advantage over conspecifics lacking

them, cooperation may begin when several birds acquire the genes—through random spreading or population growth, for example—and those which mutually benefit may spread the genes through the whole population.

Escape is a question of method as well as distance. Birds not only attempt to fly away as fast as possible, or resort to manoeuvring. They also try to hide on land, particularly if they have a protective camouflage, as, for instance, many immature gulls do. Hiding, often in an immobile hunched posture, is remarkably frequent among immatures before fledging. Seabirds that can dive are often seen to escape aerial enemies by diving, and such semiaquatic birds escape aquatic predators by flying up into the air. In the case of flightless birds, climbing onto land is a normal means of escape from enemies in the water. Penguins gain high speed underwater and may jump up onto land or ice when pursued by leopard seals.

Communication

Much of the interaction between seabirds is communicative in character, mainly within the same species. Signs used for communication, as mentioned already, have a definite function if they possess value for both the transmitting and receiving individuals. One animal gives off signs which affect another animal, and the latter adjusts to them by reacting in appropriate ways. Warning signs are a common example among birds, being of different kinds according to whether they warn attackers or, in many cases, warn conspecifics about enemies. These signs may be sounds, and sometimes visual patterns or colours, with a meaning like "don't touch—I bite!". Signal behaviour as a threat or aggressive display is most frequent in communication between species. By such messages a bird announces its readiness for attack or defence if another fails to react suitably.

It is not always easy to distinguish communication from other types of interaction. For instance, if two birds are fighting, the reactions in a receiver of signs may be obscured

by violent movements, due to energy transferred from the opponent. Communication involves events in a receiver that do not depend directly on the amounts of energy transferred. Instead, these events are dependent on the form of signs and the properties, or internal condition, of the receiver. Only when certain signs match a receiver's properties can it "understand" them by responding accordingly.

In order to examine the varied messages of seabirds, some more general principles of communication are needed. A sign is basically a difference, or contrast, which must be sufficiently clear to release a response in a receiver. Highly evolved animals may use many signs that must also differ clearly from each other to prevent confusion. One or several signs can make up a communicative unit called a "message". If a bird adopts a threatening posture with a particular structure, and with a given intensity of the threatening behaviour, its message contains these two elements, contrasting with the possible postures and behaviour it does not show. What determine the choices for each element are, of course, the sender's skills and the receiver's discriminating abilities. The well-developed visual senses of seabirds allow a notable range in the intensity of threats.

Here, too, is illustrated a distinction between two main types of communication: *digital* and *analog*. In the first, a sign is an all-or-nothing choice, and does not resemble the reaction which it induces in the receiver. Thus, a posture might be like a yes-or-no answer to the question "am I threatening you?" Analog communication, however, involves messages and reactions which may change in degree and are similar. The intensity of a threat is proportional to the readiness for attack, and is normally followed by a reaction of analogous intensity.

The functions of messages

There are two different kinds of messages according to the reactions they produce. One is a *cognitive* reaction in which an animal comes to know something. This results from a *reference message* that denotes, or is about, something. Exactly

what birds "know" may seem rather speculative, but their behaviour frequently reveals the information they have obtained through such messages.

Ocean birds presumably communicate little or nothing about the past, whereas the present and the immediate future apparently account for all of their reference messages. These can also be divided into messages about the environment, and others about the animal which is transmitting the message. Less advanced communicators like birds do not convey much environmental information, although examples exist—as with food calls by gulls, or warning calls to inform conspecifics about predators. The reference messages in birds are mostly about the birds themselves, denoting their situations at the time and their probable future states and activities.

Noncognitive reactions, such as observable behaviour and internal processes, are due to a second kind known as *regulative (coordinative) messages*. Their function is to regulate, or mutually adjust, activities of communicating animals. This is particularly important for conspecifics during reproduction. With animals at the evolutionary level of seabirds, a great part of their communication involves such regulative messages. These are of both *inhibitory* (negative) and *excitatory* (positive) types, which respectively hinder or encourage activities.

Mutual coordination shows that communication seldom has a one-way character. Transmitting animals are often subsequently sent signs by the receiving animals, forming a sequence of *feedback*. The feedback messages may be either positive or negative, and frequently occur in very rapid exchanges—as when movements signal intentions. Two or more animals can thereby make up large systems of communication, with circular chains of cause-and-effect that are difficult to isolate and describe.

Regulation may be temporary, but some communication deals with more permanent behavioural modifications. The permanent bonds in pairs of mates are established by such means. There are also various kinds of "sanctioning",

Red-billed Tropic-bird *(Phaethon aethereus)*   **Great Frigate-birds** *(Fregata minor)*
Kittiwake *(Rissa tridactyla)*

Magnificent Frigate-bird *(Fregata magnificens)*

(Above) Two Great Frigate-birds harass a Red-billed Tropic-bird in an attempt to make it regurgigate food. This feeding method, normal among frigate-birds, forces the tropic-bird to make escape manoeuvres. The tropic-bird is also induced to give warning calls which announce its readiness to fight back—an example of interspecific communication.

(Opposite bottom) The red gape of the Kittiwake is usually invisible but, when demonstrated, it serves as a threat signal. This releases aggression when neighbours fight on cliff ledges during breeding.

(Right) As is common in its order of seabirds, the Magnificent Frigate-bird chick feeds from the parent's throat. Such feeding behaviour requires coordination of the actions by parent and offspring, involving communicative "feedback" of signals.

A Great Skua, long-calling with its neck held obliquely forward, also raises its wings so that their flashes of white colour function as signals. White/black differences are often used in communication between animals, although one or the other colour may serve as the sign according to the circumstances.

in which conspecifics communicate rewards and punishments—positive and negative reinforcements—that bring about lasting changes in behaviour. Teaching can occur through sanctioning and enable traditions to be passed from one generation of animals to the next, in addition to "teaching by example" with observation and imitation. The extent of these learning processes in seabirds has not yet been studied closely, and it may be significant in some species where traditions prevail.

A message having more than one effect on a receiver is called *multifunctional*. Warning calls may produce cognitive reactions, of understanding what the warning is about, but they can also directly result in protective reactions or states of alarm. Further, a message may produce different effects in different individuals. The displays used during courtship often yield dissimilar reactions according to sex. For instance, it has been found that certain male displays, such as long-calls by Herring Gulls, attract females but repel males.

Another observation is that some types of signs have effects, or meanings, which vary with their environmental circumstances or external *contexts*. In a message, the meaning of each sign may depend on the signs that it is combined with. Context-dependence plays many roles in communication through elaborate behaviour. Indeed, the omission of a sign can also be meaningful in particular contexts, where the sign's occurrence is expected and its absence thus makes a "difference". A sudden silence in a seabird colony may give an alarm which is equivalent to the usual function of alarm calls.

Phenomena of context-dependence, multifunctionality, and analog communication indicate that signalling and the regulation of behaviour can be very complex. Without taking such details into account, one could easily underestimate the number of messages in use by seabirds. Modern "information theory" is able to calculate amounts of communication, and a comparison of other communicating creatures would doubtless show that seabird behaviour is informative to a surprisingly high degree.

Behaviour among conspecifics

A great part of the interactions between seabirds in the same species is concerned with reproduction. Before considering its behavioural aspects, several other kinds of social activity should be noted, sometimes having ecological importance as well. Perhaps the most obvious example is gregarious, as opposed to solitary, behaviour. Whether a group of birds has been formed for distinctly social reasons is, however, often hard to determine.

Certain species, such as many gadfly petrels and tropic-birds, consist of birds that live mainly alone—but these are occasionally attracted together, as when resting on water. Resting in flocks, at sea and on land, is common among other seabirds. In most species, they also often form large aggregates when attracted to a single resource, like a big fish shoal. Further, a group of birds may be driven to a coastal area by wind or bad weather. These instances do not necessarily involve social behaviour in the gathering of individual birds. Yet a particular attraction to conspecifics is clearly at work in numerous cases, as with seabirds flying in groups to seek food, to move between feeding and breeding areas, or to migrate. Here, they tend to form anonymous flocks, without individual recognition or social hierarchies. Only if adults accompany their offspring for some time after fledging, as in some terns and auks, are temporary family groups of a more social nature found.

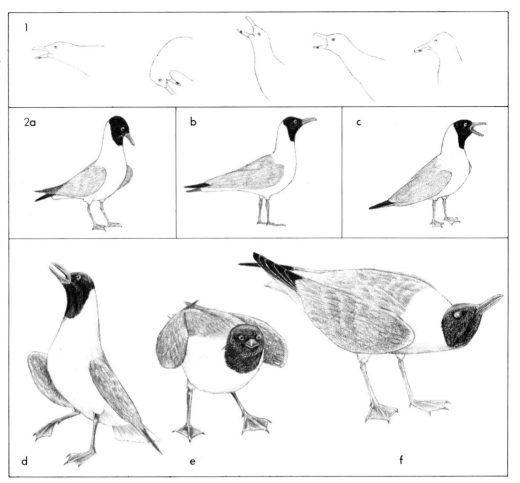

(1) The multifunctionality of signals is illustrated by the long-calling display of the Herring Gull. It serves as a long-distance threat to repel males, but in the early stage of pair formation it also attracts unpaired females.

(2) A Northern Black-headed Gull forms messages by combining the signs of head and bill positions, neck posture, and calls, while the meaning of the messages depends on the context. *(a)* Neck upright with downward-pointing bill means a threat. *(b)* The same neck posture with uplifted bill means anxiety, and generally inhibits aggression. *(c)* With the bill forward, the gull may call menacingly. *(d)* The same call with uplifted bill and neck withdrawn indicates fear. *(e)* Males threaten by facing each other with the neck held forward. *(f)* A very similar posture is used during pair formation, but the male and female stand parallel with their bills more uplifted: this inhibits aggression and forges the pair together.

Why have various seabird species become extremely gregarious? A well-known advantage of flocking is protection against predators. Enemies are not only more readily detected by birds that live in groups and can communicate warnings to each other. As was pointed out previously, an attacker also has greater difficulty in separating any bird from a dense group, and such groups are even formed during aerial manoeuvres by many gulls and terns when under attack. But the information which can be exchanged in a group may have valuable results of additional kinds.

It is believed, for instance, that seabirds signal the presence of good food resources when they return to a nearby colony. Young and inexperienced individuals might learn to find food by following older ones to traditional feeding areas. Techniques of feeding and choices of prey could also improve through learning from conspecifics, as does recognition of the species' own enemies. Training of young birds to understand mutual behaviour, to use signals, and to recognize sexes, are further possible advantages of group living, which may increase the chances of finding sexual partners as well.

Many of the modifications in behaviour caused by group living are evidently requirements of the latter, not directly advantageous for the individual's survival. A striking example is the mechanism by which gregarious seabirds are spaced apart in a group. Generally, there is a definite *individual distance* for a given species, the birds being kept apart by some kind of aggressive or threatening activity. In a crowded place with little room for resting, the consequence may be a very neat arrangement of birds sitting at almost equal intervals.

Breeding behaviour

The astonishing quantity of behaviour that seabirds need for successful reproduction illustrates how complicated an animal's nervous system can be. Breeding frequently includes a long sequence of activities, and fails if any of them is incorrect. Some of them constitute procedures that must be performed properly before others may begin. These processes involve much communication, often with feedback between mates. They might thus be visualized as a "spiral" chain of mutual behaviour, leading gradually through several stages: establishment of a breeding site, formation and maintenance of a pair, copulation and egg-laying, incubation, and the rearing of young.

Sites and territoriality

The difficulty of finding a site is not great in certain cases, as with seabirds breeding on flat open ground that has ample space, like terns on sandbars. Many seabirds, however, breed in places such as cliff ledges, natural holes, or crevices, where optimal sites are in limited supply. Sites in the centre of a colony are commonly preferred, and investigations have shown that breeding success is often highest there, probably because predation and other problems render sites on the edge of the colony suboptimal. Competition for sites is frequent in a dense colony whose old and experienced birds occupy the best sites. Adults tend to be very faithful to their sites year after year, and they are at an advantage in defending home territory.

The relative times at which a site is established and a pair is formed are variable among species. Male frigate-birds, for instance, first display and, after acquiring a mate, find a breeding site. Sandwich Terns and Royal Albatrosses occasionally form pairs that later seek a site together. But some male seabirds establish a site first, then look for a female outside it, notably among burrow-nesting petrels, shearwaters, and tropic-birds. Particularly in the clearly

American White Pelican *(Pelecanus erythrorhynchus)*
White-chinned Petrel *(Procellaria aequinoctialis)*

(Top) American White Pelicans feed and rest in groups. With a raised posture, straight neck, and lifted bill, they communicate readiness to take off in flight.

(Opposite) White-chinned Petrels, though rather solitary when flying about in search of food, often rest in groups on water. Here they are taking off at the windward side of a wave.

(Above) Royal Albatrosses show some striking behaviour during pair formation. In the early stages, they stand together and "sky-point" dramatically, with their enormous wings outspread. Mutual billing is a further, very common display, and sometimes one bird nibbles the other's neck.

(Right) Pair-bonding behaviour in Herring Gulls may take many days. *(a)* A male's upright threat posture attracts an unpaired female. *(b)* She courts him by approaching in a hunched, submissive posture, tilting her bill upward at times. *(c)* If he accepts her, both birds stand together and head-flag to inhibit aggression. *(d)* Later, she may beg food which the male regurgitates. *(e)* The mates also often call together. *(f)* Finally, their "choking" display shows agreement on a nest site.

(1) In a colony of King Penguins, a bird of either sex which has recently arrived *(a)* announces its presence with an "advertising" call. Older birds may thereby find prior mates as they recognize each other's sounds and look for former nest sites. Unmated birds also attract partners with this call. *(b)* When mates come together, they may head-flag, each turning its head by more than ninety degrees. *(c)* Courting birds also often stand breast-to-breast in a posture of "high-pointing", and bow while making a rattling sound with their bills *(d)*.

territorial seabirds, a site is found by the male and he subsequently attracts a female to it by displaying.

Most seabirds breed in colonies and primarily choose those of the same bird species, often the same colonies in which they were born. Seabirds breeding for the first time in their lives may inspect a number of adjacent colonies before they settle down in one. Such birds are probably the pioneers when new breeding colonies are founded. If the species has great fidelity to the site that will be used, the birds normally spend a long interval in seeking and establishing the site before they breed. Fulmar petrels and many other tubenoses may visit a future site one or two breeding seasons before their own breeding begins. There are also seabirds which easily abandon their breeding grounds if disturbed, a valuable anti-predator device. These usually spend a short time on the site before laying eggs, such as two or three days in the case of Sandwich Terns.

The procedure for establishing a site depends on its character, which differs greatly between species. Typical examples are the elaborate nests constructed by many pelicans and cormorants, the burrows dug by numerous tubenoses, and the diverse territories defended on open breeding grounds by skuas, terns, and gulls. Territoriality is common among birds, generally involving both displays and violent defensive behaviour. Seabirds are no exception to this rule, but the nature of displays and the degree of aggressiveness vary according to the site and breeding strategy.

All species strongly defend an area around the nest. Most are content to snap, bite, or lunge at intruders without inflicting much injury. They also respect the territories of neighbours if these have been established at the beginning of the breeding season. Newcomers to breeding grounds often announce uncertainty by means of anxiety postures,

and tend to flee instantly if attacked by the occupants of sites. Nevertheless, very violent fights are frequent in some species, such as tropic-birds and gannets. This seems to be connected with a commonly limited availability of breeding sites for the species.

What can be called the normal size of territory also varies according to the species. Large gulls have quite extensive territories and defend them well—probably as an evolutionary result of protection against predators and, in part, against conspecifics that endanger chicks. Many species, in which territorial defence is important, minimize the need for actual aggression, by exhibiting ritualized *territorial displays*. Wide territories are generally announced through long-distance threats, like the songs of songbirds. Oblique postures by gulls serve as a long-distance territorial display, in addition to their long-calls. On the whole, however, seabirds have rather small territories because they feed at sea outside these areas, and their long-distance ownership displays are relatively poorly developed.

It is interesting to compare territorial activities in the different seabird orders. Among penguins, those breeding in burrows defend them, partly with threats, but generally lack territorial displays. Of the open-ground breeders, the King and Emperor Penguins build no nests, but males sometimes fight by beating each other with the hard edges of their flippers, as do females in occasional competition over attractive males. Nest-builders usually defend a small, static territory around the nest with threat postures and actual fights.

Such a posture, among male crested penguins of the genus *Eudyptes*, involves bowing toward the feet and uttering loud throbs, then swaying the head and foreneck between the upraised flippers with a series of braying cries. The size and frequency of head and neck movements differ somewhat

(2) Mutual preening is a common form of behaviour which maintains pair-bonds in many species of seabirds. Shown here are Erect-crested Penguins, which also have a habit of pirouetting around their nest in a "shoulders-hunched" attitude during the formation of pairs.

d

between species of the genus. This display seems mainly to show ownership of the nest site, but probably also has a pair-bonding function. A clearer threat posture is to gape and utter deep growls, stretching the head forward and moving it up and down. Moreover, an "appeasement" posture is often used by penguins to avoid attack when crossing others' territories between the nest and the sea, since penguins cannot fly and many species nest densely. The crested penguins then frequently adopt a "slender walk" with the head and neck lowered, feathers sleeked, and flippers held forward roughly parallel to each other. A bird attacked in that posture normally does not retaliate but hurries along.

Tubenoses have developed little territoriality with clear borders, and almost totally lack formal displays announcing ownership. But many use cackling sounds as threats, in addition to the threatening and biting of intruders too near nests, and the oil-spitting defence by fulmars, petrels, and shearwaters. Giant petrels have an aggressive display of outspread wings, swaying the head in great arcs and holding the fanned tail forward.

Territoriality is common among the *Pelecaniformes*, although chiefly near the nests for those which build them in bushes and trees. Boobies are much less violent than the hole-nesting tropic-birds and the gannets. As well as a threat display, gannets have a highly stylized "bow" which announces site ownership, as does a bowing display of Brown Pelicans. Ritualized threats, mainly for intruders, are used by numerous cormorants, such as the Shag which gapes and shakes its head sideways.

In the order *Charadriiformes*, refined displays of site ownership are illustrated by the long-calls of skuas while they glide in a stiff ritualized manner, and those of gulls in an oblique posture. Such displays also have a pair-bonding

function. Terns are far less territorial, fighting and threatening each other little, although they defend an area around the nest and a few species exhibit aerial pursuits. Most auks nest rather densely and lead a peaceful colonial life, occasionally fighting with vigour but lacking the clearly aggressive displays found in gulls.

Formation of pairs

In order to reproduce, a bird must not only be fit for breeding but also find a fit partner. This selection is usually even more important for a female than for males, since she may suffer serious consequences from mating with unsuitable partners. She tends to invest greater resources in the offspring than do males, and the production of eggs requires large amounts of protein that strain her own resources. Ineffective copulation by a male is less costly, as the investments of energy and protein in sperm are small.

Partner selection is, however, of importance for the male as well. He normally contributes to incubation and feeding over a very long period, and this investment will be wasted if he makes such a bad partner choice that the offspring are not raised to independence. Probably because the parental investment is greater for females, the evolution of reproductive behaviour has in many cases had the result that the male only advertises to attract a partner, whereas the female makes the crucial selection to form a pair. The subsequent establishment of a pair bond also involves much behaviour to ensure that the mates have compatible properties.

Various communicative activities are devoted to these purposes. First, a bird must correctly determine the species, sex, readiness to breed, and fitness of a possible mate. This is done through colours, structures, and other characteristics with signal functions, which birds carry continuously—

177

(*Above*) Threatening behaviour may be shown by immature Red-footed Boobies, and has the effect of spreading them out on a site, while also allowing them to test each other's strength. Such communicative acts are a less drastic kind of aggressiveness than violent fights. The latter, nevertheless, occur in many ways among seabirds, both within and between species. Often, violence does not even involve anger and cannot be called aggressive—as with predation and parasitism. Violent behaviour results from *interference competition* among animals, as opposed to nonviolent *resource competition* of a less direct nature. Since animals invest energy when interfering with each other, the benefits of doing so must have been greater than the costs when such behaviour evolved. Yet for these immature seabirds, signalling

of threats is even more beneficial than attempts at violence.

(*Opposite top*) The "individual distance" between birds, which is characteristic in most species, regulates their density in groups so that conflicts do not occur. At maximum densities, they sometimes spread out quite regularly, as shown by these immature Red-footed Boobies in the author's company. Also visible is their remarkably short "escape distance" from man. This distance, too, is usually peculiar to the species, although varying with the kind of animal which they meet. Some seabirds are renowned for such fearlessness, particularly in areas where they have long been undisturbed, as in the Galapagos Islands where the photographs on these pages were taken.

(*Opposite bottom*) Behavioural interactions between parents and offspring are prominent in the reproduction of the species. An adult Red-footed Booby must take constant care of its small chick while nesting in bushes or trees in the tropics, where overheating is a great risk.

Red-footed Booby *(Sula sula)*

as well as through behavioural signals transmitted during the pair formation. A mate must also be able to identify its partner, in order to perform proper behaviour afterward and, especially, to avoid aggressive behaviour towards the partner. It is known that many seabirds can identify their partners by both visual and auditory means. The aggressiveness of a male defending a site is normally overcome by an approaching female, in early stages of pair formation, with appeasing behaviour. This seems to be particularly important in overcoming the "individual distance" between young birds which are breeding for the first time.

Pair formation is gradual in many seabird species and involves numerous displays. Albatrosses may even display a couple of seasons before the bond is established and breeding begins. A bond must also be maintained through at least one breeding season, often requiring special displays, mutual preening, and greeting ceremonies. The gannets copulate from January to May although eggs are not laid until April, a habit which probably has a pair-bonding function. But among the many seabirds that pair for life, displaying tends to be less frequent after the bond has been established. Albatrosses seldom meet after their egg is hatched, as they stay mainly at sea while the chick waits to be fed. When pairing is not for life, seabirds frequently still breed with the same mate in subsequent seasons if the pair was successful earlier. However, pairs may break apart if breeding has failed due to incorrect behaviour by one of the mates.

Some other functions of displays occur at the onset of breeding. Among gulls and terns, the male commonly feeds the female during courtship, and this helps not only pair-bonding but also egg-production, in which much protein is needed. Communication is of value for the stimulation of hormonal production, gonad development, and other physiological processes in reproduction. Sometimes, social stimulation by conspecifics is equally prominent, as when gulls or terns coordinate their egg-laying so exactly that a whole colony completes it within a few days. This probably decreases the loss of eggs due to predators, which cannot find and take more than a limited number of eggs each day.

Choosing a place to lay the eggs may be easy after a site is established, in birds such as burrow-nesters. In other cases, notably where both of the mates build a nest, agreement on the nest site may have to be communicated. Some species do this by a certain display, such as "choking" in gulls.

As a rule, seabirds copulate when all their physiological processes have been coordinated and the female is ready for egg-production. The act usually begins with inciting movements by the female. As the male and female have

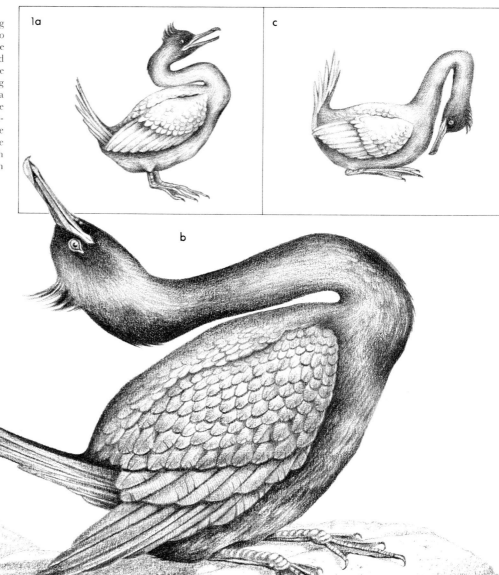

(1) Pair formation in the Shag begins with a lone male trying to attract a female by means of three main displays. *(a)* He darts his head forward and upward, at the same time opening his bill and exhibiting his vivid yellow gape. *(b)* When a prospective mate approaches, he tosses his head over his back, vibrating his throat-pouch. *(c)* When she comes closer, he starts to bow. If she accepts him, other displays by both partners will follow, forging them into a firm pair.

cloacae which must be juxtaposed so that sperm can be transferred, some rather difficult balancing performances and tail-movements are necessary. Only a few days are normally devoted to copulation and, subsequently, to the laying of eggs if there are more than one.

Behaviour during pair formation varies considerably between the seabird orders. Penguins use loud vocal displays along with their stereotyped movements, making large colonies very noisy. When they reach the breeding grounds at the beginning of the season, many advertise their readiness to start breeding by means of displays, such as the head-swinging of crested penguins. Birds of opposite sex, once attracted together, usually display in unison, with head-flagging by King Penguins and bowing by numerous other species. Loud trumpeting calls with the head held vertically are common, and normally occur throughout the breeding season—particularly when paired birds reunite and, probably, use these sounds for purposes of mutual recognition.

Most tubenoses are also quite vocal, but less given to ritualized visual displays, although the opposite is true of the relatively silent albatrosses. Billing and preening are employed as pair-bonding displays in the entire order. The many nocturnal species frequently sing or call, both while flying over the colony and when in their burrows.

In contrast to the preceding orders, *Pelecaniformes* are generally rather silent. The hole-breeding tropic-birds use vocal displays in courtship flights, often of small groups. As for visual displays, these birds do not use them much on nest sites, but others in the order have many complex displays during pair formation. Notable is the head-swaying of a male Brown Pelican when attracting females to the nest, followed for example by bowing and head-turning of both sexes after a female has adopted the site. Gannets and boobies use sky-pointing displays, and some engage in symbolic nest-building, as well as in mutual preening. Greeting ceremonies are particularly common throughout the breeding season among gannets, which pair for life. Fascinating, too, is the male frigate-bird, sitting on a potential nest site with spread wings and showing his inflated throat-pouch. When females fly over, he tries to attract them with various movements and some sounds. If a female joins him, the two may proceed by waving their heads and passing them over each other's necks.

Among the *Charadriiformes*, the behaviour of certain gulls is well-known and has been illustrated here in regard to several general principles. Its inclusion of both vocal and visual displays is typical of the entire order. Some terns and auks also take courtship flights, and auks even display communally on land and water, occasionally with under-

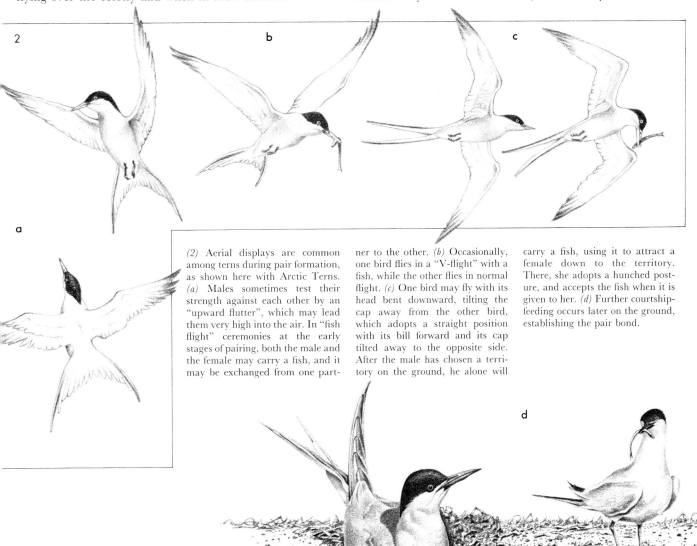

(2) Aerial displays are common among terns during pair formation, as shown here with Arctic Terns. (a) Males sometimes test their strength against each other by an "upward flutter", which may lead them very high into the air. In "fish flight" ceremonies at the early stages of pairing, both the male and the female may carry a fish, and it may be exchanged from one partner to the other. (b) Occasionally, one bird flies in a "V-flight" with a fish, while the other flies in normal flight. (c) One bird may fly with its head bent downward, tilting the cap away from the other bird, which adopts a straight position with its bill forward and its cap tilted away to the opposite side. After the male has chosen a territory on the ground, he alone will carry a fish, using it to attract a female down to the territory. There, she adopts a hunched posture, and accepts the fish when it is given to her. (d) Further courtship-feeding occurs later on the ground, establishing the pair bond.

Waved Albatross (*Diomedea irrorata*)
Blue-footed Booby (*Sula nebouxii*)

(Above) Behaviour during formation of pairs in the Waved Albatross includes billing, as seen here, and displays such as "sway-walks". They occur mainly at the end of the breeding season, a year before the birds actually begin to breed. The pair bond usually lasts for life.

(Left) Sky-pointing is one of the conspicuous displays used by the Blue-footed Booby in establishing a pair and maintaining the bond. Other boobies employ variants of this behaviour which are typical of their species. Such short sequences of innate, stereotyped behaviour are good instances of the "fixed action patterns" that are studied by ethologists.

(Opposite) Non-stereotyped kinds of behaviour are frequent among the diverse interactions in pairs during breeding, as in this case with Swallow-tailed Gulls. Yet the development of these kinds, too, may depend on inheritance.

Swallow-tailed Gull
Creagrus furcatus

(1) After a pair has been formed, copulation will follow when the mates' physiological processes are coordinated and the female is ready for egg production, as with these Lesser Black-backed Gulls.
(a) Copulation may begin with enticing movements by the female, tilting her head upward.
(b) This may be followed by the birds biting each other's bills.
(c) The male mounts the standing female, and their tails manoeuvre so that their cloacae meet.

water pursuits. During courtship, many auks touch, rub, or grasp each other's bills, and a number of them have brightly coloured gapes. Indeed, a few species such as the puffins copulate on water far from the sites where eggs will be laid.

Incubation

In practically all seabirds, both sexes share incubation. Exceptions are the Emperor Penguin and phalaropes, in which only males incubate. Some coastal seabirds have very short intervals for incubation, often only a few hours—but the truly oceanic seabirds are renowned for their lengthy periods. Tubenoses alternate extremely long foraging flights with incubation shifts which, in many species, often last more than a week. Shifts of 19–22 days are common for the Waved Albatross, and 17 days is an average for the Great-winged Petrel. However, the coastal diving-petrels usually relieve each other daily.

In the seabirds that lay more than one egg, some species—such as boobies—start incubating immediately after the first egg has been laid, although many begin only when all the eggs are laid. The incubating bird provides necessary warmth to the egg, transferring heat from its brood patches or, in cormorants, pelicans, gannets, boobies, and tropic-birds, from the webs. But chilling is seldom a danger at the outset of incubation. Overheating may threaten eggs that lie exposed to the sun for long periods, and another role of the incubating bird is sometimes to shade them. Since a little water is lost from the egg during incubation, control of its humidity is important. Protection of the egg from predators may be essential.

Displays such as greeting ceremonies are frequently performed when parents relieve one another at a nest. The returning bird may well show some appeasement behaviour to inhibit aggression by the incubating bird. A Flightless Cormorant normally greets its mate by handing over some seaweed when it returns—and in an experiment, when its seaweed was taken away, a bird was attacked by its incubating mate. Such ceremonies are most important in species that strongly defend territories, like gannets. On the other hand, frigate-birds scarcely display during nest relief: the incubating bird simply slips off the nest and flies away.

Rearing

When a seabird egg hatches, the chick always has to get out of it with no help from the parents. Yet many adult gulls and terns remove the shells soon after hatching, so that predators will not be attracted to the vicinity of chicks. During a certain period after hatching, which varies greatly in length between species, the chick is vulnerable to starvation and bad weather, requiring constant care by at least one parent. Birds breeding in protected sites, such as burrows or natural holes, leave the chicks unguarded relatively soon. Many tubenoses do so as early as three or four days after hatching, since the chicks are fed with energy-rich proventricular oil and can eventually withstand hunger for long intervals. Open-ground nesting requires more protection, and chicks can easily die by overheating or chilling if not shaded or covered.

The frequency of feeding is another behavioural adaptation that depends on the species. In tubenoses, days may pass between visits by parents, particularly at the end of the breeding season when fledging is near and the young—having briefly weighed more than the adults—

2a

2b

(2) Greeting ceremonies, when the mates reunite at the nest, are common among seabirds and probably help to maintain the pair bond. Gannets perform such ceremonies throughout the breeding season.
(a) A returning male normally bites the female's nape, and she faces away as an appeasement. The females appear to like this male aggressiveness, and it may have evolved because of such males' ability to defend good nest sites.
(b) "Mutual fencing" occurs often.

normally decrease in weight. Coastal seabirds generally feed the chicks daily, often several times. Terns seldom fly far and, like many alcids, they usually carry food in their bills when returning to the colony from a feeding area. But the pelagic Sooty Tern feeds the young with partly digested food. Most seabird species carry the food in the crop, and regurgitate it after exchanging some communicatory behaviour between the parent and the young. Commonly, the young peck at the parent's bill to release feeding. Some, as among gulls, eat food that is regurgitated on the ground, while tubenoses and others eat directly from the parent's bill, and the *Pelecaniformes* tend to take food from deep in the parent's throat.

The fledged young may go through a difficult period as they begin to feed for themselves. In certain species, they are fed temporarily by the parents, for an unusually long time in the case of many terns and frigate-birds. Some auks fledge before they can fly, and are followed awhile by the parents. Guillemots and Razorbills leave their cliffs a few weeks after hatching, normally late in the evening when they are less vulnerable to predators, and it has been found that they frequently accompany adults which are not even their own parents. The young of Craveri's and Xantus's Murrelets, in the Pacific Ocean, leave the nest only 2–4 days after hatching, and are subsequently followed by their parents.

The evolution of displays

From the foregoing survey it is clear that a great number of genes has been involved in the evolution of very complex

behaviour among seabirds for reproduction as well as for survival. Birds differing in such genes may vary in their breeding behaviour and thus in reproductive success, so that their genes spread differently in a population. This evolutionary process helps to account for the genes which control, for example, announcements of partner fitness and the understanding of displays. There remains, however, much to learn about the genetic causes of each form of seabird behaviour, particularly displays, and ethology has given some notable explanations.

A familiar phenomenon in evolution is that a single species may give rise to two or more distinct species. This can happen only if, in some way, populations have become isolated from each other, usually in their geographical distribution with localized conditions leading to differences in their properties. But sometimes such populations come together again, with two possible main results. They may interbreed until all the differences have disappeared, or they may somehow be kept separate as distinct species. In the latter event, we must discover what keeps them apart and why properties separating them have evolved.

The hybrids produced by interbreeding are often more viable than their parents, due to the "heterosis" effects of mixed genes. A merging of the populations will then result, and this can occur even without such a difference in viability. However, hybrids are frequently less viable than the parents, for example if the populations have previously diverged much in properties: a random mixture of these may yield offspring that do not function adequately. If the populations have become ecologically specialized, the hybrids may simply be less well adapted, as a specialist type may use limited environmental resources more efficiently than a

185

Communicative behaviour of extreme variety can be found among Adélie Penguins, whose distribution and smaller breeding range are shown here on the map of the Antarctic. Some of the regular displays in a large colony are as follows.

(a) The "sideways stare" may be given by a bird whose territory is approached, or by a female coming towards a possible male partner.

(b) A bird "gapes", in an extended posture and usually while calling harshly, to protect the boundaries of its territory from neighbours.

(c) An "ecstatic" display is given in varying degrees, with sounds, mainly by males attracting mates.

(d) A male and female "bow" at a nest site to establish or maintain a bond.

(e) The "bill-to-axilla" display, usually by a bird left alone at the nest, is mildly threatening.

(f) A "loud mutual" display tends to occur in pairs for recognition, as when one bird returns to the nest. Parents and chicks, or two birds fighting, also use variants of it.

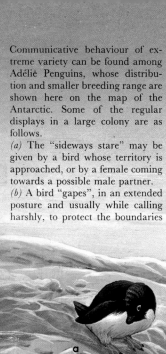

generalist type with intermediate properties. Thus, the hybrids may have lower survival chances and reproductive success than do their parents, particularly if food resources limit population sizes.

There is always some variation in properties among the individuals in populations. Some may be less prone to hybridizing than others, because of the character of displays and responses. If hybrids are less viable than normal offspring, natural selection favouring greater differences in behaviour may begin, with a spreading of genes which inhibit hybridization. In this manner, homologous reproductive behaviour in closely related species can be modified. Genes conditioning displays, fixed action patterns, and innate releasing mechanisms may all change in their relative frequencies.

Seabirds abundantly illustrate the latter process. Many gull species have similar threats which are not very important for pair-bonding and hybridization, but they differ in regard to other displays that play a key role in pair-bonding, for example the long-calls serving to aid attraction between mates. The colour of eye rings is also often different in closely related gull species, and it has been

proven in certain cases to effectively inhibit hybridization. Such calls and colours might be compared to traffic signals that would have become identical if a complete mingling of vehicles were safe.

The fact that every signal involves contrasts is a clue to the character of genes which have spread by conditioning clear displays. This character has three main aspects, according to ethology and evolutionary theory. First, a display should be clear and conspicuous in its contrast to nonsignalling behaviour. It may be exaggerated, as with the sway-walk of the Waved Albatross and braking by the feet in Blue-footed Boobies, or it may have a rhythmical feature. Often, it is quantitatively different from normal behaviour, being obviously faster or slower. Displays in general are so stereotyped that only one degree of such a contrast is used, and the fixed activity commonly depends on a connection between motor elements which are otherwise independent in the bird.

Secondly, a display should be in striking contrast to other signals employed by the species, preventing confusion with them. Threats and appeasements, for instance, are normally made through the use of opposite kinds of behaviour.

(1) Skuas long-call during flight with their wings held in a stiff, conspicuous way. This display is territorial but also has functions in pair-bonding. The four species of skuas seen here differ in their manner of holding the wings.
(a) The Great Skua exhibits a distinctive "V-flight".
(b) The Pomarine Skua keeps a similar but lower wing-position.
(c) The Arctic Skua's wings are slightly below the horizontal.
(d) The Long-tailed Skua's wings are lowest, in an inverted "V".

Thirdly, each signal should have a clear function, releasing a distinctive activity in the receiver. The sense organs of receivers, along with the breeding strategies adopted by species, are evidently related to the nature of their displays. If, like most tubenoses, they are nocturnal on breeding grounds, visual signals are of little value and vocal displays prevail.

Additional links can be found between displays and breeding strategy. Albatrosses, which seldom meet after the young has reached a fair age, consistently devote much energy to pair-bonding behaviour but very little to maintenance of the established pair. The reverse is true for numerous other species that meet daily while rearing the young and use, for example, greeting ceremonies or mutual preening to maintain the pair-bond. Cost-benefit relations seem to have played a role in the evolution of certain behaviour, as with species having a limited supply of nest sites. These tend to defend the sites aggressively and, despite the cost of violent behaviour, its apparent advantages have enabled the conditioning genes to spread.

Some signals have obtained their character through a process of *ritualization*. Here, a normally occurring movement is adopted and modified as a display. Selection favours genes that make such movements more clear and exaggerated, until they may no longer resemble those from which they originated, although the latter are detectable by comparison of related species. Movements associated with intentions have frequently become ritualized into displays. A Herring Gull holds its wings slightly away from the body as an "upright" aggressive display, which plainly originates in movements of intention to fly.

Behaviour in conflict situations is the probable origin of many displays. Redirected responses and "displacement activities" are of this character, as has already been illustrated. A kind of compromise between competing tendencies can be seen in some ambivalent postures of seabirds, as when a threat is made instead of actually attacking or escaping. Their behaviour used for pair-bonding, too, often appears to be a ritualized result of conflict between pairing, aggressiveness, and escape. It is perhaps in these cases, where animals act creatively yet in a manner reminiscent of noncreative or self-destructive behaviour, that the work of evolution in keeping them alive has been most essential.

1c

1d

(2) Appeasement postures are often clearly opposite in form to threat postures. In the Herring Gull, both (a) immatures and (b) females adopt an appeasing hunched posture with the neck withdrawn, and the female tilts her bill upward. This is in contrast to (c) a threat with the neck upright and the bill pointing downward. In such cases, the possibility of confusion between different kinds of signals would be disadvantageous to the species.

Kittiwake *(Rissa tridactyla)*
Masked Booby *(Sula dactylatra)*

(Above) Kittiwakes normally breed on cliff ledges, where they build nests of mud. But such breeding habitats are sometimes scarce.

(Opposite) An alternative breeding site of Kittiwakes may be a low island, such as Nidingen on the west coast of Sweden. Here, the birds try to obey their normal habits by building the nests close together on a navigation mark. The young are also following usual rules by staying in the nest until they are fledged—although they could easily hide on the ground, as the young of most species of gulls do.

(Right) The Masked Booby brings small objects to the nest during one of its pair-bonding displays. The evolutionary origin of this habit, however, seems to be nest-building. Such a process, in which behaviour acquires a new function, is called "ritualization" by ethologists.

Intention movements have often become ritualized into displays, during the course of evolution in numerous seabird species. As seen here, a Common Cormorant lifts its wings upward as a display in courtship. Such wing-waving or fluttering is also performed in various ways by other cormorants when breeding. It originates in movements of intention for flight.

Chapter Seven
SEABIRD
REPRODUCTION

Relationships between the life of an ocean bird and the means by which it comes to be alive have often been noted in the preceding chapters. Reproduction is so central and curious a feature of the seabird world that we must now try to clarify the underlying processes and their real measure of effectiveness. This is done chiefly by observing and analyzing what can be called "reproductive strategy", the mixture of choices and conditions which allow each type of animal to replace its individuals with a certain degree of "reproductive success".

In general, a population has a rate of replacement that depends on its birth rate and death rate—nativity and mortality. These, in turn, may differ between subtypes of animals, or parts of the population. If so, the comparative sizes of the parts change with time, and variations can occur in the genetic constitution and evolutionary history of the population. Its reproductive strategy is thus both a cause and an effect of its degree of success.

A leading example, as will be illustrated later on, is the frequent difference in birth and death rates according to age. Very young seabirds normally have low nativity and high mortality, but the opposite is true for older birds of reproductive ages. Some types of animals have low nativity and, for instance through considerable parental investment, may keep mortality in offspring low as well. Others maintain high nativity, their mortality being also quite high and, usually, highest at young age. The latter strategy is commonly found in animals whose population size is largely controlled by factors apart from food resources, such as great predatory pressure or recurrent bad weather.

Reproductive strategies vary widely among species of seabirds. Their description must take into account the entire life cycle, including not only age groups but also longevity and the duration of immaturity. An extremely important element is the *breeding strategy* with its many biological and environmental aspects. These concern the places and times of breeding, influence by climate and food supplies, investment in diverse phases of the breeding cycle, the role of sexes, the characteristics of breeding colonies, and solutions to the problems of egg-laying and incubation.

Places of breeding

Given the fact that seabirds need land for breeding, their choice of a place can be divided into three stages. The first involves selection of an ecological habitat and of some position in an ecosystem during breeding. Secondly, a macroscopical location must be found, such as an island, steep cliff, or mountaintop. Within those limits, the third requirement is to determine a site for laying eggs—as in a hole, crevice, tree, on flat ground or ledges—along with the manner of building a nest, or digging a burrow, and other preparations.

While every seabird survives by being generally adapted to a certain niche in an ecosystem, some species differ to an extent in their ecology between breeding and non-breeding periods, as a result of the first stage. The second stage depends mainly on feeding and weather conditions. There is, of course, enough land on earth to hold the nests of all breeding birds which are supported by the oceans' production. Many places are unsuitable, however, in terms of the food in surrounding waters, the foraging distances demanded, and hazards such as strong wind or predation.

These factors have often resulted in extraordinary, although successful, adaptations by seabirds. Species like some alcids in the Arctic, and Grey Gulls in the Chilean deserts, go dozens of miles (km) from the nearest sea to breed. The Snow Petrel has been found breeding almost 200 miles (300 km) from the coast on the Antarctic mainland, while the Emperor Penguin even breeds on ice. Certain petrels and shearwaters particularly exemplify a phenomenon of breeding on mountaintops, which may be as high as 6,500 feet (2,000 metres) above sea level. On the other hand, oceanic islands are commonly used for breeding because they shorten foraging distances and increase protection from predators. Smaller islands and sandbars are frequently employed near coasts, notably by gulls and terns. Many seabirds breed on steep cliffs and slopes at coasts, where updrafts aid those which have difficulty in landing or taking off, such as albatrosses and auks.

The choice of a site for eggs, too, reflects factors like weather and predation. It is not unusual that different types of site occur within the same macroscopical breeding habitat. On cliffs, for example, some auks put their eggs directly on ledges, yet gannets and kittiwakes make a nest there. Various auks, tubenoses, and penguins, as well as tropic-birds and the Inca Tern, breed in crevices and natural holes, whereas a burrow is made by certain penguins and medium-sized tubenoses. Such holes and burrows are occasionally found under high vegetation and, as may be the case with shearwaters and petrels, even in forests.

Similarly, along the western coast of South America, birds like the Peruvian Diving-Petrel and the Humboldt Penguin dig in guano or sand. The Marbled Murrelet, and a race of the White-tailed Tropic-bird on Christmas Island, breed in tree holes. Hole-nesting protects birds not only against predators, but also from both hot and cold weather. Where overheating is a danger, evaporation of body fluids easily results in dehydration, and young birds that are not shaded by parents can perish if not sheltered in holes. This kind of protection is especially important in the immediate post-hatching period for seabirds that breed on open ground in the tropics. The parents themselves often lose much fluid in such conditions, and Sooty Terns may actually fly away at intervals to cool off by soaking their feet and feathers in sea water.

A number of seabirds build nests in trees, as among boobies, cormorants, frigate-birds, noddy terns, and gulls. The White Tern lays its egg directly on branches. Tree-nesting is of value for landing and taking off, in addition to avoiding predators or, in the tropics, very hot ground. But nesting on flat ground is used by many species as of penguins, the larger tubenoses, pelicans, boobies, cormorants, skuas, gulls, and terns. This tends to occur where terrestrial predators are few or absent, mainly on islands. Skuas and gulls may succeed in such breeding partly because of their active joint defence, relatively large territories, and camouflaged chicks which wander away from the nest soon after hatching and generally hide if warned by the parents.

Site fidelity

It is particularly the seabirds building elaborate nests, digging burrows, and breeding in natural holes that are faithful to their sites year after year. The evolution of site fidelity is understandable in view of the great efforts and costs which are often needed to establish such sites. This fidelity is commonly shown by both of the mates and is accompanied by strong mutual faithfulness.

However, in species with little or no nest-building, plenty of breeding space, and difficulty in identifying the same sites from one year to the next, there is seldom much site fidelity. Birds that breed upon sandbars, such as some pelicans, gulls, and terns—as well as penguins breeding on ice—have few constant characteristics in their surroundings between years, although their colonies are frequently in more or less the same places during successive seasons. A few species, like gulls and terns, are prone to relocating whole colonies when disturbed. The Waved Albatrosses breeding on Hood Island in the Galapagos build no nest, laying the egg directly on the ground, and often shift it for a distance of several feet (metres) even during the incubation period.

Colonial breeding

What is meant by a seabird "colony" has not always been clear, although some kind of gregarious breeding is implied. The Long-tailed Skua may be called colonial, yet it feeds in a very large territory, despite the occasional use of a limited area with good feeding conditions for a number of birds. We should, rather, define any bird colony as a place of congregation by breeding birds which obtain their food outside the breeding area.

The colony's size can range from only a few pairs to the million-headed assemblages in certain seabird species. A question whether one or more colonies are present may arise in some cases, as when seabirds breed in adjacent groups along a cliff, but there need not be doubt that the breeding habit is colonial. Another characteristic of a colony is social interaction between individuals. While seabirds do not form very hierarchical groups with leaders and recognition of each member, their colonies do involve

Elliot's Storm-petrel *(Oceanites gracilis)*

complex interrelationships and some differences of status, the older experienced birds often occupying the best sites at the centre.

Around 95% of seabird species have adopted colonial breeding, with great variations in colony size between species and, sometimes, even within a species. One cause of a small colony is the establishment of a new breeding place by an expanding population. Fulmar petrels and gannets have increased enormously in the eastern North Atlantic during the past century, regularly founding new colonies. Such a foundation tends to be made by a single pair or a few pioneering pairs, and the subsequent growth is frequently great. But some species normally breed in tiny colonies, which may have only 10 pairs or less. Examples are Flightless Cormorants and certain gulls and terns. These colonies, however, can be numerous along a coastline. There are additional species, like the Waved Albatross, in which all the birds breed in the same colony.

It is found ecologically in such cases that the colony size reflects the type of food, its availability, and maximum foraging distances. When the food is quite widespread or abundant, seabirds commonly have huge colonies. This is well illustrated among penguins in the Antarctic, and a colony on Zavodevski Island contains an astonishing population of ten million Chinstrap Penguins. Further colonies reaching a million or more individuals belong to the Adélie Penguin, the Great, Sooty, and Short-tailed Shearwaters, Wilson's Storm-petrel, the Guanay Cormorant, Sooty Tern, Atlantic Puffin, and Little Auk. In some colonies, though, the size is also determined by the amount of space, or supply of holes and crevices, which limits

growth. Many crowded gannetries have remained at the same size for decades in spite of an increase in the species' total population.

The origins of colonies

In explaining why predominantly colonial habits have evolved, their disadvantages to seabirds must be noted. A disturbance in a colony may cause panic and the loss of many eggs and chicks. Interference between the breeding birds is often costly. Hygiene becomes a problem in very dense colonies, and diseases spread easily. Predators can detect a large colony from far away and profit by its high concentration of birds and eggs. Nonetheless, birds with genes or traditions that condition colonial breeding must have reproduced more successfully than solitary breeding birds, in order for the habit to have spread so widely.

A possible explanation is that suitable habitats for breeding are in limited supply, forcing birds to breed together in these areas regardless of the disadvantages. This might be why colonial habits began to evolve in some species. But there seem to be few examples today of such extreme habitat limitation, and many well-known colonial seabirds appear to be attracted to each other rather than to sites. In fact, colonial breeding has been found to possess clear advantages over solitary breeding. As was mentioned earlier, protection against predators is aided by the many watchful eyes and the evolution of alarm calls in a group of birds. Skuas, gulls, and terns are notable for joint harassment and attacks which compel predators to waste energy in avoidance manoeuvres.

Synchronized laying of eggs is common among colonial

Grey-backed Shearwater (Puffinus bulleri)

(Opposite) The breeding grounds of some seabirds are still unknown because of their strange breeding habits. An example is Elliot's Storm-petrel, shown here off the Galapagos Islands.

(Right) The Grey-backed Shearwater breeds in New Zealand, but this specimen was observed off the coast of Chile in the middle of the breeding season. Being in moult, it is unlikely to breed.

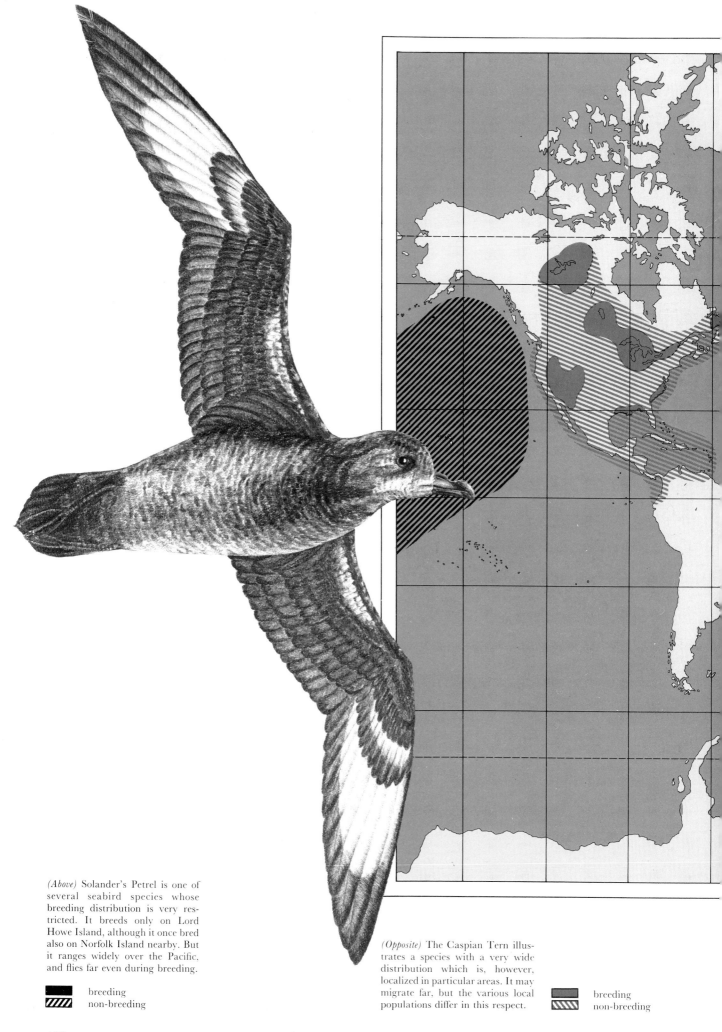

(*Above*) Solander's Petrel is one of several seabird species whose breeding distribution is very restricted. It breeds only on Lord Howe Island, although it once bred also on Norfolk Island nearby. But it ranges widely over the Pacific, and flies far even during breeding.

▰▰ breeding
▨▨ non-breeding

(*Opposite*) The Caspian Tern illustrates a species with a very wide distribution which is, however, localized in particular areas. It may migrate far, but the various local populations differ in this respect.

▨ breeding
▨ non-breeding

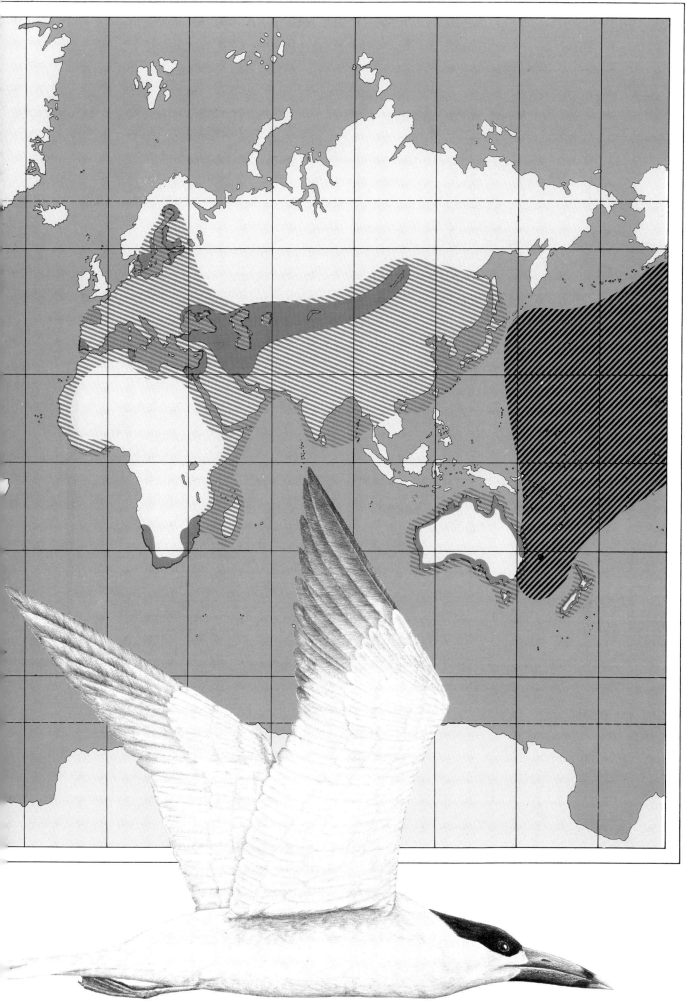

Nocturnal breeding habits

Many seabird species are surprisingly active at night on breeding grounds. As long as sunlight lasts, one may pass through such a colony without seeing or hearing a single bird. But as soon as it is totally dark, the air may fill with birds, while weird sounds come from all directions. Smaller tubenoses are notably hard to observe, and they may breed among large boulders or in scree. The burrow-digging species may dig among the roots of large trees in forested areas, making whole colonies difficult to find.

Hornby's Storm-petrel (above) is fairly common in Humboldt Current waters, but no colony is known today. However, it may breed in the northern desert of Chile where mummified nestlings have been found in holes—one of them about 30 miles (50 km) from the coast at an altitude of 5,000 feet (1,500 metres)—as well

as in southern Peru where fledged immatures have been found. Another enigmatic species is the Marbled Murrelet (opposite), not uncommon in the North Pacific. Only some years ago was it discovered to breed in holes in large trees, sometimes rather far from the coast. It, too, is active at night in such places.

Less mysterious is the Little Penguin (below). It is not the only penguin which breeds in burrows, but most of the others do not need to hide from predators with as much care as this bird. Smallest of all penguins, it breeds along many coasts of New Zealand and Australia, often on islands near the shore, landing at dusk and departing at dawn. The nest is placed in cavities or burrows, which the birds themselves may make if the ground is soft. Such sites are sometimes close to the high-water mark, but may be several hundred metres inland.

seabirds. This phenomenon has been shown to decrease the loss of eggs and chicks. Firstly, it minimizes their vulnerability to predators, since these can take only a limited quantity of food each day. Thus, on the average, taking of eggs and young is greatest with birds that start to breed earlier or later than do the synchronized members of a colony. Moreover, on islands that lie deserted for part of the year, predators specializing in such seabirds have been unable to evolve, because they would starve between breeding periods. A rather similar strategy occurs among other types of organisms, like bamboos and conifer trees, which have a synchronized production of seeds at certain times.

A second benefit of synchronized egg-laying is to diminish the occasional loss of eggs and chicks through interference between seabirds that compete over breeding sites. Competition occurs mainly before the birds begin to lay, and is thus most harmful to those which lay relatively early. Thirdly, it is possible to exploit a sudden rise of food production in surrounding seas during breeding, principally in the tropics and other areas where food conditions change rapidly. Such synchronization, including that of feeding, requires communication between conspecifics. This is facilitated by colonial, rather than solitary, breeding.

Seabird species vary as to how precisely egg-laying is synchronized. Black-headed Gulls and Sandwich Terns lay most of their eggs within a few days. More common is laying over a period of a few weeks, or sometimes longer. Certain tropical colonies, as of the Masked Booby, have eggs all the year round, although a maximum is reached in particular periods of a few months. It is interesting that even tropical seabirds without annual breeding seasons exhibit synchronization. There are species in the Galapagos Islands, like the Swallow-tailed Gull, which breed during the entire year, yet lay eggs at much the same time in local colonies.

Colonial breeding is often thought to have a "social advantage". For example, the activities and displays of birds in a colony stimulate their hormone production, gonad development, and other preparations for breeding, so that reproductive success is favoured. This helps to account for the spread of genes which influence such stimulation, especially when the benefits of synchronized egg-laying are recalled. But a further social advantage of colonial breeding probably lies in the communicative sharing of information, whose general value has also been described in Chapter 6 as regards social behaviour.

Birds breeding together are not only able to improve their knowledge of food supplies, learning of traditions, and finding of partners. As a species, they must also be reproductively isolated and, to some extent, ecologically specialized. This is achieved partly through a periodic return of birds to the colonies where they were born. The pelagic seabirds, normally far-flung over the oceans during non-breeding periods, have good reason to reunite in breeding colonies and maintain the full compatibility of all their properties, avoiding the risks of hybridization.

In the terms of seabird conservation, however, there is an unfortunate consequence of the fact that colonial breeding has so many advantages. Animals can be wiped out easily if they become dependent on a highly organized activity which is quite vulnerable to disturbances. When the size of a seabird colony is reduced too far by human encroachment, such a factor as social stimulation may no longer be strong enough to motivate the birds to breed, even though it might appear for a time that the colony is still viable.

Nest density and territorial habits

The amount of area occupied by seabirds when breeding, and the spacing of nests within it, are characteristic in many species but hard to explain. For birds using holes and crevices or digging burrows, the nest density may be due simply to the nature of the ground and the problem of burrows collapsing when dug too close together. In the latter case, we sometimes find several burrows with a common entrance, which has enabled the birds to maximize their density. But even birds that breed on flat ground often exhibit a particular density of nests. A definite territorial area is established by some species, and it can be fairly large although—as with Herring Gulls—the birds still feed outside the breeding area.

Instances of extreme density occur among penguins, gannets, cormorants, and terns. Frequently, the spacing is just enough for safe landings and take-offs, or seems to be determined by how far the birds on nests may reach without touching each other. If the population decreases in such dense nesters, they normally do not spread out, but keep the same density as the colony's area shrinks. Guanay Cormorants breed with a density of about three pairs per square yard (metre), and this remains constant when their population crashes during "El Niño" conditions, of warm water flowing south along the Peruvian coast. In many places where guillemot colonies have declined considerably in numbers, the birds continue to breed with about the same density on a smaller part of their cliff ledges, rather than dispersing across the original areas.

Some terns nest quite densely on sandbars in spite of additional space there for nests. Since they breed in places with mainly avian predators, protection from these is apparently the reason for dense nesting. This makes joint defence more effective and, if egg-robbers such as big gulls arrive, the terns stay on the nests to protect their eggs. But terns breeding where mammalian predators are a danger have been found to space their nests more widely than do conspecifics breeding on offshore islands. Herring Gulls—which also occasionally breed in areas with, for example, foxes—have large territories making their chicks and eggs hard to find. A further reason for the extensive territories of birds like skuas and bigger gulls, however, seems to be prevention of "cannibalistic" feeding on eggs and chicks by conspecific neighbours. It is known, at least, that this is a major cause of death among Herring Gull chicks.

Thus, a species' normal nest density and territorial size have probably often evolved through a dynamic balance between advantages and disadvantages. A breeding habitat might once have possessed both abundant food and limited nesting space, so that it could continue in use only with the evolution of a territorial habit or aggressive nest-defence by a moderate number of birds, rather than under the difficult conditions of nesting very densely.

Times of breeding

A seabird's life cycle, like that of other organisms, includes a period of dependence on the parents, a period of independence while maturing, and a period of breeding in adulthood. The duration of these periods is part of the reproductive strategy of each species. Adult life itself is characterized by cycles of breeding and non-breeding, within which there are intervals of moult, migration, and wintering in most species.

Maturation

In comparison to land-birds, seabirds tend to have a long adolescence. The tubenoses, in particular, normally take many years to mature. Age of first breeding is 10 years or more for the two large albatrosses, somewhat less for the smaller albatrosses and fulmar petrels, and 5–8 years for most petrels and shearwaters. In this order, only the diving-petrels mature rapidly, as soon as 2 years. The penguins and, probably, frigate-birds also take 5–10 years to reach maturity. Other seabirds generally start breeding at 3–6 years, although 2 years may suffice in some cases as among Cape Gannets, guillemots, gulls, and terns. In certain species, the age of first breeding is rather variable, such as 7–11 years for the Fulmar, 3–8 years for the Kittiwake, 4–8 years for the Sooty Tern, and 3–6 years for the Razorbill.

Why maturity is occasionally deferred to so great an extent is not quite clear. It presumably reflects annual differences in food supply, and individual differences in ability to acquire the feeding skills needed for survival and reproduction. Many seabirds rear only one offspring in a protracted breeding process, and unskilled birds may have trouble in caring for even a single chick. Problems of finding a nest site in crowded colonies with older and more experienced birds can delay breeding. Adult birds, too, often take a rest without breeding in years when the food supply is unusually low. A well-studied example is the Laysan Albatross, whose breeders are as few as 40% of the adult population in some years, but 100% in years with a high breeding success. Pomarine and Long-tailed Skuas breed chiefly at four-year intervals, raising two chicks, in the tundra where their supply of rodent prey varies in a four-year cycle.

Compensating for seabirds' long adolescence and low reproductive rates are their low annual adult mortality and long average life-span. Less than 10–15% of seabirds die each year in the majority of investigated species, and the figure is just 3–5% for some tubenoses. When it has been possible to identify individuals, often through banding, certain ones prove to be 20–30 years old in many species, and up to 40–50 years old among tubenoses. The albatrosses are notably long-lived and, in view of such findings, seem able to reach 80 years or more.

Annual and seasonal breeding

The frequency of a seabird's breeding cycle, and the time of year at which it occurs, are further important aspects of its reproductive strategy. Most adult seabirds breed once each year, but other cycles are not uncommon. While the duration of breeding cycles is closely related to the annual variation in climate and productivity, additional factors arise in the case of non-annual cycles. A few species need more than a year for all activities from the onset of breeding until the young are independent—such as the Wandering and Royal Albatrosses, Abbott's Booby, and frigate-birds, which breed biennially, or the King Penguins with an eighteen-month cycle.

In tropical areas where climate and productivity are nearly constant throughout the year, diverse seabirds have adapted to them with a sub-annual breeding cycle. Many species breed annually as well, though at different times of the year in different colonies. Within some species, the duration of breeding also varies greatly, depending on local conditions in breeding areas. For example, the Brown Booby breeds annually in numerous parts of the tropics, yet has a cycle of 9 months on Ascension Island. Here, too, the Sooty Tern has a cycle of 9.3 months, but it breeds every 6 months on Phoenix and Line Islands. Like this bird, the Silver Gull in Australia and New Zealand, and Cassin's Auklet in the North Pacific, breed regularly in two seasons.

Most seabird species breed in summer, exploiting the great food production at high latitudes. But there are tubenoses, mainly gadfly petrels, which consistently breed in winter, as a rule in subtropical waters. This divergence of breeding seasons may have resulted, in some cases, from a lack of protected nesting sites as on the Madeira and Salvage Islands where the breeding of Little Shearwaters in late winter is followed by that of Cory's Shearwaters in summer. However, such winter-breeding could also be due to ecological factors that are not adequately known. As an instance, the productivity of subtropical seas is greatest in springtime, with a rather smaller peak in autumn. Since the young of winter-breeding species become fledged in early spring, their survival chances at the beginning of independent life may thus be maximized.

In general, peaks of productivity at high latitudes do not last very long, and tubenoses with extended breeding cycles may have had difficulty in evolving an optimal strategy. Most of the seabird species breeding at high latitudes adjust their cycle so that the rearing of young coincides with peaks of productivity, and the plankton-feeding species often breed somewhat earlier than do those which feed on other animals. Certain species, like the winter-breeding Emperor Penguin, bring the young to independence during peaks of productivity. On the other hand, many of the smaller tubenoses are affected by the fact that the sun shines all day long in summer at high latitudes, making a nocturnal habit on breeding grounds useless for protection against predators. This probably explains why the Leach's and British Storm-petrels, on Lofoten in northern Norway, begin their breeding as late as August, the young fledging in November or December.

Stages in the breeding cycle

The breeding activities can be divided conveniently into four periods: those of pre-laying, incubation, fledging, and post-fledging. Their durations, and the amounts of investment in them by parents, vary greatly among seabird species. A couple of months may be enough for the entire process, as with many gulls, terns, and phalaropes, while the large albatrosses and some others need over a year.

Several species put on reserves of fat before their breeding begins, and may complete their breeding rapidly. Most, however, subsist wholly on the food obtained during breeding, which makes it a protracted process in certain cases. Among Emperor Penguins, the male lives on a huge reserve of fat during incubation in the Antarctic winter, and the female continues to feed at sea until the eggs hatch. But the King Penguins, of similar size, rely upon feeding as they breed, and have been forced to adopt a long cycle of eighteen months. No flying seabirds put on such heavy layers of fat as do some penguins, for a heavy bird needs more energy and manoeuvres less easily than a lighter bird does.

The roles of the sexes when rearing young are fairly distinct in seabirds, although usually less so than in many other animals. Some ecological separation between the sexes during breeding exists in a few seabird species but is not as common as among terrestrial creatures. For example, males of the Blue-footed Booby tend to feed farther inshore, and on smaller fish, than do the larger females, and it is the males which supply all food to the chicks immediately after

◄ **Common Cormorant** *(Phalacrocorax carbo)*

White-capped Noddy *(Anous minutus)*
Bulwer's Petrel *(Bulweria bulwerii)*

(Opposite) Among many seabirds that breed in trees is the Common Cormorant. This widespread species feeds both in freshwater areas and at sea. Its tree-breeding habit is found inland as well as along sea coasts. Trees which have been used for a long time die because of the birds' excretion, and the trees then usually fall down, forcing the birds to move to surrounding trees or to new localities.

(Above) The White-capped Noddy also tends to put its nest in trees. It is a warm-water species, breeding mainly on tropical islands.

(Right) Bulwer's Petrel is extensively distributed in warmer waters of the Atlantic and Pacific Oceans. It resembles the larger storm-petrels and is nearly as small as they. Most birds of this species breed on subtropical islands, chiefly among boulders or in natural cavities, where they have nocturnal habits.

hatching, despite the two sexes' greater similarity in life when not breeding.

An evident sexual difference, mentioned in the last chapter, is that the female lays eggs. Their size, relative to hers, is dependent on the species and, in some, she incurs a high material cost through egg-laying. Many gulls and terns use courtship feeding of the female by the male as a compensation, but the latter can occur in additional forms. Male seabirds commonly contribute most to establishing and defending a territory and a nest site, as well as to building a nest or digging a burrow if this is the habit, thus liberating the female to feed at sea and gather essential proteins for the eggs. Tasks of incubation and feeding the young are shared rather equally by the seabird sexes—with exceptions such as the Emperor Penguin and phalaropes, whose males perform all incubation, or the frigate-birds whose females are mainly responsible for feeding the young after fledging.

The pre-laying period

The time until egg-laying is often short, particularly in high latitudes where seabirds are eager to take advantage of a brief peak in food productivity. Certain boobies and other tropical seabirds also undergo relatively short pre-laying periods. This is probably an adaptation of sub-annually breeding birds to a utilization of temporary favourable conditions that occur irregularly there.

Yet the pre-laying period is quite long for some species in temperate and warm latitudes. These usually devote much effort to establishment and defence of sites, as do guillemots and gannets which frequently attend their sites for three or four months before laying eggs. Such investments may be profitable if optimal sites are in limited supply. The same appears to be true of, for example, the Galapagos Storm-petrel on Tower Island, where up to 80% or so of the birds in the colony are found to be attending sites without having either eggs or young. Long pre-laying periods tend

The Peruvian Diving-petrel *(above)* digs burrows to nest in *(below)*. Nowadays, it does so primarily in soft ground on the islands along the coast of Peru and northern Chile. It formerly burrowed in guano beds, which could become literally honeycombed with such burrows. The exploitation of guano by man left this species, to a large extent, without suitable breeding places.

to be spent largely in pair interactions, leading to gonad development and to preparations for copulating and, finally, egg-laying. Tubenoses normally pass through a "honeymoon" interval after the pair has been formed, during which the females stay chiefly at sea in order to catch sufficient food for egg production.

Incubation

Primarily because their great foraging distances make it impossible to rear many young, seabirds lay few eggs in a clutch by comparison with numerous land-birds. Sea ducks are an exception to this rule, but do not invest in feeding, as the chicks are nidifugous and feed independently under guard by the females. Only one egg is laid by the *Procellariiformes*, the large penguins, and various species in other orders, like some boobies, tropic-birds, frigate-birds, and alcids, the Swallow-tailed Gull, and the Sooty Tern. Apart from these, a clutch of two or three eggs is most common, although certain pelicans and cormorants may have four.

The duration of the incubation period is related to the size of eggs. It is longest for albatrosses, being somewhat over two months in the smaller species, and reaching a maximum average of 79 days with the Royal Albatross, while other tubenoses usually take 40–60 days. The male Emperor Penguin spends around 64 days incubating alone in the winter, but the smaller penguin species need only 33–40 days. The shortest incubation periods are of about 3 weeks for most species of phalaropes and terns, and of 3–4 weeks for most gulls. As regards the egg size in proportion to the female's body weight, it amounts to only 3.4% for gannets, and is smallest for penguins, but makes up some 25% for British Storm-petrels. In species laying more than one egg, the investment may also be very great, as with certain gulls whose clutch weighs 25% as much as the female.

The size of an egg itself reflects the degree of the chick's development when hatched. Eggs are comparatively small in most of the *Pelecaniformes* order, whose chicks are born naked and are dependent on parental care at first. The eggs are larger in most gulls, for example, which have down-covered chicks that soon leave the nest and are fairly independent of parents. Large eggs occur in the *Procellariiformes*, too, where the downy chick is born with an ample supply of yolk to prevent starvation just after hatching.

Hole-nesting seabirds generally have white eggs, but coloured ones are laid by many species breeding in the open. The colouring serves either for camouflage, or as a pattern enabling parents to recognize their eggs—which may be necessary among densely nesting birds, such as the guillemots on cliffs or the terns on sandbars. There is also a variation in the thickness of the shell protecting the egg. It is very thick in some alcids laying on bare rock, and in the Northern Gannet which sits directly on the egg while incubating with the webbed feet.

Fledging

What is usually called the fledging period, from the time of hatching until the young fledge, is a busy one for the parents. Indeed, it tends to take longest and to demand most labour among all the stages of the breeding cycle. It is affected, however, by several factors such as the size of birds, their foraging distances, and food sources in the surrounding seas.

King Penguins and the two largest albatrosses have the longest fledging periods, and need more than a year to complete the whole breeding cycle. In the first case, 10–13 months normally pass after hatching until the young begins its independent life in the sea. By then, it is fed so little in wintertime that it nearly starves, but its weight increases again in the spring when food productivity rises in the sea. The Wandering Albatrosses forage very far from the breeding site, and their chick takes 38–43 weeks to fledge. It has to starve for weeks when feeding conditions are bad, although its reserves of fat are usually sufficient to withstand such an interval. Frigate-birds also have difficult feeding methods and require around 6 months to fledge a chick.

A wider variation with food supplies is seen among the smaller albatross species, whose young need between 16 and 26 weeks to fledge. Of the other tubenoses, a few take nearly 4 months, such as the winter-breeding Great-winged Petrel or the Galapagos Storm-petrel, and most require at least 2–3 months, but the Northern Fulmar takes about 6 weeks. The period is considerably shorter for some coastal seabirds: terns usually fledge in 23–28 days, although the pelagic Sooty Tern needs 56–63 days, while most gulls take 35–45 days. Certain alcids, like guillemots and the Razorbill, have very short fledging periods because the young leave the nest before they can fly. The shortest periods may be found in Craveri's and Xantus' Murrelets, whose chicks leave the nest only 2–4 days after hatching. These nidifugous chicks are fed to some extent by their parents at sea, but they also feed themselves once they are able to swim freely.

According to their size and development at hatching, the chicks have a limited ability to regulate their body temperature, move about, and resist starvation, independently of the parents. In the *Procellariiformes*, some of the yolk remains to be used after hatching, for the chicks are adapted to infrequent oceanic feeding. When they are a few days old, the chicks are usually left unguarded by parents in holes or burrows. The larger species such as albatrosses or giant petrels, breeding on oceanic islands safe from predation, may leave chicks sitting alone in the open for days. Eventually, the chicks tend to become very fat, those of the Manx Shearwater weighing up to twice as much as their parents. However, their weight decreases at the end of the fledging period when they are fully mature and their down is replaced by a true plumage with flight feathers. Nidifugous chicks, as of skuas and gulls, are fairly developed at hatching and can soon walk well, generally having camouflaged down. Among the *Pelecaniformes*, only the chicks of tropic-birds are clad in down at the time of hatching.

Not all parts of a chick grow at the same rate, and growth patterns vary somewhat between the species. Wings and wing-quills are developed at a late stage, and the bill is perfected at the end of the fledging period. But the digestive organs develop quite early, as do the feet and leg muscles in nidifugous birds. Many species have immature plumages that are duller than those of adults.

Post-fledging

The only seabirds which care for their fledged young are a number of species in the *Pelecaniformes* order—with the exception of pelicans, tropic-birds, and gannets—and in the *Charadriiformes*. A few give prolonged feeding. In some cases, the immatures return regularly to the nest or remain in the breeding area to be fed by parents, while occasionally also foraging nearby. In other cases, such as many terns and gulls, the immatures acompany one or both of the parents to feeding areas, or when migrating to wintering areas, and are fed by them during this time. Among the

Common Gull (*Larus canus*)

White Tern (*Gygis alba*)

(Above left) Breeding on roofs has spread rapidly among gulls of Northern Europe, both in Common Gulls as shown here and in other species. This demonstrates that traditions may play a large role in breeding habits.

(Above right) The White Tern breeds in trees on tropical islands. Without building a nest, it places the single egg directly on a branch. This habit can be as risky as that of seabirds which lay eggs on cliff ledges.

(Below) The Northern Gannet breeds in temperate waters on both the western and the eastern sides of the North Atlantic. Its nests are usually built on rocky islands, with the nests close together as seen here.

(Opposite top) Common Guillemots choose cliff ledges for breeding. The birds generally stand close together when incubating their single eggs. Such collective security seems to enhance their breeding success.

Northern Gannet (*Sula bassana*)

Common Guillemot *(Uria aalge)*

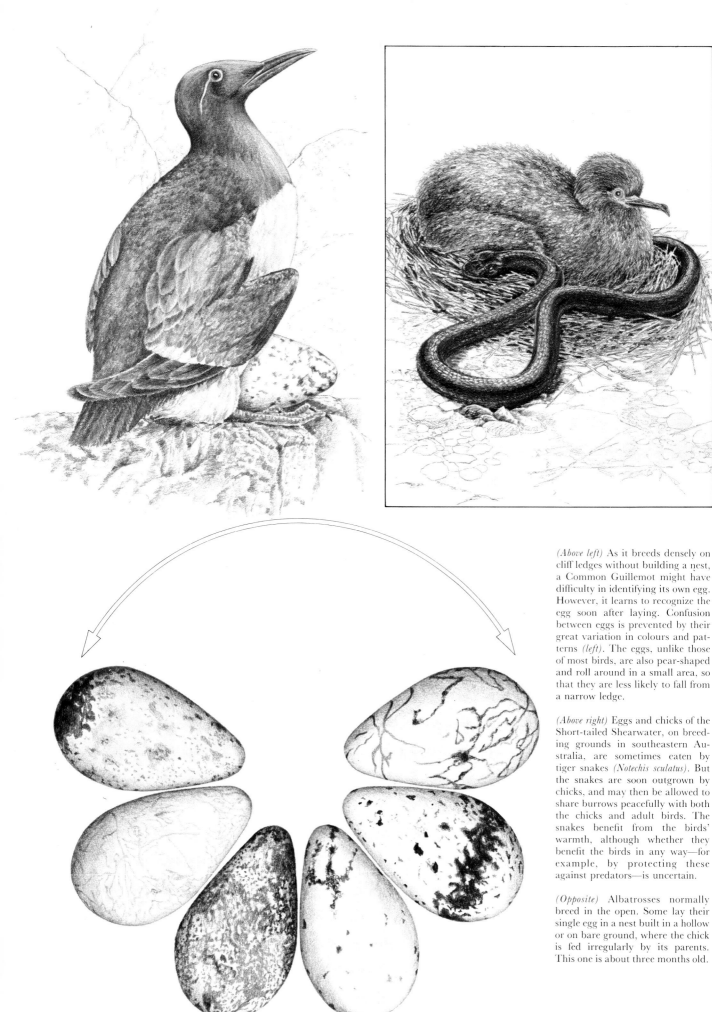

(*Above left*) As it breeds densely on cliff ledges without building a nest, a Common Guillemot might have difficulty in identifying its own egg. However, it learns to recognize the egg soon after laying. Confusion between eggs is prevented by their great variation in colours and patterns (*left*). The eggs, unlike those of most birds, are also pear-shaped and roll around in a small area, so that they are less likely to fall from a narrow ledge.

(*Above right*) Eggs and chicks of the Short-tailed Shearwater, on breeding grounds in southeastern Australia, are sometimes eaten by tiger snakes (*Notechis sculatus*). But the snakes are soon outgrown by chicks, and may then be allowed to share burrows peacefully with both the chicks and adult birds. The snakes benefit from the birds' warmth, although whether they benefit the birds in any way—for example, by protecting these against predators—is uncertain.

(*Opposite*) Albatrosses normally breed in the open. Some lay their single egg in a nest built in a hollow or on bare ground, where the chick is fed irregularly by its parents. This one is about three months old.

Laysan Albatross *(Diomedea immutabilis)*
Galapagos Storm-petrel *(Oceanodroma tethys)*

Madeiran Storm-petrel (*Oceanodroma castro*)

(*Opposite top*) The Laysan Albatross is a winter-breeder of the North Pacific. Almost all breed in the Leeward Islands west of Hawaii.

(*Left*) The only storm-petrel with diurnal habits on breeding grounds is the Galapagos Storm-petrel. It appears here on Tower Island where most of the species breed.

(*Opposite bottom*) The chick of the Masked Booby is hatched naked—a normal occurrence in the order *Pelecaniformes*, tropic-birds being the only exception. The chick is therefore strongly dependent on protection by its parents, which shade it by day and cover it during cool nights if necessary.

(*Above*) Madeiran Storm-petrels breed in natural holes or burrows used by other species. This frequently occurs in Madeira during the winter when larger tubenoses have left their nests for an oceanic life.

(*Below*) As is normal among the tubenoses, this Little Shearwater chick has grown to a size which markedly exceeds the weight of its parents. But its flight feathers will soon begin to grow, and its weight will gradually decrease until it is fledged.

Little Shearwater (*Puffinus assimilis*)

Breeding on the Antarctic ice, the Emperor Penguin may be the only bird on earth which almost never sets foot on solid land. The male stands incubating for 62–64 days, with no relief throughout the long polar darkness. Finally, when the well-fed female returns sliding across the ice, she must find her mate among a host of others that huddle together for protection against the cold winds. The same problem arises when the young grow up, collecting in crèches once they are several weeks old. All probably rely on sounds to some extend for recognition. The young take about four months to reach independence, which occurs in early December at the onset of a very productive period in the Antarctic seas.

nidifugous alcids, parents and immatures swim together at sea.

When a gannet chick leaves the nest, it is heavy with fat and flaps down to the sea, where it begins an independent life by swimming until it becomes lighter and perfects its flying abilities. Cormorants and shags normally feed their young for several weeks after fledging, as do many boobies. Record lengths of post-fledging care among such *Pelecaniformes* are found in the frigate-birds: the young are fed chiefly by the females for up to 6–9 months after fledging, an adaptation to the necessity of perfecting their difficult feeding methods.

Reproductive success

Animals with a certain combination of genes will become relatively common in a population if they have a higher reproductive success, and survive better, than do animals with other genotypes. The "reproductive strategy", as the preceding discussion has shown, involves many factors and possibilities of change. Every such factor is the evolutionary result of a delicate balance between costs and benefits, for the parents as well as the young.

For example, greater investments in reproduction may diminish survival chances for the parents, so that a gene combination which conditions these investments may become less frequent than other combinations. This could happen if birds start to breed too early in life, so that their mortality is excessive in comparison to nativity, making deferred sexual maturity a better strategy. Similarly, an increase in the number of eggs laid may raise the mortality of females, or of chicks when the parents cannot gather enough food for them, thus diminishing the number of fledged young. The Grey Gull, breeding far from the sea in Chilean deserts, with a clutch varying between one and two eggs, is thought to be evolving towards a clutch of only one egg for such reasons.

Reproductive success as a whole means that each bird in a population should be able to replace itself with another bird which can also reproduce. The degree of success, therefore, is a product of three general factors or probabilities: that the bird's eggs will hatch, that the hatched young will fledge, and that the fledged young will live until they reproduce.

The first two factors are usually known as "hatching success" (the number of eggs hatched per eggs laid) and

"fledging success" (the number of young fledged per eggs hatched), whose product is called "breeding success" (the number of young fledged per eggs laid). These factors refer to the periods of incubation and rearing of young, which involve diverse circumstances. Some eggs never hatch because they are not fertilized, and other failures result from parental inadequacy, accidents, predatory pressure, weather, or interference by conspecifics.

Hatching and fledging successes vary considerably among seabirds, and may have opposite relative sizes in different species. The net breeding success also varies, but it is normally somewhat higher for seabirds than for land-birds (due partly to breeding sites where predators are fewer, and partly to a greater parental investment in breeding), although it is presently quite low in certain seabird colonies because of local conditions. Since the weather and productivity in the seas fluctuate widely in many areas, breeding success often differs between years and, at times, it may be virtually zero in some colonies, even if the average population remains substantial during the long lives of such birds.

The third factor, or "post-fledging success", is no less important and variable. For instance, gannets tend to have

a very high breeding success, 75–85% being common in numerous colonies, but their success as measured until full independence seems to be relatively low. By contrast, Abbott's Booby on Christmas Island has a breeding success of under 10%, which appears to be alarmingly low, yet the survival of fledged young is increased through their being fed by parents for half a year.

Further understanding of the efficiency with which seabirds reproduce can be gained by dividing a population into age groups. Mortality rates differ between these, as well as from one species to another, and such rates directly affect the total number of birds of a particular type that are able to reproduce. Moreover, the degree of reproductive success depends on the parent's age, and is generally greatest among the experienced birds of middle age, which also tend to have the largest eggs. Research on this level of detail makes it possible to foresee how seabird populations will change in size and composition, despite the complexity of their reproductive processes.

213

Seabirds of the northernmost Pacific

Around the Aleutian Islands and in the Bering Sea between Asia and North America, seabirds and their breeding places are abundant. In particular, the family of alcids has its centre of distribution there, forming rich communities of species that occupy a wide variety of ecological niches. Small plankton-feeding auklets occur in vast numbers, and often range far from their breeding colonies to find tiny plankton, which they carry back to the offspring in their comparatively big throat-pouches. The Horned Puffin also wanders extensively, feeding mainly on lesser fish, while the Pigeon Guillemot and the cormorants stay nearer land. More peculiar are the murrelets, whose chicks leave their nests a few days after hatching and follow their parents by swimming at sea. The Red-legged Kittiwake is not as plentiful as the other Kittiwake species, but both breed in the area. Of the seabirds shown here, only the Mottled Petrel breeds elsewhere—in New Zealand—although it is a frequent visitor to this region.

(1) Red-legged Kittiwake
(2) Ancient Murrelet
(3) Cassin's Auklet
(4) Parakeet Auklet
(5) Least Auklet
(6) Aleutian Tern
(7) Glaucous Gull
(8) Mottled Petrel
(9) Pigeon Guillemot
(10) Crested Auklet
(11) Horned Puffin
(12) Red-faced Cormorant
(13) Pelagic Cormorant
(14) Brandt's Cormorant

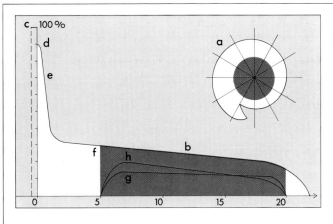

Population dynamics and reproductive success

How the number of seabirds in a population varies with age and time can be studied in detail. An idealized example is given graphically here. (a) Total population size, during a year, is shown by the radius of a curve from its centre. The radius changes as one moves clockwise along the curve during twelve months. The curve spirals inward due to mortality, as the population declines between the end of a breeding period and the beginning of the next. But new birds are gradually added during the breeding period—an annual season in this typical case. The number of birds able to breed (shaded area) is comparatively constant, since some birds mature while others become too old or die.

At a given time, the population's percentage of birds of each age in years may be counted (b). *The rate of falling in this "age-structure" curve is the mortality rate, which is greatest for the youngest and oldest birds. One may also compare the proportion of eggs laid* (c) *with the eggs that hatch* (d), *the young which fledge* (e), *and the adults reaching reproductive age* (f). *Each proportion, compared to the last, shows respectively the* degrees of success in hatching, fledging, and post-fledging, *as discussed in our main text. These degrees may differ for several reasons.* Breeding success, *the product of hatching and fledging success, depends on the age and capability of the parents. Thus, the number of fledged chicks per breeding pair at each age in the reproductive time-span* (g) *shows least success for the youngest and oldest parents. But the total number of fledged chicks for each age of parents* (h) *indicates that fairly young parents make the biggest contribution, because they are most abundant.*

The age curve may vary greatly from year to year in actual seabird populations, as changing environmental conditions affect reproductive success. There may even be a steadily shrinking population with very few young birds, or else a growing one with very few old birds. It is also often hard in practice to measure numbers of birds at each age. Further, species differ in life-span, which is 40–70 years for many tubenoses but is seldom 25 years for birds such as gulls and phalaropes. This diversity is probably related to the higher metabolic rates in smaller animals, and to the evolution of optimum reproductive strategies.

Chapter Eight
OCEAN BIRDS AND MANKIND

People have long known that they depend on the environment for their existence. But the fact that some important properties of the environment are dependent upon the existence of living things has been widely recognized only during the last few decades. Just as the air's oxygen and the sea's nitrates are produced and controlled mainly by organic processes, so does human activity influence nature while being influenced by it. Life on earth forms a united biosphere whose ecosystems can never be isolated from one another, although there are border areas where exchange between these is limited.

Seabirds are as much a part of this global whole as is man. Since they do not live permanently in the water, they are often overlooked by oceanographic studies and by research on marine ecosystems. Ecological investigations in general, however, reveal their role of interconnecting many ecosystems of land and sea. Interactions between human and seabird populations are difficult to determine exactly, yet several aspects are clear enough. Man and seabirds have predator/prey relations, in places where birds are a food resource for people. Indirectly, the two compete with each other for resources, by exploiting the same types of marine organisms. Numerous other indirect environmental relations exist that show the value of seabirds to man, as well as the reverse: human effects on seabirds have been not only detrimental but, in some cases, helpful or even mutualistic.

Seabirds in world ecology

The most crucial comparisons to be made between seabirds and man concern their dependence on food from the oceans. To begin with, the total annual production of marine plants and animals has been estimated by various means, as has the total annual consumption by seabirds. While the results are very different and uncertain, it seems that seabirds consume rather little of the marine animal production. According to one study, they probably take less than 0.3%, about as much as the total catch of fish and invertebrates by man.

Seabirds tend to feed on types of marine animals that are seldom caught by man—relatively small fish, crustaceans and squid whose exploitation is not yet highly developed. In spite of this contrast and the low global human consumption, fish populations have been extensively depleted by man in a number of areas, and some of these are greatly overfished as in the Mediterranean, the North Atlantic, and waters off Japan and Peru. In particular localities, human fishing certainly takes a significant share of all secondary production of marine life. Consumption by seabirds

apparently does so as well, and the scale of their feeding can be quite impressive.

For example, among the many penguin colonies which contain at least a million birds, that of Adélie Penguins breeding on Lawrie Island has been estimated to eat 9,000 tons of marine animals each day. The daily consumption by a Cape or Guanay Cormorant is about 1 lb (0.5 kg), and such guano-producing seabirds once numbered in tens of millions. Local fishing industries often regard seabirds as important competitors, and pleas have been made to reduce their populations when fish are becoming scarce due to human fishing, as in the Barents Sea, Peruvian, and South African waters. Consumption by seabirds near huge colonies is sometimes thought to be as high as 25–33% of local secondary production. Evidently, predation by seabirds has even affected the past evolution of diverse marine creatures, which have acquired protective adaptations in their behaviour and physical properties.

Most secondary production occurs through herbivores, including plankton, that are too small to be eaten much by seabirds. The birds' modest consumption of world marine animals is thus understandable. But some herbivores such as krill, and anchoveta in the Humboldt Current, are comparatively large. In the Antarctic, seabirds eat considerable amounts of krill, although about half of these are believed to be taken by squid. A substantial part of anchoveta production was probably consumed by seabirds in the past.

Nutrient flows

The role of seabirds in nutrient cycling is also of great interest, particularly since they take a fair toll of the total secondary production in local areas. Such a role can easily be underestimated in the case of warm-blooded animals like seabirds, with a long life and few offspring each year—for their high food needs are not reflected by large changes in population. Their consumption primarily involves a flow of nutrients through populations and back into the environments by excretion.

In contrast to numerous aquatic animals, seabirds excrete chiefly at the water surface, in the same layers where nutrients are required by the primary producers. Diving seabirds which feed in deeper water layers thereby bring nutrients to the surface and contribute to greater primary production. Moreover, seabirds of a big breeding colony feed at long distances from it, but excrete on the way back to it, increasing the food production in nearby waters. The process is often circular: seabirds abound in a colony because the surrounding ocean is productive, and their very abundance is a cause of high productivity. In such a place, seabirds might indeed seem to be competing against human

Giant Petrel (Macronectes sp.)
Chilean Pelican (Pelecanus thagus)

(Above) An immature Giant Petrel is seen over an Argentine river mouth, where it sometimes ranges into fresh waters near large human population centres. Being a scavenger on dead animals, it plays an important ecological role at high trophic levels.

Nutrients flowing through seabirds return to the environment in many ways, such as vast deposits of guano on breeding islands *(below)*. Examples are those of birds like Chilean Pelicans *(left)* and Peruvian Boobies *(opposite, centre right)* in the Humboldt Current, where the Simeon Gull is also common *(opposite, lower right)*.

Breeding seabirds also enrich surrounding land, as do Kittiwakes *(opposite top)*, or fresh water as in the case of the Northern Black-headed Gull which feeds in agricultural areas *(opposite, centre left)*. Birds even transport nutrients from the open sea to the surface waters near a breeding colony, as in this illustration of a tropical colony *(bottom)*. Its species are *(left to right)*: Sooty Tern, Red-footed and Masked Booby, Great Frigate-bird, and Brown Noddy.

Kittiwake *(Rissa tridactyla)*

Northern Black-headed Gull *(Larus ridibundus)*

Peruvian Booby *(Sula variegata)*

Simeon Gull *(Larus belcheri)*

Few people today recall that the increased agricultural production in early industrial societies was stimulated by ancient deposits of seabird guano in Peru. Some guano first reached England in 1840, and it was soon recognized to be the most valuable known fertilizer. The Peruvian Indians had used it since time immemorial, but now its fame spread around the world. Only a decade or so later, imports of guano to North America had risen to 200,000 tons per year. The deposits were estimated to be sufficient to supply the world for 170 years, and whole fleets of guano carriers could be seen in 1860 (below). Yet even then, the layers on the Chincha Islands had dwindled from a thickness of over 180 feet (55 metres) to mere residues (right). All the guano was gone by 1874, and no deposits as rich as the Peruvian ones were found by the empty vessels which visited every major seabird colony in suitable climates.

fishing, yet their extermination would lead to diminished production in the waters.

Nutrients flow continually from the land into the oceans through rivers and streams. Seabirds, however, return a good deal of nutrients to the land on which they breed, excrete, die, and yield eggs or offspring to terrestrial predators. The productivity of land near their colonies is frequently greater than what it would be without them, and the addition of nutrients by seabirds is essential in many poor areas. Some plants are specially adapted to the high nutrient contents of the soil near such colonies and are rarely to be found elsewhere. Certain animals on barren land survive only through predation, scavenging, or decomposing of seabirds—for example, along the desert coasts where all rich upwelling waters occur, and at very high latitudes like those of the Arctic Basin where even humans have commonly depended on seabirds for food.

Guano, the accumulated excrement of seabirds on dry land, is most plentiful in upwelling regions and on some tropical islands. It has been exploited for centuries by man, and was long important as a fertilizer in domestic ecosystems. Such systematic work, in several instances, has made use of very old guano deposits that began over two thousand years ago. Around half a million tons of these were shipped annually from western South America in the nineteenth century, improving agricultural production in industrialized countries.

Man's abuse of seabirds

The direct influences of man upon seabirds have, in large part, pursued a sad course with severe reduction of many bird populations and the complete extermination of a few species. There are, to be sure, cases in which predation by man is limited and a balance is maintained with the numbers of seabirds. People like the Eskimos, Samoyeds, and islanders of the Faeroes and St. Kilda, have normally understood the need to regulate catches of seabirds as an important food resource. Supplementation of human diets is illustrated by the traditional "harvesting", in southeastern Australia and Tasmania, of fledgling Short-tailed Shearwaters that weigh around 2 lb (1 kg) each. This is also strictly regulated today, and the annual taking of about half a million "mutton-birds" has not affected their population size. Such control, however, is still the exception rather than the rule.

Various kinds of seabird eggs are collected all over the world, especially those of gulls, terns, and alcids. Chicks have been taken as well, usually at a time just before fledging when they are fat and almost full-grown, as with penguins, certain tubenoses, and (occasionally only for fish-bait) gannets. Adults, too, have been killed on a massive scale, for example by being dragged out of their burrows or caught in the air with a net on a pole. Such predation was easiest when people spread into previously

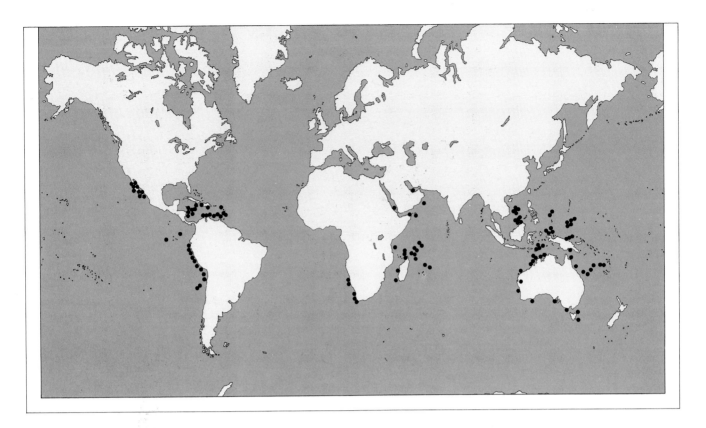

Shown above are the locations of islands with significant guano deposits in the middle of this century. Exploitation of guano has been regular in many places other than Peru, although only in southwest Africa has it been of greater economic value. The early lack of planning in Peru was exchanged for strict control after 1900, leading to good results. Protection of seabird breeding grounds, and limitations on digging, enabled guano to maintain its value in sales and agriculture up to the beginning of the 1970s.

Important guano deposits are formed only at desert coasts. In rainy areas, the guano is washed away from the breeding grounds. Rain also causes a chemical reduction of the nitrates in guano, leaving phosphates as the main substance of value for use as fertilizer.

However, some guano has been exploited in places with relatively great precipitation, such as the Falkland Islands during the last century.

uninhabited places and discovered seabirds that had not evolved a fear of man. Colonies of these "naive" species have frequently been wiped out, while some birds—notably among the tubenoses—have withdrawn to inaccessible areas for safe breeding.

The numbers of seabirds involved have been enormous. Up to two million Sooty Tern eggs were collected annually in the Seychelles Islands during the recent past. Alcids have suffered similar losses until lately, sometimes even without reduction of their populations. Thus, each year, Little Auks have been caught by the million, and Eskimos once took around 750,000 of the Brünnich's Guillemots in Greenland. Extensive killing of penguins occurred in the nineteenth century, mainly for extraction of oil, and it greatly reduced many colonies, although these are widely recovering now.

The original "penguin"—the Great Auk, or Garefowl, *Alca impennis*—became totally extinct in this manner. It might have been saved by an awareness of conservation, as some of the last ones were killed simply for museum collections. Easily caught due to its flightlessness, it was hunted chiefly for food throughout its range in the North Atlantic. Since June 3, 1844, when two specimens were taken at Eldey Rock off Iceland, only a few doubtful sightings have been reported.

Also brought to extinction at about that date was the Spectacled Cormorant, *Phalacrocorax perspicillatus*, ranging primarily near Bering and Komandorski Islands in the North Pacific. This big, clumsy, almost flightless bird was persecuted for food by both natives and visitors. People spreading to oceanic islands during prehistoric times may have wiped out other seabirds. For example, the people of Chatham Island, who long ago eliminated certain landbirds there, left behind bones of the Magenta Petrel—a species which, however, apparently survives according to recent records.

Exploitation of seabirds by man has included the use of feathers and down to stuff bedding, and of feathers or skins for clothing. Plume-hunters have wrought terrible havoc among bird populations, and they nearly put an end to the Short-tailed Albatross. Some five million of this species were killed between 1887 and 1903, when volcanic eruptions buried the last hunters themselves. The people of Tori Shima killed another 3,000 in December, 1932, and most of the remaining albatrosses succumbed to eruptions in 1933 and 1941, while a few stayed at sea and the 10 breeding pairs known in 1955 had increased to 57 in 1973. Sailors in the past have occasionally caught albatrosses to make feather-rugs from the skins, tobacco pouches from the webs of the feet, and pipe-stems from the long hollow bones. Another instance of feather-hunting for aesthetic purposes involves the Red-tailed Tropic-bird, whose beautiful red tail-streamers were taken by Polynesians, although they often released birds from captivity soon after removing the streamers.

(Right) The Humboldt Penguin used to dig burrows in old guano deposits, along with the Peruvian Diving-petrel and the Inca Tern. These species were once abundant as producers of guano, but its exploitation left them with little suitable ground to breed in. Their populations were soon reduced to a fraction of earlier levels and are still comparatively low.

(Bottom left) The Grey-headed Gull can be a delight to the human eye, and many people appreciate the beauty of gulls although some regard them as a nuisance. The enjoyable atmosphere of coasts is due partly to seabird life and gives them an importance for man in addition to economic advantages.

(Bottom right) The Black-browed Albatross has a subspecies named *impavida* which breeds only in the New Zealand area. Its yellow iris differs from the dark one of other populations. Such small marks of identification make the observation of seabirds particularly interesting and challenging to the ever-growing ranks of amateur ornithologists.

Humboldt Penguin *(Spheniscus humboldti)*

Grey-headed Gull *(Larus cirrocephalus)*

Black-browed Albatross *(Diomedea melanophris)*

(Right) The eggs of penguins, like this Rock-hopper species, were once collected indiscriminately by the Falkland Islanders. Alcids were particularly exploited in a similar way. But some regulation was later introduced, so that only a bird's first egg was taken.

(Below) A large-scale problem that grows yearly is illustrated by a Common Guillemot struggling to free itself from a fishing net. Millions of diving seabirds drown in such nets annually.

Common Guillemot *(Uria aalge)*

Environmental conflicts

Even more serious than predation may be man's expanding impact on the natural resources needed by seabirds. This is particularly obvious in regard to fishing. The mere fact that man and seabirds tend to seek different kinds of marine prey cannot ensure adequate food for seabirds, since man's overfishing impoverishes the seas in general. One might imagine that man helps seabirds by catching a large fish which would otherwise eat small fish that they require. But a large fish's detritus is a source of nutrients, its young may be edible by seabirds, and its own prey may live on smaller animals which seabirds hunt. Thus, its death weakens the entire food-chain, and such interference has repeatedly affected seabirds.

Competition over exactly the same kind of food has occurred between man and seabirds, at a drastic cost to the latter. Some alcids are becoming much less numerous in the northeastern Atlantic, probably due to its heavy over-fishing. A fish-meal industry off California destroyed supplies of sardines for seabirds. When this industry was transferred to Peru, the local "anchoveta" were soon reduced, and all guano-producing seabirds in the Humboldt Current—Guanay Cormorants, Peruvian Boobies, and Chilean Pelicans—declined steadily in population from the end of the 1950s. Here, annual fishing eventually reached 10–11 million metric tons, exceeding the total catch by vessels of European countries!

These Peruvian anchoveta, with the onset of the warm "El Niño" current in 1972, formed shoals and retreated into the colder water of coastal bays, becoming easy prey for the fishing fleet. Their virtual eradication stopped a huge local industry supplying cheap fish-meal to animal factories abroad, which had to substitute soya protein at soaring prices. Meanwhile, starving seabirds littered the ocean and drifted ashore in heaps. Guanay Cormorants suffered most, being highly dependent on the anchoveta: a population of tens of millions in the 1950s now dwindled to tens of thousands, and only a few birds could be seen in areas that they had once darkened from horizon to horizon. Some anchoveta survived, and fishing began to recover at the end of the 1970s, although both fish and Guanay Cormorants are still relatively scarce.

Modern fishing versus seabirds

Marine-food industry is growing in refinement as well as in scale. Giant "purse seine" nets now have a smaller mesh size, increasing the catch of tiny fish like capelin and sand-eels, which nourish many kinds of seabirds. The effects are already noticeable. Very few Atlantic Puffins have fledged in northern Norwegian colonies since 1975, coinciding with this innovation, despite uncertainty as to why the young die prematurely. Fishing on krill, too, is at an experimental stage and will probably soon expand rapidly, competing with numerous seabird species for food.

Even cruder techniques such as underwater dynamiting have often helped to destroy local supplies of fish, as in the Mediterranean area and lately in the Bay of Siam. Similarly, breeding grounds for fish are ruined by construc-

The Faeroe Islanders used to catch alcids, mostly puffins, in numbers which provided a significant food resource. This "fleyging" was done with a net on a long pole, from boats or—more often—by standing on the steep slopes of breeding colonies. It required considerable strength, and is now usually done only as a hobby.

Herring Gull *(Larus argentatus)*
Kittiwake *(Rissa tridactyla)*

Olivaceous Cormorant (*Phalacrocorax olivaceus*)

Herring Gull (*Larus argentatus*)

Hawaiian Petrel (*Pterodroma phaeopygia*)
Southern Black-backed Gull (*Larus dominicanus*)

Herring Gulls, like many other seabirds, profit from human activities by feeding on the offal thrown overboard from fishing vessels *(opposite top)* or by eating garbage *(top right)*.

(Opposite bottom) Kittiwakes breed on the ledges of buildings in various places. They may have been forced to do so by a lack of natural breeding sites. But they are thereby protected from predators which hesitate to approach such structures, and they are usually tolerated by people. Many seabirds also benefit from man-made structures by resting on these, as does the Olivaceous Cormorant *(above)*.

(Centre right) The Hawaiian Petrel has, however, suffered heavily from human expansion. It has been almost wiped out on the islands for which it is named, and its breeding success on Santa Cruz in the Galapagos Islands is as low as 2–3% today, due mainly to the spreading of rats.

(Right) Countless seabirds have died from diverse effects of the oil which man spills at sea. A little oil in the plumage, as on this Southern Black-backed Gull, may not be lethal. But such birds may meet a slow death through chilling or poisoning.

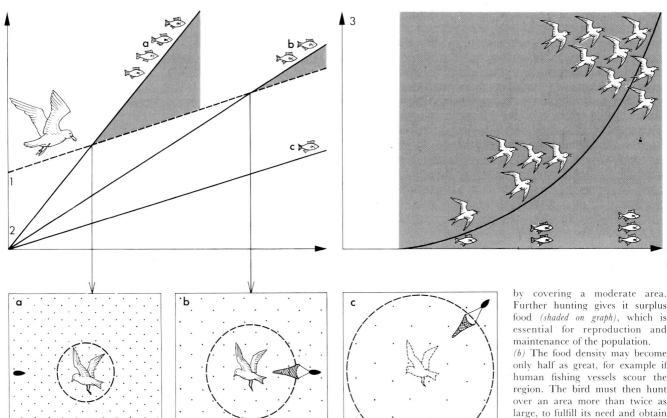

The survival of a seabird depends largely on its need and supply of food, as shown here in simplified form. On the first graph above, food is measured vertically, and the bird's hunting range for food is measured horizontally.

(1) Like other animals, a bird needs food even when not hunting, and its need increases with activities such as hunting. The farther it must go to catch food, the more food it has to eat, as indicated by this sloping line.

(2) The food supply available to the bird also increases with its hunting range. But the rate of increase depends on the density of food in the environment.
(a) With a relatively high food density, the bird can fulfill its need

by covering a moderate area. Further hunting gives it surplus food (shaded on graph), which is essential for reproduction and maintenance of the population.
(b) The food density may become only half as great, for example if human fishing vessels scour the region. The bird must then hunt over an area more than twice as large, to fulfill its need and obtain surplus food (shaded).
(c) If the food density becomes still lower, the bird may not even be able to fulfill its need with long-range hunting, so it dies.
(3) The effect on seabirds can be seen by comparing a population's size (vertical on this graph) with the food supply (horizontal). The number of birds often grows exponentially with more food, but they all die out if the supply falls below a certain minimum.

tion activities in shallow waters, and terns living on small fry—a conspicuous example—cannot feed where harbours dominate shores or estuaries. Large numbers of birds, particularly diving birds like alcids and loons, also drown in fishing nets. It is estimated that around half a million Brünnich's Guillemots do so in Greenland waters alone each year.

A main danger of these recent developments is that, by lowering the concentration of food in the environment, man forces seabirds and other predators to spend more energy in search of food for survival and reproduction. As illustrated here, the viable population of seabirds is thus lowered even faster. This problem is still worse—because the energy needs are greater—for underwater than for aerial hunting. Indeed, it occurs not only in direct competition over fish.

Man's market in whales, dolphins, and tuna conflicts indirectly with various seabirds. These creatures bring prey to the ocean surface in dense concentrations which birds feed upon. Storm-petrels often follow whales that stir up plankton while swimming—and in the Bering Sea, the Humpback Whale weaves a "net" of bubbles around fish and krill when releasing air through its blowhole as it swims upward in a spiral. Equally valuable are the "meat balls" of smaller fish driven up by dolphins and, notably in warm waters, by tuna. Some seabirds also feed on the dung of whales or scavenge on those that die naturally.

Yet man has reduced most species of the great baleen whales to 2–5% of their original populations. Probably half of the Spinner Dolphins in the Pacific were killed before a change of methods decreased the annual toll of dolphins to about ten thousand. Thirty times as many dolphins were drowned every year during the 1960s in the nets of Pacific tuna fleets, since certain tuna and dolphins swim together. Only a few percent remain of the big tuna in the Atlantic, and overfishing threatens tuna elsewhere as well. Seabirds have thereby lost countless meals.

Water pollution

Feeding conditions for seabirds are aggravated by human destruction of the marine environment with toxic material that enters it through intention or accident. Chemical outlets from industry, sewage and rubbish from cities on coasts or rivers, and oil spillage from giant tankers or drilling sites, are common examples. The chemicals often directly harm seabirds, as in Holland where much of the tern population has been wiped out.

The pesticides DDT and PCB are extremely dangerous, since they cannot easily be broken down in nature. Such substances become ever more concentrated at higher levels in a food-chain until they may kill predators like birds, as is illustrated in the present chapter. DDT and its derivatives also affect the reproduction of birds by causing thinner

(4) The quality of seabird food is as important as its quantity, and is affected by the phenomenon of *food-chain concentration*. Some elements in the environment may become concentrated with each link in a food-chain. Toxic elements can reach lethal proportions at high trophic levels, even if they are very dispersed at low levels. Thus, certain insecticides which were once thought harmless to vertebrates have proved dangerous. The persistent DDT was long used before its effects on birds and mammals were discovered. Shown here is a food-chain *(with main links shaded)* in the salt marshes of Long Island on the northeast coast of the United States. DDT concentration (parts per million) is given for: *(a)* marsh water, *(b)* plankton, *(c)* shrimps, *(d)* silversides, *(e)* clams, *(f)* minnows, *(g)* pickerel, *(h)* needlefish, *(i)* Little Tern, *(j)* Common Terns and *(k)* their abandoned eggs, *(l)* immature Double-crested Cormorant, *(m)* Osprey or "fish hawk" egg, *(n)* Herring Gulls (one moribund), *(o)* immature Ring-billed Gull. The concentration in carnivorous birds was thus found to be as much as 100 times greater than in their prey, and a million times greater than in the water. Scavenging seabirds like gulls are especially vulnerable, since they may eat animals which have already died from pollution.

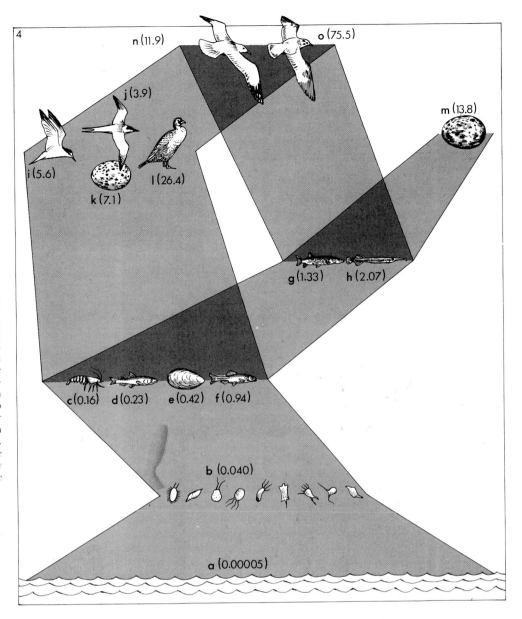

n (11.9) o (75.5) m (13.8) j (3.9) i (5.6) k (7.1) l (26.4) g (1.33) h (2.07) c (0.16) d (0.23) e (0.42) f (0.94) b (0.040) a (0.00005)

eggshells, which may be crushed during incubation. Brown Pelicans in Florida were thus markedly decimated for some time. Even pelagic Cahows, facing extinction, suffered from DDT in the 1960s, and it has reached as far as Antarctic penguins.

Birds are poisoned by oil on occasion, especially if they happen to ingest it while preening. But oil-smeared feathers usually lead to death in other ways, as through chilling. In fact, rather small amounts of oil may prove lethal by ruining the insulating properties of plumage. Why seabirds fail to avoid oil is understandable: they have not had time to evolve reactions against it, and too few of them survive an encounter with it to teach others about its risks. Oil has the property of smoothing water surfaces, luring birds to rest there and become polluted. When a moving ship releases a long oil slick that drifts shoreward, coastal birds find it hard to escape.

Accidents involving oil tankers such as the *Torrey Canyon* and *Amoco Cadiz* are but a few of those which have killed hundreds of thousands of seabirds—and which are little publicized when they occur far from the industrial world, as was once shown by a wreck in the Strait of Magellan. Some offshore oil-drilling mishaps and "blow-outs" have also been catastrophic, as in California and the Gulf of Mexico. Yet more dangerous than oil are frequently the detergent chemicals used to clean it up.

A "normal" source of oil in the ocean is continual leakage or flushing from tankers and other vessels. This occurs in small amounts that add up to huge ones, greatly exceeding accidental oil spillage. The long-term effects of such pollution on marine life and reproduction are hard to determine but may be disastrous. Heavy usage of artificial fertilizers in agriculture also allows them to enter rivers and streams constantly. These chemicals, and sewage outlets, can overfertilize coastal areas, so that the decomposition exhausts oxygen in the water, killing organisms on which seabirds depend. Cold waters are most vulnerable, since the chemicals break down slowly in them.

Encroachment on colonies

Breeding among seabirds is disrupted in many ways by man. To begin with, people spread diverse animals that have wiped out, or severely reduced, breeding colonies. Brown and black rats are very damaging in some areas, where adult seabirds can escape from them but are not efficient enough to defend eggs or young. The Kiore Rat, spread by seafaring Polynesians, thus ruined numerous colonies in New Zealand and on Pacific islands—and it has even been seen to attack adult albatrosses, which are not adapted to such a threat.

Cats and dogs also take adult seabirds, while pigs are able to root out the burrows of seabirds. Donkeys, goats,

White-tailed Tropic-bird *(Phaethon lepturus)*

Brown Pelican *(Pelecanus occidentalis)*
Glaucous-winged Gull *(Larus glaucescens)*

(Left) Seabirds like the adult Brown Pelican have a firm place in human culture due to their beauty and curious habits.

(Above) Exhausted or sick seabirds sometimes come to rest on ships, as has this White-tailed Tropic-bird in the Bismarck Archipelago.

(Below) Vessels at sea often provide a normal resting site for seabirds. Here, a Glaucous-winged Gull prepares to take off from a freighter.

(Opposite top) The Wandering Albatross is seldom seen, although it is among the most legendary of birds. Yet seabirds are becoming increasingly accessible, and one may witness the fearlessness and individuality of some species, like immatures of the Masked Booby and the Great Frigate-bird *(opposite, centre and bottom)*.

Wandering Albatross *(Diomedea exulans)*
Great Frigate-bird *(Fregata minor)*

and rabbits destroy the vegetation needed for nest-building, as on South Trinidade Island where a large colony of Red-footed Boobies was ruined in this manner. These animals multiply rapidly in newly occupied places that lack predators, and man has tried to control them by introducing predators like weasels and stoats, but the latter have often become dangerous for seabirds as well.

An immediate human menace to seabird colonies is the building of adjacent harbours, airports, roads, and other works. On breeding islands, settlements are sometimes erected and import domesticated animals, or devastating fires have been caused, or tourism is developing the land used by gulls and terns. The exploitation of guano in the nineteenth century had awful effects on populations of the Humboldt Penguin and the Peruvian Diving-petrel, which dug their burrows in guano deposits due to a lack of suitable soil, and they have not recovered.

Human visits to such areas for a variety of reasons frequently result in the loss of eggs and chicks. For instance, Sandwich Terns may entirely desert a colony in the midst of breeding activities if they are disturbed, and guillemots easily panic so that their eggs fall from cliff ledges. Once the adults have fled, eggs and chicks are readily accessible to predators such as skuas, gulls, and frigate-birds. Indeed, breeding failures are sometimes caused by amateur ornithologists and scientists during research in colonies.

Conservation and coexistence

Some awareness of the need to protect nature and wildlife arose already in the nineteenth century, leading to a number of measures for the benefit of seabirds. The main effort was to prohibit hunting, and disturbance or egg-collecting on breeding grounds, of certain endangered species. This is one reason for the increased populations of the Northern Gannet and the Great Skua in the North Atlantic. In such cases, the bird populations would probably have been great if man had never existed, and conservation may have merely stopped their decline rather than actually increasing them. Yet the value of these early steps taken by individuals and organizations must be acknowledged; without them, the situation for seabirds would have been very different today.

Seabird breeding grounds now enjoy a limited degree of protection in many areas, but only a small proportion of the world's species is involved. In addition to this passive conservation, there have been active measures such as the extermination of animals introduced by man to seabird habitats. Pigs that were spread to Clipperton Island in the eastern Pacific ruined many large colonies of tropical seabirds, which are recovering strongly since the pigs were killed a couple of decades ago. Another example is the Cahow, probably saved from extinction by human assistance. Its few remaining pairs suffered disturbance and competition for nesting holes, from the sturdy White-tailed Tropic-birds which sometimes simply threw these petrels and their young out of holes. When artificial nests were built with narrow openings that could not be entered by tropic-birds, the breeding success of the petrels was considerably enhanced.

One may hope that protection of seabirds will grow in the future. Generally, the importance of conservation has increased along with human populations and with their mobility, including tourism in leisure time created by an industrialized world. However, awareness of ecology and the living conditions of birds has arrived late, only as man begins to notice that he is destroying the conditions for his own survival. A thorough ecological management of the environment is urgently required, but it may take long to develop. The delay is enormously profitable for unscrupulous individuals and organizations which exploit nature harmfully, and whose economic power makes them difficult to oppose. The fact that they will eventually bring ruin upon themselves—as we know from the many incidents of overfishing—cannot console us, since the damage they do is often irreparable.

Indirect aid to seabirds

Human activities have also had unintentional effects of value to seabirds. By overexploiting the environment, man is adding huge quantities of waste material to it. Much of this is dangerous, but some can be eaten, and opportunist seabirds scavenging on such offal in various places have greatly multiplied their populations. Gulls have benefited particularly, growing in numbers around coastal settlements. Vast amounts of fish offal, too, are spread by the large fishing fleets and become food for seabirds. This new source, as well as protection of breeding grounds, probably explains the proliferation of Northern Fulmars in the southeastern part of their range in the North Atlantic.

Every ocean-voyager has had an opportunity to watch seabirds following in a ship's wake, feeding on galley refuse thrown overboard—and, to some extent, even on marine animals brought to the surface in water stirred by a ship's propeller, which may stun or injure them so that they are more easily caught. Here we find seabirds of the most varied kinds, from small plankton-feeding storm-petrels to skuas, gulls, fulmars, and very large albatrosses. Some even take advantage of updrafts at a ship's sides to save energy while searching for food. In a few areas, such as Panama Bay, the Brown Booby has made a habit of hang-gliding at the ship's bow: it catches the flying fish that are frightened into the air as the ship advances.

Human structures, from boats to buildings, provide seabirds occasionally with resting sites, which can give protection from ground predators and may be conveniently close to feeding places. Certain species, notably gulls, have started to breed on constructions that have proven to be relatively safe. These are sometimes also near sources of food, and thus lower the energy costs of foraging in breeding periods. But supplies of food and sites for seabirds depend still more heavily on another such "structure", the legal system. Wherever acts like marine overfishing, water pollution, and encroachment on wild nature are forbidden by man—although usually for selfish reasons—seabirds tend to share the benefits.

One contrary result, to be sure, is the population explosion among gulls. Vigorous and voracious, they are presenting a threat to the breeding grounds of less competitive seabirds, ousting many terns from small islands in areas where these are scarce, or feeding on the eggs and chicks of other species. Some successful efforts to diminish gull populations have enhanced those of terns, sea ducks, and various coastal birds. But persistent control is often necessary, as gulls reproduce rapidly and have long lives. It has, in general, been impossible to stop the spread of offal that makes gulls so numerous.

Mutualistic relations

While man and seabirds live in basically different kinds of environments, a few activities are directly beneficial to both. For instance, the guano production at the Peruvian coast was already important to the native Incas, who consequently protected the breeding areas of seabirds and regulated the exploitation of guano. This balanced relationship ceased during the decline of culture which followed European colonization. Yet, with uncontrolled removal of guano in the nineteenth century, it became the chief source of Peruvian state income for over a hundred years, requiring further protection. Armed guards kept unwelcome visitors away from the breeding islands, hunted predators such as condors, and sometimes built walls to improve the conditions for breeding. Similar measures in South Africa enabled seabirds to rest and breed on wooden platforms built by guano exploiters.

Domestication is a common type of mutualism between man and other organisms, but it has seldom overcome the oceanic habits of seabirds. There are cases of people holding seabirds in captivity so as to make use of them, although real stocks have never developed. Cormorants were once widely kept in China and Japan for fishing—a practice which, however, has by now almost disappeared. These birds, tied to strings on a boat, could be let into the water and catch fish, with rings around their necks to prevent them from swallowing the fish. The cormorants were not allowed to breed in captivity, and this is not a strong example of mutual benefits for distinct species. Likewise, Polynesian islanders in the past have utilized frigate-birds as "carrier pigeons" to convey messages.

Man's control of gull populations is sometimes motivated by his desire to improve the hunting of other birds such as sea ducks. The latter may even benefit alongside man, if their numbers are thus maintained at a higher level than would otherwise be possible. Sea ducks are also protected when down is gathered from their nests for commercial purposes. In parts of Norway, small wooden boxes are customarily built for eiders to nest in, giving them better protection and facilitating the collection of down after the chicks have left.

Information is often of great economic value, and there have been remarkable benefits of the role of seabirds in showing fishermen the locations of fish shoals at long distances. The tuna fishermen on Madeira Island, aware of their debt to Cory's Shearwaters which point the way to such dispersed prey, have actually taken steps to protect the breeding grounds of these birds on nearby isles. The birds' fate would probably have been much worse in other circumstances, since unscrupulous people frequently go ashore to exploit them.

The spiritual dimension of seabirds

A fundamental orientation of all the preceding chapters has been particularly evident in the present one—towards knowledge of material kinds about seabirds. If we study their properties and lives in order to identify them on the ocean, or to understand them more scientifically, or to learn about the environment as a whole, our knowledge may well have a useful and measurable value. But it is especially when considering seabirds in the human context that we should also expect them to be known, experienced, or appreciated in nonmaterialistic ways, which are not as objective and utilitarian. Without emphasizing the need for such a higher consciousness of nature, our discussion of man's role would certainly be incomplete.

In our industrialized age, nature is viewed chiefly as an instrument for the economic and physical benefit of mankind. This is not only due to the effects of industry and

modern life upon the environment. It owes as much to the dependence of industry on advanced technology, of the latter on scientific research, and of science on physical aspects of nature. Moreover, pragmatic exploitation of the environment has usually been intended to benefit people immediately, not future generations. The long-run goals of industry and science are hard to predict or to choose. They require us to think in terms which are not entirely materialistic, but take account of possibilities such as the destruction of nature until we are left alone and are ourselves ultimately eradicated.

There are many additional reasons why man, even today, feels an emotional or spiritual connection with nature. It may seem puzzling that we take any positive, sympathetic interest in other types of living organisms, since they seldom appear to share this interest. Their self-concern and freedom, however, are some of the very features which fascinate us, particularly in the case of animals like seabirds that roam over vast tracts of wilderness. If these creatures did not appeal deeply to us, we might have no hesitation in wiping them out. The dilemma is that man, while recognizing a danger, is not always able and willing to avoid it.

Already in the pursuit of knowledge about nature, a high spiritual value is felt whenever we become intrigued by questions and excited by discoveries. This is a main motivation for organized research, and is also important to amateur naturalists. Seabirds receive close attention from amateurs all around the world, and tourism is growing rapidly to places where thrilling observations may be made, such as many breeding colonies, tropical islands, and the Antarctic. These experiences do not simply involve learning of facts and theories, but include an admiration of enormous beauty, wonderful elegance, and the teeming richness of life.

Cultural expressions of our attachment to seabirds have ranged from lore, myth, and local names for birds to great literature, paintings, photography, and recordings of birds' sounds. Every new seafarer must long to see an albatross in flight—and what could have been more normal among ancient sailors than to believe that the soul of a dead voyager continued to exist in such a bird, ensuring eternal and free life? Even with less imagination, we exhibit a similar regard for nature through the tradition of cultivating domestic plants and animals to gain a more sensitive awareness of life in general. It remains true, nonetheless, that cultivation can easily be turned into exploitation. If nature is treated simply as a garden of objects to be owned, manipulated, and traded, then the value of uncontrollable creatures like seabirds will soon be forgotten and possibly lost forever.

The time has come for mankind to view life in total, holistic terms, without excluding any of nature's aspects or values. The scientific study of seabirds—which has been prominent in the progress of biological knowledge, from evolutionary theory to ethology and ecology—gives strong support to this goal by showing the interrelationships of oceanic organisms and the unity of the earth's biosphere. We now understand that individuals are parts of entire processes, and that their properties are both taken from the environment and added to it. They must act with caution if the conditions for their survival are to be preserved, using as much knowledge of the whole as of themselves. Seabirds and many other animals may seem distant or strange to us, but only a reverence for all life can enable each kind of life to flourish. Hopefully, in the future, we will be guided by such a new "eco-ethic" in our relations with nature.

A picture of a seabird may be seen as an illustration of a species, but essentially it represents an individual in a certain situation. Such portraits may have infinite variations, some of them yielding information or understanding, and others clearly communicating the aesthetic values to be found in nature. Viewing a bird alive in its characteristic surroundings, in different conditions of light and weather, offers unlimited opportunities of appreciation, and nature-photography now engages large numbers of enthusiasts.

(Right) A Laughing Gull, faintly illuminated against dark and shaded water, seems to float in empty space. The tropical sun makes the translucent wings of a White Tern glimmer *(opposite top)*. Evening light reveals a Chilean Pelican *(below)* and a Brown Booby *(opposite bottom)* at their finest.

Laughing Gull *(Larus atricilla)*
Chilean Pelican *(Pelecanus thagus)*

White Tern *(Gygis alba)*
Brown Booby *(Sula leucogaster)*

BIBLIOGRAPHY

The preparation of this book has involved consultation of many scientific works, both of general kinds and with special regard to ocean birds. A number of the illustrations are based upon several sources, some being cited on page 4, but it has not been feasible to acknowledge them all. What follows is a selection of the literature about seabirds which is of relatively wide interest and may be useful to anyone who explores the subject further.

Alexander, W. B. 1955. *Birds of the Ocean*. London.

Ashmole, N. P. 1963. "The regulation of numbers of tropical oceanic birds." *Ibis*, 103b, pp. 458-473.

Ashmole, N. P. 1971. "Seabird ecology and the marine environment," in **D.S. Farner** (ed.), *Avian Biology*, Vol. 1. London.

Ashmole, N. P. and Ashmole, M. J. 1967. "Comparative feeding ecology of seabirds of a tropical oceanic island." *Yale Peabody Museum Nat. Hist. Bull.*, 24.

Bourne, W. R. P. 1963. "A review of oceanic studies of the biology of seabirds." *Proceedings of the XIII International Ornithological Congress*, pp. 831-854.

Cramp, S., Bourne, W. R. P., and Saunders, D. 1974. *The Seabirds of Britain and Ireland*. London.

De Schauensee, R. M. 1971. *A Guide to the Birds of South America*. London and Edinburgh.

Falla, R. A., Sibson, R. B., and Turbott, E. B. 1975. *A Field Guide to the Birds of New Zealand*. London.

Fisher, H. I. 1976. "Some dynamics of a breeding colony of Laysan Albatrosses." *Wilson Bulletin*, 88.

Fisher, J. 1952. *The Fulmar*. London.

Fisher, J. and Lockley, R. M. 1954. *Seabirds*. London.

Harper, P. C. and Kinsky, F. C. 1978. *Southern Albatrosses and Petrels: an Identification Guide*. Victoria.

Harris, M. 1974. *A Field Guide to the Birds of the Galapagos*. London.

Harrison, P. 1983. *Seabirds: an Identification Guide*. Beckenham.

Johnson, A. W. 1965 and 1967. *The Birds of Chile and Adjacent Regions of Argentina, Bolivia and Peru*. Vols. 1 and 2. Buenos Aires.

King, W. B. 1967. *Seabirds of the Tropical Pacific Ocean*. (Preliminary Smithsonian Identification Manual.) Washington, D. C.

Lack, D. 1945. "Ecology of closely related species with special reference to Cormorant *(Phalacrocorax carbo)* and Shag *(P. aristotelis)*." *Journal of Animal Ecology*, 14, pp. 12-16.

Lack, D. 1967. "Interrelationships in breeding adaptations as shown by marine birds." *Proceedings of the XIV International Ornithological Congress*, 1966, pp. 3-42.

Lack, D. 1968. *Ecological Adaptations for Breeding in Birds*. London.

Lockley, R. M. 1961. *Shearwaters*. New York.

Lockley, R. M. 1974. *Ocean Wanderers*. Newton Abbot.

Matthews, G. V. T. 1968. *Bird Navigation*. Cambridge.

Murphy, R. C. 1936. *Oceanic Birds of South America*. Vols. 1 and 2. New York.

Nelson, J. B. 1970. "The relationship between behaviour and ecology in the *Sulidae* with reference to other seabirds." *Oceanogr. Mar. Biol. Annual Review*, 8.

Nelson, J. B. 1978. *The Gannet*. Berkhamsted.

Nelson, J. B. 1980. *Seabirds: their Biology and Ecology*. Feltham.

Palmer, R. S. 1962. *Handbook of North American Birds*. Vol. 1. New Haven.

Pearson, T. H. 1968. "The feeding biology of seabird species breeding on the Farne Islands, Northumberland." *Journal of Animal Ecology*, 37, pp. 521-552.

Peterson, R. T. 1961. *A Field Guide to Western Birds*. Boston.

Saunders, D. 1971. *Havsfåglar*. Stockholm.

Serventy, D. L., Serventy, V., and Warham, J. 1971. *The Handbook of Australian Seabirds*. Sydney.

Shackleton, K. and Stokes, T. 1968. *Birds of the Atlantic Ocean*. Feltham.

Shallenberger, R. J. 1978. *Hawaii's Birds*. Audubon Society Publication.

Shuntov, V. P. 1974. "Seabirds and the biological structure of the ocean." (From *Dalnevostochnoe Knizhnoe Isdatelstvo*, Vladivostok, 1972.) Translation by the Bureau of Sport Fisheries and Wildlife, U. S. Dept. of Interior, Washington, D. C.

Slater, P. 1970. *A Field Guide to Australian Birds: Non-passerines*. Adelaide.

Stonehouse, B. 1972. *Animals of the Antarctic—the Ecology of the Far South*. London.

Stonehouse, B. (ed.) 1975. *The Biology of Penguins*. London.

Tickell, W. L. N. 1968. "The biology of the great albatrosses, *Diomedea exulans* and *Diomedea epomophora*." *Antarct. Res. Ser.* 12, pp. 1-55.

Tinbergen, N. 1953. *The Herring Gull's World*. London.

Tuck, G. S. and Heinzel, H. 1978. *A Field Guide to the Seabirds of Britain and the World*. London.

Tuck, L. M. 1961. "The murres: their distribution, populations and biology." *Canadian Wildlife Service Rep. Series*, 1. Ottawa.

Vaurie, C. 1965. *The Birds of the Palearctic Fauna: Non-passeriformes*. London.

Watson, G. E. 1966. *Seabirds of the Tropical Atlantic Ocean*. (Smithsonian Identification Manual.) Washington, D. C.

Watson, G. E. 1975. *Birds of the Antarctic and Sub-Antarctic*. Washington, D. C.

Watson, G. E., Zusi, L. R., and Storer, R. E. 1963. *Preliminary Field Guide to the Birds of the Indian Ocean*. Washington, D. C.

Woodwell, G. M., Wurster, C. F., and Isaacson, P. A. 1967. "DDT residues in an east coast estuary: a case of biological concentration of a persistent insecticide." *Science*, 156, pp. 821-824.

Wynne-Edwards, V. C. 1935. "On the habits and distribution of birds on the North Atlantic." *Proceedings of Boston Soc. of Nat. History*, 40 (4), pp. 233-346.

Page numbers in italics indicate illustrations. Included here are many additional Latin and common names of seabirds, with reference to the nearest equivalent names used in this book.